OPRAH WINFREY UP CLOSE

In October 1993, *Forbes* magazine published its list of "The 40 Top-Earning Entertainers," and the big news was that Oprah Winfrey topped the list. At thirty-nine, she has outdistanced early mentors Steven Spielberg and Bill Cosby, and now controls a personal fortune worth $250 million dollars.

Not bad for a self-described "nappy-headed little colored girl" who was born on a dirt-poor Mississippi farm, grew up in poverty, was raped at nine, and at fourteen bore a child who died at birth.

Today she is an international star, a woman who speaks to the United States Senate about the issues of child abuse, but who is not too lofty to listen to the cries of the homeless.

And she enjoys every minute of her success.

OPRAH!

UP CLOSE AND DOWN HOME

NELLIE BLY

ZEBRA BOOKS
KENSINGTON PUBLISHING CORP.

ZEBRA BOOKS are published by

Kensington Publishing Corp.
475 Park Avenue South
New York, NY 10016

Zebra and the Z logo Reg. U.S. Pat. & TM Off.

First Printing: December, 1993

Printed in the United States of America

I press toward the mark for the prize of the high calling of God. . . .

—*Philippians, 3:14,*
Oprah Winfrey's favorite biblical verse

THANKS . . .

. . . to Susan Lippe for her invaluable assistance

. . . to Ann La Farge, Paul Dinas and Tracy Bernstein for editorial guidance generously given

. . . to Ruth Harris, Lynn Brown, Ernie Petrillo and Eileen Bertelli for early enthusiasm and support

. . . to Kevin Bohan and Joyce Kaplan for reality checks

. . . to Clark for showing me the light

. . . to Sarah Gallick for making it all happen

TABLE OF CONTENTS

"A Very Dear Friend is Living with AIDS"
Her Generosity
"I Have Arrived!"

Oprah Works Out with Schwarzenegger
"My Husband Is So Cheap . . ."
"After Nine Years, I Found Out My Son Isn't Mine"
"Family Photo Foiled My Two-Timing Lover"
"I Was a Target at a Shooting Contest"
A Woman Saved His Life after He Was Raped
by Three Men
"Why I Forgive My Daughter's Killer"
"A Psychic Voice Saved My Life"
The "Other Woman" Was a Man!
"My Grubby Look Drives Women Wild"
Successful Dentist Freeloads Off His Mom
Robin Williams: "What Makes Me Tick"
Great-Granny Gives Homeless Her House
"I Left My Wife and Went Home to Mom"
Marla Won't Miss The Donald's Money
Barry Manilow: "My Nightmares About the Nazis"
Rapist Torments Victim—from Behind Bars
Coma Mom's Strange Awakening
Jilted Wife Fights Fire with Fire
King of Cads Bares His Soul
Mom Pays Price for Spoiled Son
The Girl Who Loved Daddy Too Much . . .
"My Husband Left Me—for Another Man"
Trapped at Home—Because She Feels So Ugly
Guests Who Hoaxed the Show
An Apology
Another Phony Guest Cons Oprah Twice!

Chapter One
Mississippi to Milwaukee

I remember going to the interview process where they treat you like you're already a known convict and thinking to myself, how in the world is this happening to me? I was fourteen and I knew that I was a smart person; I knew I wasn't a bad person, and I remember thinking: How did this happen? How did I get here?

—Oprah Winfrey, recalling her mother's attempt
to have her put in a juvenile detention center,
1968

In May of 1953, a slim and handsome twenty-year-old soldier named Vernon Winfrey, on leave from Fort Rucker, passed through Kosciusko, Mississippi, which folks who live there like to point out is seventy miles from Jackson. One of the first people young Vernon encountered in the tiny hamlet was pretty, bored, nineteen-year-old Vernita Lee, whose family, descendants of slaves, had farmed in the area for two hundred years.

In the sultry languor of a Mississippi spring, Vernon and Vernita experienced what their daughter would later describe as a "one-day fling under an oak tree." Young Winfrey returned to his army base and thought no more about the lovely Vernita until the following February, when he received a newspaper clipping announcing that Oprah Gail Winfrey had been born in Kosciusko on January 29, 1954.

Attached was a brief note saying: "Send clothes."

The baby girl's unusual first name came from the Old Testament. Orpah was Ruth's sister-in-law in the Book of Ruth. It was a bumbling (or dyslexic) bureaucrat who misspelled it, creating the unique, distinctive, and unforgettable Oprah.

Like her name, Oprah is one of a kind.

There wasn't much to offer a young woman in Kosciusko in 1954, and Vernita soon joined the epic 1950's migration of blacks to the northern industrial states, leaving her mother's farm for the bright lights of Milwaukee.

Baby Oprah was left in the care of her grandparents, the former Hattie May Bullock and Earless Lee. Hattie was a strict disciplinarian who believed in the laying on of hands, in all ways. In other words, Hattie did not spare the rod.

"When my grandmother used to whip my behind, she'd say, 'I'm doing this because I love you,' " Oprah recalls. "And I'd say, 'If you loved me, you'd get that switch off my butt.' "

But her grandmother's corporal punishment is not Oprah's most terrifying memory of that time. She knew that Hattie acted out of love. Perhaps she was overreacting to the departure of Vernita; perhaps she felt she had made mistakes with Vernita and that was why Vernita had not only given birth without benefit of marriage, but compounded the sin by leaving the baby behind. Whatever Hattie's reasons, deep in her heart little Oprah knew that her grandmother acted out of love.

Oprah's grandfather, Earless Lee, was another story entirely. He was the first of what would become a long parade of negative experiences with men in Oprah's life.

"I feared him," Oprah recalls. "Always a dark presence. I remember him always throwing things at me or trying to shoo me away with his cane."

Life was hard on the farm. Oprah shared a bed with

her grandmother. The house had no indoor plumbing, and it was her job to empty the slop jar in the morning.

"One night, my grandfather came into my room, and he was looming over the bed and my grandma was saying to him, 'You got to get back into bed now, come on, get back into bed.' "

Oprah was only four years old, and she was scared that Earless would kill them both. Even years later, as she recalled the episode, it was chilling:

"She couldn't get him back in his room. And there was an old blind man who lived down the road, and I remember my grandma going out on the porch and screaming, 'Henry! Henry!' And when I saw his light going on I knew that we were going to be saved."

For years, Oprah had nightmares that her grandfather would come in the dark and strangle her.

In spite of episodes like that, Oprah's early years were happy. Certainly, they were much better than what was to come in Milwaukee.

Hattie May believed in prayers and that God answered prayers. Together, she and Oprah knelt nightly to thank God for His protection and generosity, for His guidance and forgiveness.

Her grandmother taught Oprah to read and write by the time she was three, and together they read and studied the Bible, a habit Oprah continues to this day.

Much of their life revolved around the Baptist church, especially the Sunday school performances that Oprah loved.

"At a Sunday school performance—all weekend, they'd say, 'And little Mistress Winfrey is here to do the recitation' . . . and I'd have these little, little patent leather shoes. Oh, *very* proper."

It was the first sign that Oprah had a tremendous rapport with a crowd, and the warm, loving relationship little

Oprah developed with those churchgoers would be the same enthusiasm she would generate years later in her talk show audiences.

Most of all, Hattie May gave Oprah a deep and abiding faith in God and a conviction that God is the center of the universe. "Once you understand that," Oprah says, "it's all really simple."

Her grandmother taught Oprah to pray, telling her, "As long as you have the power to bow your head and bend your knees, you do it and God will hear you better."

To this day, that is how Oprah prays. "I have not been able to get that out of my brain," she says.

Then suddenly, Oprah's world changed. Vernita Lee had settled in Milwaukee and she wanted her little girl with her. Vernita sent for Oprah, and at five she said goodbye to the sweet joys of rural Mississippi and her grandmother, and hello to the rough streets of inner-city Milwaukee.

The culture shock was immediate.

Oprah was only in her Milwaukee kindergarten for a couple of weeks when she wrote her teacher a note that said: "Dear Miss New: I don't think I belong here."

Impressed with her precocious little student, the teacher had Oprah moved up a grade. A year later, Oprah recalls, "I didn't think it was necessary to go to second grade, so I told my teacher and was moved into third grade. I couldn't stand to be bored."

But while Oprah was doing well in school, her home life was difficult. By 1960, Vernita Lee had two more children, Patricia and Jeffrey Lee, and was struggling as a single mother.

When Oprah was eight, her mother had had enough and sent her to stay with her father, Vernon, who had married and was living in Nashville. She was bounced back to her mother when she turned nine.

Oprah and her family disagree dramatically about just how bad things were during those Milwaukee years.

In the 1980s, when Oprah's career began to take off, she would claim in interviews that she had been raised in grinding poverty. She told one magazine: "We were so poor we couldn't afford a dog or cat, so I made pets out of two cockroaches." She told another publication that her mother was on welfare and living in a three-room flat.

But her sister Patricia Lee scoffs at this idea.

"Sure, we weren't rich," Patricia says. "But she exaggerated how bad we had it, I guess to get sympathy from her viewers and widen her audience."

Patricia denies Oprah ever had cockroaches for pets. "She always had a dog. She also had a white cat, an eel in an aquarium, and a parakeet called Bo-Peep that she tried to teach to talk."

Patricia recalls that Oprah played with her dogs for hours, holding and kissing them and sharing lollipops with them. Oprah's favorite was a little poodle named Simone. She would cuddle her and tell her all her secrets.

As for the "pet" cockroaches, Patricia insists that "Oprah hated insects. If she had to even touch a cockroach, she'd jump out of her skin!"

Other statments Oprah has made over the years have bothered her little sister greatly. "She also said she was a welfare child, with only one pair of shoes and no decent clothes while growing up." Patricia protests, "That's just not true."

Patricia Lee insists: "Our mom worked like the devil at two jobs to provide for us. Oprah had seven or eight pairs of shoes and a closetful of nice clothes. Mom always dressed us beautifully."

"Oprah's later lies broke my mother's heart and made

her cry,'' Patricia says. ''Mom had tried so hard for us kids.''

Finally, according to Patricia, ''After quietly enduring this heartbreak, my mother told Oprah that if she didn't stop lying, Mom was going to the press herself and tell the truth. That's the only reason Oprah stopped telling those tales.''

Maybe Oprah has exaggerated how badly off her family was. Maybe she was compensating for her terrible secret: From the age of nine she was being sexually abused by her own relatives.

"I SOLD MY SILENCE FOR AN ICE CREAM CONE AND A TRIP TO THE ZOO"

The photographs of Oprah Winfrey at age nine show a wide-eyed little girl, her black hair in neat pigtails tied with bright ribbons. She looks at the world curiously, intelligently, as if she is eager to learn all about it. Tragically, she was to learn too much, too soon.

The pictures give no hint of what Oprah had begun to endure at home, for it was at the age of nine that Oprah was raped by a nineteen-year-old cousin, the beginning of a long nightmare of sexual abuse that would last until she was fourteen and would leave scars that would last a lifetime.

The abuse began the summer that Oprah was nine. Looking back on the experience, Oprah says that ''I had no idea it was a sexual thing, because I didn't have a name for it.'' And she acknowledges that she was grateful for the attention of the cousin, thankful when he bribed her with presents. As she puts it: ''I sold my silence for an ice cream cone and a trip to the zoo.''

When Oprah returned to school in September, classmates told her the facts of life and how babies were made.

"I was horrified," she admits, "because someone had done that to me."

But the horror had only begun. The following year, another cousin's boyfriend began to notice the little girl, to encourage her reading and studiousness. Little Oprah responded to rare praise and affection and became his favorite.

One day, in his car, he began to fondle her. "Over a period of time, I became his pet," she recalls. "And every time he was around, people would try to put him with me, even though I began to try to be scarce with myself around him. I began to wonder: 'Don't they know this is happening?'"

Whether or not family members realized what was happening, the outside world certainly didn't. Her life often seemed painfully normal, even to clashes with her little sister, Patricia.

There was the time when thirteen-year-old Oprah tried to teach seven-year-old Patricia how to put on eye makeup.

"She put eyeliner and mascara and stuff around my eyes," Patricia recalls. "But then she didn't know how to get it off, and Mom was going to be home soon.

"So Oprah went and got some Comet cleanser and rubbed the make-up off. It hurt and I ended up with sores around my eyes. I've still got the scar!"

In spite of episodes like that, little Patricia admired her big sister enormously.

"She had big dreams, even when Oprah was little," Patricia recalls. "She told me many times, 'I'm going to be a star.'

"She just *knew* she was going to succeed. She always had drive and ambition.

"She was head and shoulders above everybody else when it came to brainpower."

23

And even though Oprah was often a handful, Vernita agreed that her oldest child was special. "Mom said, 'That girl just frightens me, she's so intelligent. She's just like a sponge. Everything the teachers tell her she takes in.'"

Patricia recalls that when Oprah was about twelve "she was so far ahead of the rest of the kids that she had nobody to push her." Fortunately, a very special teacher, Eugene H. Abrams, took an interest in her.

Dr. Abrams discovered Oprah through a program called "Upward Bound" which was designed to help high-school students from low-income families develop the skills needed for success in college. Abrams arranged for Oprah to get a scholarship to enter Nicolet High School in Fox Point, a Milwaukee suburb.

Abrams went on to become a professor at the University of Wisconsin in Milwaukee. When he passed away in 1991, Oprah said that he had been "one of those great teachers who had the ability to make you believe in yourself. I know there are many former students like myself whose lives have been touched. We're going to miss him."

According to Patricia, "Oprah's teacher saw she was bored and knew she needed competition from other bright kids. He arranged for her to go to a nearly all-white school. I believe she was one of the few black kids there.

"Oprah was working alongside kids whose well-to-do parents were higly educated, kids who had encyclopedias at home to help them with their homework. The other kids had every advantage going, but Oprah still excelled," says Patricia.

There was a price to pay for her excellence, however. Oprah's special gifts set her apart, and sometimes it could be lonely to be set apart.

"Oprah was so bright she ended up not having friends.

She couldn't relate to many ordinary kids. That made her even more independent—and more determined to succeed.''

It is remarkable that Oprah's little sister thought that she could not relate well to "ordinary" kids. Even if it is true, it means that Oprah made enormous strides in the next few years, for there's no doubt Oprah has built her talk show career on her ability to relate well to "ordinary" people.

Patricia's big sister was always encouraging her to make the most of herself. "Oprah was always after me to be successful in school, too," Patricia recalls. "She made sure I did my homework as soon as I got home in the afternoon.''

After I did my math lessons, Oprah would always quiz me to make sure I'd learned the lessons. She taught me better than my teachers!''

But Oprah was living a double life: bright student in school, incest victim at home, and the struggle and conflict was beginning to show.

By now she was also being abused by a favorite uncle. "I started to feel," she says, "like I had a banner on my head.

"I adored this uncle," she would later recall. "Just adored him. And I could not, in my mind, make him be the bad guy.''

As Oprah described it years later, "We had started this conversation, we were talking about boys in school, the conversation went to kissing boys and 'Have you kissed boys?' and the next thing I know, he was taking my panties off. My uncle, whom I adored.''

Little Mistress Winfrey, who had wowed the Baptist Sunday School with her recitations, the little kindergarten student who had written a note to her teacher suggesting that "I don't think I belong here," the teenager who had been singled out to attend a special program for gifted, underprivileged students, suddenly began to run wild.

Vernita struggled to keep Oprah under control. "But Oprah was a wild child," Patricia says now. "She was very promiscuous. She was a 'bad girl.' "

"When Oprah was thirteen or fourteen, she invited men over during the day while my mother was working as a domestic," Patricia recalls.

"Her boyfriends were all much older than her, about nineteen or in their early twenties. Whenever a guy arrived at our door, Oprah would give Popsicles to me and our younger brother Jeffrey and say, 'You two go out on the porch and play now.'

"Oprah then would go inside with her boyfriend, and Jeffrey and I would sit on the porch stoop with our Popsicles for hours, laughing and playing with a ball or toys," Patricia says with no trace of resentment for her big sister.

"I was so young at the time—about eight years old—that I had no idea then what Oprah was doing inside the house.

"We might be out there on the porch for two hours at a time—and finally Oprah's man would walk out the door. He would smile at us and then Oprah would come out and tell us, 'Come on in now. Mom's going to be home soon.'

"I didn't find out what Oprah was doing until I was older and she showed me how she did 'The Horse'—which is what she called the sex act. She said that's what she used to do—and I realized that all those afternoons she was making out with her men!"

Patricia remembers when Oprah was fourteen and had a pair of glasses with ugly frames she hated. "So she broke the glasses," Patricia says, "and when Mom came home, Oprah told her that a robber had come in and knocked her in the head, breaking her glasses!''

Oprah even acted as if she had amnesia and couldn't remember who her mother was or anything about what had happened to her glasses.

"Oprah was always a big actress. She had a wild imagination," says Patricia. "Mom suspected Oprah was making up a story, but took her to a hospital just in case she really was hurt. The doctors said there was nothing wrong, just as Mom suspected. Mom was furious. Now, on top of having to pay to get the glasses fixed, she had to pay for the hospital visit!''

Patricia claims that in her sister's wild days Oprah was not even above stealing from her hardworking mother and then telling outright lies to cover her thefts.

"Around the same time, Oprah stole one of Mom's rings and pawned it," says Patricia. "Oprah said she'd taken the ring to have it cleaned. But Mom found the pawn ticket in a pillowcase and made Oprah get the ring.''

Oprah was lying, stealing, and destructive, but those weren't the only things that were driving her mother batty. When Oprah was fourteen, she ran away from home and was gone a week. Vernita was a nervous wreck, not knowing if Oprah was dead or alive.

"Mom was frantic and called all Oprah's friends looking for her, with no luck," Patricia recalls.

"Oprah finally went to our pastor's house and he brought her home.

"I was so happy and excited when Oprah came back. But Mom was just mad. She picked up a small chair and was going to hit Oprah with it.''

Patricia recalls the night vividly. Oprah was crying and cowering. "I was screaming and begging Mom, 'Please don't kill Oprah!' Mom finally calmed down and put the chair down.''

Another time, Oprah narrowly escaped death when a thug threatened to beat her brains out in her own home. And she brought the trouble on herself, according to Patricia.

"Oprah bought record albums from this guy, then didn't pay him,'' Patricia recalls. "He came to our house and tried to attack Oprah. I remember this huge guy coming in. He seemed like Godzilla to me and our younger brother Jeffrey because he was so big and angry. Oprah ran and locked herself in the bathroom to escape.''

But a mere bathroom door did not intimidate the hulking behemoth. He battered on the door, almost breaking it down as he yelled, "I want my money!''

A frightened Oprah screamed, "Get away from me!''

Patricia, who was only about seven years old at the time, and Jeffrey, who was six, hid and watched the violent scene. Jeffrey, especially, was frantic.

Fortunately, the door resisted the giant's battering. When he saw that he could not break it down, he gave up and left. Only then did Oprah come out of the bathroom. "She begged me not to tell Mama,'' Patricia recalls, "but Jeffrey told. Mom was hysterical.''

But even that terrifying incident did not reform Oprah. According to Patricia, she continued to be a holy terror, once even stealing $200 from her mother's purse.

"That $200 was all the money Mom had made that week at her job as a domestic and her second job at a clothing store,'' Patricia recalls.

It's possible that Oprah was driven to steal out of fear for her life, Patricia acknowledges. "I believe Oprah took the money to pay the guy who'd tried to attack her. But for Mom it was the last straw.''

When Oprah described the following events in her

speech to the Chicago Bar Association in 1991, she recalled that her mother was on welfare at the time, had two other children to cope with, and no parenting skills. Vernita's only alternative, said Oprah, "was to put me in a detention home for girls.

"I remembered going to the interview process where they treat you like you're already a known convict and thinking to myself, how in the world is this happening to me? I was fourteen and I knew that I was a smart person. I knew I wasn't a bad person, and I remember thinking: How did this happen? How did I get here?"

Fortunately for Oprah, the Milwaukee system was terribly overburdened in 1968, and she and her mother were told that they would have to wait at least two weeks before Oprah could be admitted to the detention home.

"My mother was so fed up with me at the time that she said, 'I can't wait two weeks. You've got to get out of the house now.' "

Vernita called Vernon Winfrey in Nashville, and told him she couldn't handle their problem child anymore.

Patricia recalls that "the next thing I knew, Vernon was in Milwaukee to take Oprah home with him. Oprah didn't want to go. She was crying and hugging me before she got into Vernon's car."

As Oprah puts it: "I was sent to live with my father in Nashville, and he changed my life."

About four months after Oprah left for Nashville, Vernita's Milwaukee home was broken into.

"Mom was scared the robber might come back, so we all moved in with her cousin Alice," says Patricia. "And it was there, a couple of nights later, that I learned about Oprah having a baby."

Vernita was working late that night, and it was Alice who got the late night phone call, which little Patricia overheard.

29

"I heard Alice say, 'Hi Vernon.' Then she said, 'What? Oh, my God—Oprah's had a baby? And it died? It was born premature? Oh no—the poor thing! Is Oprah O.K.?'

"There was a silence and then Alice said, 'So Oprah was six months along? Oh, it was a little boy . . .' "

After Vernita got home from work even later that night, Alice gave her the disturbing news about Oprah. Vernita immediately went to Nashville to take care of Oprah and give her emotional support. She was there about a week.

One can only imagine what went throught Vernita's mind as she saw how close her gifted, rebellious daughter had come to following in her own footsteps as an unwed mother. This was not at all the future she had envisioned for Oprah. It was not why she had brought her up from Mississippi. Did she wonder if she had done the wrong thing by plucking the little girl from the rural serenity of Kosciusko and exposing her to the perils of a big city?

Like her mother, Hattie May, Vernita Lee was a religious woman, and it is likely that she made a silent prayer of thanks to the Lord for keeping the misbegotten child's life mercifully brief. Perhaps she prayed, too, that after this tragedy, Oprah would be able to turn her life around.

According to Patricia, "No one ever knew who was the father of Oprah's baby. But I know that it could have been any one of a lot of different guys."

Patricia later heard throught the family grapevine that Oprah had been devastated by the loss of her baby. "She cried and cried," Patricia says. "It broke her heart."

It remained such a painful subject, in fact, that Oprah kept it a secret for many years. When she filled out applications that asked whether she had ever been pregnant or given birth, she always answered "no." As recently as 1990, or until Patricia went public with the story, Oprah was claiming that the one pitfall of the streets that she had avoided was pregnancy.

"Oprah never talked about her lost baby, and for years it was kept hush-hush," Patricia recalls. "It was a deep family secret that was almost never discussed within the family."

And on the rare occasion when the tragic episode was brought up, someone usually observed that it just proved that if it could happen to Oprah, it could happen to anyone.

In October 1993, in an amazingly candid interview with Laura B. Randolph in *Ebony* magazine, Oprah finally spoke about what she regarded as "my greatest shame."

Oprah said that she had hidden her pregnancy until the day she gave birth. While she was pregnant, she said, she spent half the time in denial and the other half trying to hurt herself to lose the baby. When asked, she named all the men who could have been responsible, including the favorite uncle who had been abusing her. But, according to Oprah, the family simply did not want to deal with it. Because she had been promiscuous, they blamed her. The pregnancy was her fault. And she could not say definitely that her uncle was the father. Her Milwaukee relatives were not interested in discussing why the uncle had sex with her. They were more concerned with who had fathered her child than with why this fourteen-year-old child had become so wildly promiscuous.

"It wasn't because I liked running around having sex," Oprah says. "It was because once I started I didn't want the other boys to be mad at me."

Oprah shut down and did not bring the story up for many years after that. She did not think anyone would believe her, so why bother?

When her sister Patricia revealed Oprah's tragic secret, Oprah was so devastated that she took to her bed, even though she was in the middle of shooting her TV series, "Brewster Place." She would go home from work, she said, and cry. She thought the world would despise her when they learned about her baby. She felt that her sister had betrayed her by exposing her darkest secret.

Oprah acknowledged that it was years before she could bring herself to even speak to Patricia again. Finally, in 1992, she called a meeting of the women in her family: her mother Vernita, her beloved Aunt Alice, and Patricia and her two teenage daughters.

For an entire weekend, with Oprah in the role of therapist, the women occupied a log cabin on her farm and reviewed their feelings about each other.

Oprah felt that she could not go on the air and talk to people about forgiveness when she could not forgive her sister. She remembers the weekend as full of pain, but in the end they were able to go on with their lives and to accept each other. She would never have an ideal relationship with her mother or her sister, but at least they would live in the world women to women.

Eventually Oprah would go public with all the dark secrets of her Milwaukee years: not only the pregnancy, but the promiscuity and the root cause—the repeated sexual abuse from her relatives. This experience would affect all her future relationships, and it would be years before she could discuss it. Then even more years until she could take the first tentative steps toward healing and finally an activist role in the national campaign against child abuse.

Chapter Two
From Nashville to Baltimore

I had given this man the power over my life. And I will never, never—as long as I'm black!—I will never give up my power to another person.
    —Oprah Winfrey on the love affair that drove her close to suicide, 1981

Oprah has said that going to live with her father was a turning point in her life. Vernon Winfrey, a Nashville barber and city councilman, was a strict disciplinarian who insisted that his daughter memorize twenty new vocabulary words a week and give him weekly book reports. Oprah also began keeping a journal, a habit that would last to this day.

"My father turned my life around by insisting I be more than I was and by believing I could be more. His love of learning showed me the way," says Oprah. At the same time, Oprah discovered her lifelong love of books.

"Books showed me there were possibilities in life, that there were actually people like me living in a world I could not only aspire to but attain," Oprah says. "Reading gave me hope. For me, it was the open door."

As Oprah says, her father "straightened [her] out,"

and by the time she was sixteen she was an "A" student at East Nashville High School. She dated East Nashville classmate Anthony Otey, and she was reunited with him on her show on March 10, 1992.

On that show, Otey reminisced about the girl he always called by her middle name, "Gail." Even then, he had recognized that she was meant for great things: "She was a very bright, very articulate person. One thing I remember most about Gail is that she knew what she wanted . . . she said she wanted to be a movie star. She wanted to be an actress and I praise God that she's done that."

Otey reminisced that in their high-school oratory contests, while everybody else did a speech from *Inherit the Wind*, Oprah would be doing something from Margaret Walker's *Jubilee*, about a slave woman after the Civil War, or Sojourner Truth's "Ain't I a Woman?" speech. But race, she insists, "Has never been an issue with me."

In fact, she recalls, "In high school, when other black kids were organizing a bloc vote for student council, I didn't vote with them because I thought their candidate wasn't the best qualified. I was ostracized then; they called me 'Oreo.' "

Years later, Oprah would demonstrate the same fierce independence when she clashed with the NAACP over the making of *The Color Purple* and "The Women of Brewster Place." Her historic visit to all-white Forsyth County, Georgia, to explore the reasons for white racism, was also picketed and opposed by civil rights pioneer Rev. Hosea Williams. She has never hesitated to hold her ground.

Oprah graduated from East Nashville with the class of 1971 and was voted "Most Popular."

None of Oprah's classmates could have imagined that

the vivacious new transfer from Milwaukee had experienced unspeakable abuse there. How could they have associated the bubbly class leader with the angry, pregnant runaway she had been only months before?

A yearbook photo shows her with hair coiffed in a stylish flip and wearing peace-symbol earrings, one of her rare political statements. Another photo from that era shows Oprah proudly holding two trophies she won for her speaking ability. Her accomplishments in high school won her a four-year scholarship to Tennessee State University.

Oprah's broadcasting career had already begun with an after school job at WVOL radio while she was a senior in high school.

Oprah was even named "Miss WVOL" in 1971. It was not an actual beauty contest, but an honorary title bestowed by the radio station. Photos taken at the time show Oprah posing in crown and winner's sash, in a demure long dress, beaming beside her stepmother, Zelma Winfrey.

DID OPRAH STEAL A BEAUTY QUEEN'S CROWN?

If it is hard to imagine that today's stately talk show host was once a curvaceous beauty queen, it is even harder to imagine that she stole her crown, but that is what a former pageant director charges.

In 1972 Oprah made it all the way to the finals for Miss Black America on the strength of her figure, wide smile, and dramatic talent. But today onetime pageant director Gordon El-Greco Brown charges that she never should have been crowned Miss Black Nashville, and she only won the contest after judges made an error in tallying up their scores!

When Oprah was told the next day she had really finished fifth, not first, in the pageant and was asked to give back the title, she refused.

"She didn't win the beauty pageant fair and square," declares Brown, who organized and ran the contest.

"At the time, Oprah was a college student who worked part-time at a local black radio station, and that contest was a stepping-stone for the big career she so desperately wanted," says Brown. "She's kept this story a secret for all these years. But I'm telling it now because I'm angry after reading interviews in which she takes credit for winning the pageant."

Brown, now a Nashville publicist, says that he met Oprah when she was a scholarship student at Tennessee State University and she enrolled in his modeling school near the campus.

"She waltzed in one day and announced, 'Hi, I'm going to be a big star someday. Where do I sign up, baby?' She was only 17 and not beautiful. But I could tell she had something. She was very poised and had a great speaking voice.

"And when I got the franchise for the Miss Black Nashville and Miss Black Tennessee contests, I invited her to enter."

Oprah filled out an entry form indicating she was 5-foot-6½, and weighed 135 pounds, with a 36-25-37 figure and wore a dress size 11-12.

Under "Hobbies or Interests" she listed "Swimming and People," and when asked for a brief statement about "Why you are entering the Miss Black America Beauty Pageant," she wrote that "I would like to instill a sense of individual (black) pride within our people. Self dignity."

But she lied when she signed a declaration that she had "never conceived a child," for, as we now know, Oprah had already secretly delivered a baby boy who died at birth. Perhaps it was such a painful memory that she had suppressed it; perhaps she had left it behind with all the other painful experiences in Milwaukee.

Miss Black Nashville was the first real beauty pageant Oprah had competed in—and she was very set on winning it. There were twenty-two contestants. On March 10, 1972, the night of the pageant, there wasn't an empty seat in the audience at the Elks Lodge in downtown Nashville.

"Oprah gave an average showing in the evening gown and swimsuit competitions," according to Brown. "The evening dress she selected was rather schoolgirlish and her bathing suit was quite modest in its cut."

It was Oprah's talent that impressed the audience at the Nashville Elks Lodge that night.

"When Oprah's talent turn came she did a dramatic reading and sang—and she knocked the audience off their feet. She was so good, it moved her into the top five."

"There was only one girl who seemed to outshine Oprah in talent," says Brown. "Her name was Maude Mobley. Not only was Maude talented, she had a beautiful figure and scored top marks in the swimsuit and evening gown competitions. Everyone picked her as the winner as soon as her foot hit the stage."

According to Brown, there were six judges, all prominent members of Nashville's black community. Each had a handful of scorecards with which they evaluated the contestants and tabulated the final results.

When the results were handed to the emcee he read them, announcing the winners in order from fifth place to first.

"I couldn't believe it when he read the name of the fourth runner-up: Maude Mobley," Brown says today. "The emcee continued to read the winners, pausing briefly before he called out: 'The winner, and the first place Miss Black Nashville, is Oprah Gail Winfrey.' ''

Later that night people came up to Gordon El-Greco Brown and charged that the contest was fixed.

"I was confused myself," Brown says. "So I gathered up all the judges' scorecards and tallied up the votes.

"I couldn't believe what I discovered: the number four runner-up and the winner's scores had been switched! I'm convinced the scoring switch was an error. The judges were honest men and women."

All that night, Brown lay awake wondering what he could do. The following day, he resolved he would go to Oprah and throw it upon her to do the right thing.

That morning, Brown knocked on the door of Oprah's home and asked her stepmother, Zelma Winfrey, if he could talk with Oprah in private. But Zelma stayed in the room.

"I explained the mix-up," Brown says. "Then I asked Oprah if she would consider giving the crown to Maude, the rightful winner. Oprah stood up and said angrily, 'No, it's mine! My name was called and I am Miss Black Nashville!' ''

Brown claims he tried to reason with Oprah by asking her: "How would you feel if you had been in Maude's shoes?"

Oprah shot back: "I don't care."

Then Brown asked her if she would consider sharing the crown. Again she declined.

"I don't mind saying that when I left that house I left with a very cold feeling," says Brown.

As Miss Black Nashville, Oprah won the right to compete in the June 1972 Miss Black Tennessee contest. She won that pageant, too.

The next stop was the Miss Black America pageant in

Los Angeles later that year and, in spite of his feeling about her selection, Brown accompanied Oprah to the judging in Los Angeles, where Oprah's lucky streak ran out.

"As district pageant organizer, I had access to the final tallies and ascertained that she came in number 34 out of 36 contestants—almost flat bottom," says Brown.

When asked to comment on this story, Oprah's spokeswoman Colleen Raleigh said, "Oprah was never told of any alleged problems with any pageants she was in at any time."

The rightful pageant winner Maude Mobley later worked as a backup singer at Nashville's Grand Ole Opry, and is now a working mother living in Detroit. Today she's not interested in discussing the pageant.

"Oprah's a rich and powerful woman," she told a reporter. "I would rather not talk about this. It might anger her."

But Maude's mom, Clara Matthews, is not so cautious.

"I knew something wasn't right when they called out Oprah as the winner," she says today. "After I talked to Maude, I was so angry that I wrote to everybody I could think of to get the situation righted. But no one was interested. It's true that Oprah stole the crown."

It is unlikely that Oprah would have deliberately stolen a beauty queen's crown. And even Gordon El-Greco Brown does not offer any hint that she did not win the Miss Black Tennessee title fair and square.

No, it's far more likely that what he and Clara Matthews saw as a miscarriage of justice was just another example of divine intervention in Oprah's life. The confusion of the judge's cards was quite in keeping with the other lucky accidents throughout her life, beginning with the overcrowded conditions that kept Oprah out of a Milwaukee detention center for girls when she was fourteen and sent her to Nashville instead.

This is especially likely since the main result of the exposure Oprah gained from winning the titles was that by the time she was a sophomore at TSU she was tapped by WTVF-TV, the local CBS affiliate, to be an on-air reporter.

Perhaps she consulted her Bible and found one of her favorite verses in Philippians, 3:14, "I press toward the mark for the prize of the high calling of God . . ."

Even then, Oprah had her "eye on the prize" of a career in broadcasting, and winning those beauty crowns was merely a stepping-stone to getting there.

One of Oprah's most memorable moments at WTVF-TV came during a 1974 cattle call assignment to interview Priscilla Presley about her latest projects.

Oprah was shaking with fear as she waited for her five-minute audience with Priscilla, when one of Priscilla's public relations representatives came up and told her she could ask Priscilla anything. Just don't mention Elvis.

"Couldn't mention Elvis?" Oprah wailed. "Five minutes with this woman and I couldn't mention Elvis? I went in there and basically went buh, buh, buh, until they carried me out."

Nashville was nurturing several future broadcasting talents during the years Oprah was at WTVF-TV. Across town future "Entertainment Tonight" host John Tesh was anchoring the news at another Nashville station, and his weatherman was Pat Sajak!

In her senior year at TSU, Oprah was offered another job, this one in Baltimore. It was a real dilemma for her: whether she should take the job or continue with her education. Her father was very much concerned that she get her degree. Still, she chose the job.

BALTIMORE: THE DIFFICULT YEARS

It is something of a paradox that even as Oprah solidfied her career as a talk show host in Baltimore, her personal life there would be marked by two heartbreaking love affairs and a brush with suicide.

In 1976, at twenty-two, she joined Baltimore's WJZ-TV as a street reporter. But shortly after arriving, her heart was broken by the collapse of a romance with a Nashville colleague, Billy Taylor. It was Taylor, her coworker and friend at WVOL, who helped her pack up and drove her from Nashville to Baltimore, but firmly refused to stay there.

Years later, she discussed it in an interview on "Sixty Minutes": "Lord, I wanted him. Threw his keys down the toilet. I wanted him. I stood in front of the door and threatened to jump off the balcony if he didn't stay. I wanted him. I was on my knees, begging him, 'Please don't go, please don't go.' "

There was a tearful scene at Baltimore's Friendship Airport as Billy and Oprah said their goodbyes while he awaited his flight back to Nashville, but his mind was made up.

Billy Taylor today is a successful Nashville mortician, but he recalls the times he shared with Oprah with fondness and acknowledges: "We really did care for each other. We shared a deep love. A love I will never forget."

By now Oprah's wounds have healed and she can afford to laugh and say, "If he'd married me, I'd be living in Nashville now, the wife of a mortician and teaching Sunday school."

Breaking up with Billy Taylor was only the beginning of her Baltimore heartaches, for Oprah would next experience a long and frustrating romance with a married man.

A romance so disastrous that she would even consider taking her own life.

"The more he rejected me, the more I wanted him," she admits. "I felt depleted, powerless. Once I stayed in bed for three days, missing work; I just couldn't get up. Sad, isn't it?"

From Milwaukee, her family observed the effect of the relationship on Oprah and worried about her.

"After Oprah went to Baltimore, she met a married man and fell for him," her sister Patricia recalls. "He was her first real love. Then she found out he was married. That was a shock. He wouldn't leave his wife, so Oprah broke off their romance even though she loved him."

Patricia Lee believes that heartbreak hardened Oprah and drove her deeper and deeper into her career.

When Oprah recalled the romance on "Sixty Minutes," she said, "There's nothing worse than rejection. It's worse than death. I would wish sometimes for the guy to die because at least then I could go to the grave and visit."

It's probably no coincidence that it was at this point in her life, 1977, that Oprah began to develop a weight problem. And in 1978, Oprah also tried, for the first time, to discuss her childhood abuse with her family.

"But my mother said she didn't want to hear it, so I never brought it up again," she says.

On September 8, 1981, Oprah went as far as to write a suicide note. She was earning a six-figure salary, co-hosting the most popular talk show in Baltimore, but the end of her four-year relationship had left her feeling worthless.

She wrote out a note to best friend, Gayle King Bumpus, telling her where to find her important papers, and asking her to look after her plants.

Today Oprah believes that she was never really serious about taking her own life, but she acknowledges that when she recently came across the note, "I cried for the woman I was then."

"I don't think I was really serious about suicide," she claims. "That suicide note had been much overplayed. I couldn't kill myself. I would be afraid the minute I did it, something really good would happen and I'd miss it."

Today, a strong, assertive Oprah can hardly believe she ever allowed herself to be so unhappy. "I had given this man the power of my life. And I will never, never—as long as I'm black!—I will never give up my power to another person."

"YOU LEARN A LOT ABOUT YOURSELF WHEN YOU ARE BLACK AND BALD"

The pressures at WJZ-TV were enormous.

Oprah was never comfortable as a street reporter. She hated being the one to thrust a mike into the face of a recent crime victim and demand to know, "How do you feel?" But she did the job and she did it so well that she was soon promoted to co-anchor of the evening news, and then promoted to cohost of WJZ-TV's "People are Talking" show, a folksy local forerunner of the Regis & Kathie Lee format that featured a mixture of celebrity guests, local news, and service segments.

But station poo-bahs went to work "improving" Oprah's image. The good looks, poise, and intelligence that had brought the beauty queen crowns for Miss Black Nashville and Miss Black Tennessee were not enough for decision makers at WJZ-TV. As hostess of "People are Talking" they decreed that she must have a new look.

"I live my life to please other people," Oprah recalls of that period in her life. "They told me my nose was too wide, my hair too thick and long. I couldn't even decide what kind of hair I wanted. They came to me and said, 'Your eyes are too far apart, your nose is too wide, your chin is too long, and you need to do something about it.' So they sent me to New York, to a chi-chi, poo-poo, lah-de-dah salon—the kind that serves you wine so when you leave it doesn't matter what you look like.

"So this Frenchman put a French perm in my black hair. I was the kind of woman at the time—this was 1977—I sat there and let this French perm burn through my cerebral cortex, rather than tell this man, 'It's hurting!' I told myself, 'Oprah, be a good sport. This man must know what he's doing.'

"What he did was burn my hair right off.

"When I got up, the only thing holding my hair follicles in were scabs. For weeks afterward, it kept coming out in these little clumps. I began to comb it sideways, the way men do. The TV station didn't want my hair too long or too thin, but when you come back black and bald, you have a serious problem. You learn a lot about yourself when you are black and bald."

In spite of her two disastrous romances and the efforts of station executives to remake her image, Oprah moved forward professionally. Her "People are Talking" show became the most popular daytime program in Baltimore and a must-stop for authors and celebrities promoting their latest project.

James Brady, the journalist and author of several novels, recalls his first encounter with Oprah in Baltimore in 1982.

"I was there to plug a book. Frank Perdue, the chicken man, was another guest. The fan club of a soap opera star, of whom I had not previously heard, comprised the bulk of the audience. The soap opera star was not going to be on the show; he wasn't there; he had never been there; perhaps he was never, ever going to be there.

"Miss Winfrey could not have cared less. Frank Perdue and I weren't going to make anyone forget the soap opera star, but we were what she had to work with that day.

"This is what you do on talk shows: you work with the material you have. She is still working everyone just fine except that now she is famous, now everyone knows her name."

It was also in Baltimore that Oprah had to deal with horrible sex harassment on the job.

"This man was constantly propositioning me and talking foul language," she told a friend. "I was young and impressionable, and there was no excuse for his behavior. He made me feel uncomfortable and creepy. I stayed away from him and vowed to get away as soon as I could. I was so grateful when I got the chance to go to Chicago."

Oprah rarely speaks about those Baltimore days. She only recently discovered that she was suffering from depression in those days when she was diagnosed right on her show by a guest.

Stephen Arterburn, author of *Hand-Me-Down Genes and Second Hand Emotions,* helped her understand her symptoms.

"We were all talking (about depression)," Oprah said, "and somebody says, 'Well, you know, when you were sexually abused weren't you depressed?' I said, 'I don't know if I was or not.' I do remember going through a period in my twenties when I thought I was in love, but I really was just obsessed . . .

"All I would do was live for this man. And if a man wasn't around, then I was in bed . . . waiting. Couldn't get myself out of bed. But was that depression or was I just crazy?"

47

STEPHEN: "I think it was probably depression."

OPRAH: "I would get up and go to work every day and I was smiling on the evening news."

STEPHEN: "We find a way to cope with it. But that doesn't mean our life isn't painful."

It may seem that Oprah's years in Baltimore make up one horrible chapter in her life. While there was a lot of pain, there were also some good things, too.

It can be said that the two best things that came out of all the Baltimore heartbreak were that Oprah discovered her gift as a talk show host, and she met Gayle King Bumpus, who would become her best friend.

"Gayle and I met in 1976, in the newsroon of WJZ-TV," she recalls. "I was an anchorwoman, and Gayle was a production assistant. One night, there was a terrible snowstorm, so I invited Gayle, who was then living about thirty-five miles away, to stay in my house. She did— and we sat up and talked until dawn! Ever since then, we talk *every* day, sometimes three or four times!"

Oprah gives Gayle credit for supporting her move to Chicago. "When I was offered a job with a talk show in Chicago, no one thought I would take it because the show was at the bottom of the ratings and it was up against 'Donahue,' " Oprah recalls. "But Gayle said, 'Leave Baltimore! I *know* you can beat "Donahue"!' Gayle has always been supportive of me, and telling me to move to Chicago was the best advice she's ever given me."

Chapter Three
From Chicago to the World

Luck is a matter of preparation. I am highly attuned
to my divine self.

—Oprah Winfrey, 1984

After seven years at WJZ-TV in Baltimore, Oprah made the jump to another ABC affiliate, to become host of WLS-TV's struggling "AM Chicago Show." In January 1984 Oprah took over the faltering program which ranked last in town. The show was up against the invincible "Donahue," and a long line of talented hosts had already failed in the attempt to unseat him.

Except for best friend Gayle King Bumpus, just about everybody warned Oprah against tackling the mighty Phil. "They said I was black, female and overweight. They said Chicago was a racist city," Oprah recalls. There was also a feeling in the industry that the whole talk show formula was on its way out.

It was Dennis Swanson, then vice president and general manager of WLS-TV and now president of ABC-TV Sports, who took one look at an audition tape Oprah had submitted and saw the woman who could challenge Phil

Donahue. "When you've looked at as many audition tapes as I have, hers just jumped out of the stack," he recalls.

In two months, Oprah was topping "Donahue" in the local ratings. In recognition, the show was soon renamed for her and expanded from a half-hour to an hour.

Soon Oprah was living in a glamorous high-rise with marble floors and a gold swan for a bathtub faucet, with views of Lake Michigan and the Chicago skyline to die for.

Oprah believes that she was able to succeed in Chicago because for the first time in her career she was working alone. Up until then, she had always been paired with someone else.

"The thing about working with a co-anchor or a co-host is that it can be stifling, like a bad marriage," Oprah says. "Somebody has always got to surrender to the other person. And usually, the person doing the surrendering was me. But I knew that I would just bide my time and get good at this—so good that moving to the next place would be easy."

But there was more to it than working alone. Oprah soon revealed an empathy, a warmth, that was unique in the history of television. "If Jane Pauley is the prom queen, Oprah Winfrey is the dorm counselor," *The Washington Post* wrote of her. "People want to hold Barbara Walters' hand. They want to crawl into Winfrey's lap."

She was also willing to share her inner feelings with her audience and guests, openly talking about the most personal matters like her weight, then up to 190 pounds. But she was never more open than on the morning in 1985 when she finally went public with the story of her own childhood abuse.

It happened live, on the air, while Oprah was interviewing another victim of sexual abuse. Suddenly, Oprah spoke up. "The same thing happened to me," she told her guest and her audience. "The fact that I had all these unfortunate experiences permeates my life."

It's possible that of all the people who were stunned and surprised by this revelation, Oprah Winfrey was the most stunned and surprised.

"I just wanted to say 'I understand,' " she said later. "I hadn't planned to say it. It just came out."

"I JUST WANTED AN EXTRA WEEK OFF"

In 1984 Steven Spielberg cast Oprah in *The Color Purple*, his film based on Alice Walker's Pulitzer Prize-winning novel. She had no acting experience, but it was an important supporting role in a lavish production.

Once again, Oprah's fate was guided by a mystical, unseen hand. Oprah had read Alice Walker's novel and even given copies to friends. She told them she felt destined to appear in the movie version, and she coveted the role of Sofia.

She has said that when she heard about the movie, "I prayed at night, 'Dear God, find me a way to get into this movie!' I would have done anything, 'best boy,' or 'water girl.' "

Fate stepped in in the form of composer-arranger Quincy Jones who turned up in Chicago in 1984 to testify in a lawsuit. Jones was coproducing *The Color Purple*, and he was putting the production together, insisting that Steven Spielberg direct. Jones had already racked up four Academy Awards as a scorer and arranger and composer. This was his chance to fulfill a longtime dream of becoming a film producer.

Jones insisted that Steven Spielberg direct the project. The youthful director had already made a bunch of successful films including *E.T., Jaws, Raiders of the Lost Ark,* and *Close Encounters of the Third Kind.* He was considered, however, a controversial choice for this project. Many in the black community thought the project should have gone to a black director. Others were dubious about Spielberg's ability to direct a "serious," issues-oriented story.

Spielberg openly acknowledged that he regarded *The Color Purple* as his biggest challenge yet: "It's as if I've been swimming in water up to my waist all my life—and I'm great at it—but now I'm going into the deep section of the pool."

Some Hollywood wags started referring to Spielberg's project as *Close Encounters with the Third World.*

Casting had only just begun when Jones caught Oprah's show on a television in his hotel room and immediately saw her potential. Jones arranged for Oprah to audition for the role of Sofia.

It was a stroke of luck that Quincy Jones was passing through Chicago and happened to turn on Oprah's popular local show. But to Oprah, "Luck is a matter of preparation. I am highly attuned to my divine self."

But don't get the idea Oprah is not eternally grateful to Quincy Jones for "discovering" her. She told a journalist that Quincy Jones was "the first person I have unconditionally loved in my whole life. He walks in the light. If something were to happen to Quincy Jones, I would weep for the rest of my life."

Oprah was so eager to appear in the movie that she didn't care about the money at all. She's always felt that way about her talk show, which can sometimes make for interesting conversations between Oprah and her long-time attorney and business partner, Jeffrey Jacobs. A former litigator, he has been working for Oprah since 1984 when she started out in Chicago.

"As her career progressed, I was handling more and more of her business matters," says Jacobs. "It got to where I was spending 60 or 70 percent of my time working with her, so I shut down my practice, and came in-house in 1987."

One of Jeffrey Jacobs's first jobs for his new client was negotiating her deal for *The Color Purple*. And although she was an untested actress who had been "discovered" by a random flip of the television dial, he insisted on getting her star terms.

"I love getting paid, but I'd do this [the talk show] for free if I had to," Oprah has said. "When Jeff was negotiating for me to appear in *The Color Purple,* he was pushing, pushing. I said, 'Jeff, I'd do it for nothing— please, *please* don't ask for any more money!' He said, 'You're *not* doing it for free.' "

Before Oprah could begin filming in South Carolina, however, she needed to juggle her schedule in Chicago. And her bosses at WLS did not like the idea.

"I just wanted an extra week off," Oprah recalls. She was happy with her contract and with the station, but she wanted to explore her other opportunities. And being cast in a key role in an important, big budget feature film was just such an opportunity.

Oprah and Jacobs realized that the only way to have the freedom and flexibility they craved was to control the talk show themselves.

Accordingly, Oprah and Jacobs began to look for a syndication contract. "It's always been my philosophy to try and control as much as your own destiny as possible," says Jacobs. This is a philosophy he passed on to Oprah. Together they soon made a deal with King World, until then best known for the hugely successful "Wheel of Fortune" and "Jeopardy," to distribute the show nationally.

Oprah's first contract with Capital Cities/ABC and King World Productions, Inc., to syndicate "The Oprah Winfrey Show" was quite lucrative. She received approximately twenty-five percent of total revenues after production and distribution costs.

The syndication made instant history, making Oprah a multimillionaire. But it was just the beginning of a brilliant master plan, conceived by Oprah and Jacobs, which would make broadcasting and financial history even as it would one day make Oprah the richest individual in the entertainment industry.

THE COLOR PURPLE

Set in rural Georgia in the early 1900s, *The Color Purple* opens with fourteen-year-old Celie (Desreta Jackson) giving birth to her second child by the man she calls "Pa" (Leonard Jackson), a cruel farmer who gives her babies away. The grown-up Celie (Whoopi Goldberg who had just been "discovered" in New York by director Mike Nichols doing a highly acclaimed one-woman show) is "given" to a widowed farmer known as "Mister" (Danny Glover) and spends the next twenty years of her life in servitude to this selfish, wife-beating adulterer. The only bright light in her life is her close bond with her younger sister, Nettie (Akosua Busia). Mister throws Nettie out, but the sisters maintain a secret correspondence for years.

Oprah's robust, proud, and physical Sofia marries Mister's son, Harpo (Willard Pugh).

Adolph Caesar portrayed Mister's mean-tempered father. A memorable performance was also given by Margaret Avery as the lusty blues singer Shug.

Oprah recalls her experience on the North Carolina set

of *The Color Purple* with pain, mainly because she felt intimidated and had no control.

All through filming, she felt that director Spielberg treated her coldly. "I thought he doesn't like me, I'm going to get kicked off the set," she stated. Actually, Spielberg was engaging in a sophisticated directing technique. Later, at the movie premiere, he would tell Oprah: "I realized how terrified you were, and that was working for you. That's why I never gave you any reassurance."

During one scene, where Sofia goes berserk, Oprah told a journalist that she was not acting at all. "Steven [Spielberg] had them [the other actors] call me 'nigger,' but he didn't tell me what he was going to do. 'You fat nigger bitch,' they said. Now I knew this is what it sounds like and this is what it feels like. After that, I left the scene and wept for a long time."

Oprah was experiencing another ordeal off the set, for the NAACP was picketing outside, protesting (sight unseen) the film's treatment of black men.

But there were rewards: "It was a spiritual involvement," Oprah has said about the film. "I learned to love people doing that film."

And another reward was a new close friendship with Whoopi Goldberg who told her: "It—and I mean It with a capital I—doesn't even start to happen until you're thirty-six."

With those stars, Spielberg's direction, and a Quincy Jones score rich with African, gospel, blues, and jazz influences, *The Color Purple* was destined to be a blockbuster, a promise it delivered from the moment it opened in December 1985. Dozens of people picketed the Hollywood premiere, arguing that the film reinforced black stereotypes by portraying black men as sadistic brutes. Protests from the NAACP and a group calling itself the

Coalition Against Black Exploitation would continue throughout the movie's release.

The Color Purple had all the right ingredients for a box office blockbuster: outstanding performances by a talented cast, plenty of sex (including a hint of incest and lesbianism), a touch of violence, racial discrimination, good original music, and some breathtaking scenes shot on location in Kenya.

But the movie also had an abundance of negative images of black people.

Spielberg, Jones, and Walker met the criticism head-on. They insisted that the film was not just about the "black experience," and the characters and situations could be about any family, any race, any ethnic group.

Jones said, "It's impossible to put the whole story of the black race in America in one picture. That's too much of a burden for any picture to take."

The Color Purple soon became the most talked about, most controversial film of the 1985–1986 season.

Gene Shalit of the "Today" show raved, "It should be against the law not to see *The Color Purple*."

Some critics accused Oprah of playing an "Aunt Jemima" role. "At first I was very kind," she responded. "Now I'm just ready to slap them."

In an otherwise scathing critique of the novel and the film in the intellectual magazine *Antioch Review* that summer, Gerald Early unwittingly hit on exactly the qualities of the story that must have appealed to Oprah.

According to Early:

"This 'liberal' film winds up purporting a very conservative ethic: we must all pull ourselves up by our emotional bootstraps. The victim, in essence, cures herself . . . *The Color Purple* has all the historical sense of 'Cinderella' . . . a superbly realized feminist cartoon about a woman, victimized by cruel relatives, who is transformed into a princess.''

You want to grab Early by his tweedy lapels and scream out: Yes, Professor, that's the point! Oprah *is* Cinderella! She's no cartoon, she's a flesh-and-blood woman who had come from poverty and abuse and was costarring in a movie!

"HOME AND STUDIO ARE THE ONLY PLACES I FEEL TOTALLY SAFE AND SECURE"

But Oprah's home base was and would remain the talk show. In fact, at times it was difficult to tell her high-rise and TV studio apart. Oprah seemed to acknowledge this when she said, ''Home and studio are the only places I feel safe and totally secure. In my TV studio, folks are like guests in my home.'' (Although one might point out that few of us require guests in our home to go through a metal detector and a phalanx of security guards before admission.)

As 1985 drew to a close, Oprah found herself at the peak of her career. True, she still lacked a steady man in her life, and she fretted about her burgeoning weight. But her work had never been more rewarding, and she was on the brink of going national, reaching a whole new audience.

Now the rest of America would see what all of Chicago was watching and talking about: the phenomenal Oprah Winfrey.

At thirty-one, Oprah was already financially comfortable. She had been drawing a six-figure salary since her salad days at WJZ-TV in Baltimore. Now, with a twenty-five percent piece of her show, Oprah was about to discover a degree of riches and fame that the little Mississippi farm girl, the nine-year-old rape victim, the pregnant Milwaukee runaway, could never have imagined.

Oprah has always been eager to share her good fortune with those she considers her friends, and her generosity was already becoming legendary. That Christmas 1985, when WLS-TV refused raises for seven members of her staff, Oprah gave each of them a $10,000 bonus in cash, stuffed inside rolls of toilet paper.

"It was great," she observed, "everyone wept and had a wonderful time. It feels good to do things like that with no strings attached, just because I can."

Chapter Four
Make Way for Miss Winfrey!

I asked the spirit, "Lord, could you do something about this man situation in my life? I get so tired of runnin' into these no-good men who don't have a job and want my money." So I asked the spirit, "Would you send me somebody? Lord, could he be smart? Could he have some intelligence? And if you don't mind, could he be tall? And the spirit, He sent me Stedman.

—Oprah Winfrey, recalling the beginning of her romance with Stedman Graham, 1986

The year 1986 everything seemed to come together: *The Color Purple* had opened to rave reviews, especially for Oprah's luminous performance; in January she was nominated for an Academy Award, and "The Oprah Winfrey Show" was scheduled to go national in September. And by the end of the year she would be dating Stedman Graham.

But Oprah was not about to forget her roots or the troubled girl she had been. When a friend asked her to help in a Big Sisters project designed to help troubled Chicago girls, Oprah was ready, asking only that her generosity be kept a secret.

"Oprah and I had developed a slight friendship," recalls Carolyn Shelton, founder of the project. "She said 'Carolyn, if you ever start a Little Sister program with these kids, I want to get involved.' "

Carolyn had been running Employability Plus, a program for children at Chicago's Cabrini Green, one of the country's worst public housing projects. Employability Plus was designed to teach the kids the etiquette they needed to find a job and function in the world outside the projects.

She came up with the idea for a Little Sister program in 1986, designed to save the girls from the pitfalls of drugs, early pregnancy, and despair.

Oprah opened her heart and her home to the girls, even inviting them to slumber parties, ordering pizza, and sitting up all night talking and watching TV.

Sometimes she would take them shopping for a day in her limousine. Other times, she took some of the girls to meet her relatives in Nashville. She even took them on a group ski trip.

Many of the girls had never eaten in a restaurant before. They were angry and potentially violent, but they were deeply touched that this wealthy television star would care about them and their future.

The Big Sisters had only one rule: If you got pregnant, you were out. "We tell the kids that if you want affection, you don't need a baby," explained Oprah. "Get a kitten instead."

Carolyn says, "Oprah was always interested in the girls and willing to help. She came to speak several times and never hesitated to pitch in.

"I was a little in awe of her, considering the projects are very dangerous. She's a big star, and anything could happen out there."

Oprah showered love on the twenty-four girls, ten to thirteen years old, and matched two each with twelve volunteers from the Cabrini staff and her own company, Harpo, Inc. Oprah also donated money to start the program.

Her friend, Quincy Jones, came up with a name for the

program: Kidadah, which means Little Sister in Swahili. "We thought it heritage-filled and very beautiful," said Carolyn.

Oprah wanted the girls to learn to appreciate books and education. "Getting library cards was the first thing we did together, and it was Oprah's idea," said Carolyn.

"It became a rule that to be in the program you had to have a Chicago public library card. The girls had to read at least a book a week, and keep their grades up."

Oprah even invited the girls to a special screening of *The Color Purple*.

Oprah shared her feelings about God and the need to find a source of spiritual strength in their lives, but it is sad that she never shared with them one of the most painful experiences she had gone through, namely that she had given birth to a child at fourteen. For some reason, she chose to still refer to herself as among those who had escaped the trap of early pregnancy. There were no doubt feelings of shame, sorrow, and a good dose of denial contributing to her silence.

"AFRICA, PURPLE 11 SPIELBERG 0"

When the Oscar nominations were announced in January, both *Out of Africa*, which starred Meryl Streep and Robert Redford, directed by Sydney Pollack, and *The Color Purple* each snared eleven nominations, including Best Picture and Best Supporting Actress for Oprah. But Steven Spielberg was conspicuously missing from the nominations, leading to much industry chatter, and a memorable headline in the *Los Angeles Herald-Examiner*: "Africa, Purple 11 Spielberg 0."

Whoopi Goldberg, nominated for Best Actress, was among those who rushed to Spielberg's defense, pointing out that the director had drawn nomination-worthy performances from two first-timers, herself and Oprah Winfrey.

Whoopi called the Motion Picture Academy of Arts and Sciences "a small bunch of people with small minds who choose to ignore the obvious." Perhaps because of the stresses she experienced on the set, Oprah did not publicly rise to Spielberg's defense.

Oprah also chose not to campaign actively for the Academy's votes, unlike Margaret Avery who had also been nominated for Best Supporting Actress for her performance as Shug. She campaigned hard in the "trades" with ads in black English soliciting votes. The ads were controversial and probably backfired, turning off more voters than they turned on.

The Academy Awards ceremony was held in Los Angeles at the Dorothy Chandler Pavilion on March 24. The cohosts were Jane Fonda, Alan Alda, and Robin Williams. It was telecast live over the ABC network. Oprah arrived swathed in a $10,000 dyed-purple fox coat.

There was a nice moment when Marsha Mason and Richard Dreyfus prepared to announce Best Supporting Actress, and a seemingly overconfident Margaret Avery reached back to shake Oprah's hand. Or it may have been simply a moment of two sisters giving each other moral support. Alas, the winner was Anjelica Huston for *Prizzi's Honor*.

Whoopi Goldberg was up against even stiffer competition, including Jessica Lange and Meryl Streep; the Oscar went to Geraldine Page. Oprah would soon be working with Page in her next movie, *Native Son*.

The following month Oprah had another clue to how far she had come from her grandmother's dirt-poor farm in Kosciusko when she attended the star-studded wedding of Arnold Schwarzenegger and Maria Shriver in Hyannis, Massachusetts.

Oprah's talk show finally went national that September. Almost instantly, it became a ratings giant, an American institution, and the name "Oprah" became a household word.

That December Oprah's new movie premiered and disappeared almost as quickly. *Native Son* was a well-intentioned film adaptation of Richard Wright's classic novel about a poor black man who accidentally kills a white woman. A coproduction of PBS's "American Playhouse" and directed by Jerrold Freedman, it featured a cast of outstanding actors including Geraldine Page and Matt Dillon, but critics complained that changes in the script had softened the novel's disturbing truths and themes.

Native Son came to the screen and then vanished without much of a ripple. While Oprah in the role of Mrs. Thomas was singled out for praise, the project as a whole—difficult to translate from book to film—faltered in the end.

The film disappeared quickly, and remains most notable in Oprah's life because it was at the December premiere at Harlem's Apollo Theatre that the public got its first look at the new man in Oprah's life, Stedman Graham. The couple was snapped by paparazzo Ron Galella, with mink-wrapped Oprah giving the thumbs-up sign as they entered the theatre.

At thirty-two, after a lifetime of terrible relationships, Oprah had finally found the man of her dreams. Four years earlier, in the journal she has kept since her teens, Oprah had written: "I'm not married. I'm *never* going to be. Oh, my God! What's my life? My life's nothing!" And as usual, she credited her belief in "the spirit" for bringing him to her.

"I asked the spirit, 'Lord, could you do something about this man situation in my life? I get so tired of runnin' into these no-good men who don't have a job and want my money.' So I asked the spirit, 'Would you send me somebody? Lord, could he be smart? Could he have some intelligence? And if you don't mind, could he be tall?' And the spirit, He sent me Stedman.''

If Oprah's fans were able to order up the ideal man for her, he would probably look and act an awful lot like Stedman Graham. Tall, movie-star handsome, a former basketball star who is now a partner in a Winston-Salem based public relations agency, he comes across as the strong, silent type, very devoted to Oprah but very much his own man.

Stedman appreciates Oprah's celebrity status, but he is not overly impressed by it. He has been through it himself.

''I played ball all my life and went through the whole gamut—a star in grade school and high school, people yelling and screaming for me. I thought I was God's gift to humanity. Anything I did had the Midas touch,'' Stedman acknowledges. He was forced to face reality after the cheering stopped.

''I went through a transformation when the fans stopped screaming,'' he acknowledges. ''It was like, what now?''

He had known Oprah through his work with Athletes Against Drugs, a nonprofit organization he cofounded in 1985 to counsel young athletes. But a casual, pleasant acquaintance would need a little time to evolve into a serious romance.

INSIDE "THE OPRAH WINFREY SHOW"

At eight o'clock on a typical morning, armed guards would be securing the entrance to ''The Oprah Winfrey Show'' and preparing to admit her audience for the day.

Mostly women, they would flash smiles as they passed through the metal detectors. Oprah's team of producers would check out the crowd with the air of Secret Service agents guarding the President. (Producer Mary Kay Clinton has said, "I would take a bullet for her.")

Journalist James Brady, who visited the show in 1986, when it was still at the WLS-TV studios, recalls his experience:

"On the morning I was on her show, I got there very early. I like to see a studio when it's still empty and quiet. You get a feel for it. The green room where I waited had a beat-up old piano, painted red, and one end of the long, narrow was set up for makeup and hair. There were three guests that morning, Fred Gershon, who'd written a book about the world of rock music; Jackie Collins, whose latest novel was *Hollywood Husbands,* and myself."

While Brady was in the green room, Oprah was preparing for her show.

"Oprah hugged us all, reminded me I'd been on her show in Baltimore, and reviewed cardboard cue cards like the gray cardboards they put inside shirts at the laundry.

"Out in the hallway, people were lined up waiting to be let into the studio to play audience, some men among them, but mostly women, mostly white."

The studio, Brady recalls, was relatively small and narrow, with a raised platform where Oprah's guests sat and a few spindly bleachers for the audience, maybe fifty or sixty people tops.

"Oprah works standing up. Or, rather, she works moving around, mike in hand, up and down the two aisles of the bleachers, down onto the floor of the studio, back up again. If you are accustomed to talk shows of the Johnny Carson style, where the host is nailed down, this can be somewhat disconcerting, with Oprah a moving target."

Actually, of course, as media-junkies know, this was a style of talk show hosting that was pioneered by Phil Donahue. Oprah freely acknowledges her debt to Donahue in terms of the basic format, but everyone knows that not even the great Phil has Oprah's empathy with the anguished, her rapport with the rabble.

"I've done so much TV," Brady confesses, "I can usually bully a talk show host, not literally, of course, but in steering the talk and the q & a. You can't do that with Oprah. She keeps pulling you back to what she wants to talk about. And she does it deftly. I was trying to talk about myself, quoting film director Frank Perry and a funny story he tells about cocaine in Hollywood where, if you can't afford coke, you take tennis lessons.

"I felt sort of silly," Brady admits. "But not annoyed at Oprah, more at myself for not being able to yank the talk back to the book I wrote and not to the other books. Men and women in the audience stood up and, as Oprah shoved the mike under their noses, they asked questions. Other questions came in by phone, over a sort of loudspeaker system. When viewers or the studio audience weren't asking questions, Oprah was. She gives good question. And, and this is important to an author, she keeps mentioning the book, the camera keeps focusing on its dust jacket.

"During the commercials she keeps up a running patter, with the guests, with the audience, with her staffers, who keep running around with cue cards. It is genially organized chaos. But once the red light goes back on, stop the cameras, it is all business once again, amiable business, because that is Oprah's way, but business nonetheless."

Brady was especially pleased when his book sales went

up all over the country after his appearance on "The Oprah Winfrey Show."

But it was 1986, and the jury was still out on how she would fare against the mighty Donahue, although those inside Chicago's Loop knew that she had already trounced him in the ratings there. In fact, there were many of the opinion that Donahue's move from Chicago to New York had been inspired, at least in part, by a desire to get away from direct competition with Oprah.

"Will she top Donahue?" Brady asked in 1986, as the rest of the country was just discovering Oprah. "It is too early to say and Donahue too resourceful a man to be written off. But as I walked down the hallway to the elevators, I talked to some of the people who made up Oprah's audience. Was it a tough ticket? I asked. The woman I asked didn't understand the expression. 'How long did you have to wait to see Oprah?' I said.

"The woman said she had been waiting two years."

Typically, Oprah was up by six. The alarm rang and she hit the floor running, starting the day with a shower and a mental scrub down: How did she feel about the upcoming show? Was she ready? Was she "centered"?

She listened for an intuition about how to handle a touchy subject. She prepared her facts. She did her reading, but she liked to operate from her gut instead of from scripted questions. She preferred the adrenaline and added intimacy of asking "what feels right" to working from a more formal agenda.

So whenever she had tricky material, which was often, Oprah liked to meditate before tackling it. This meditating, "just getting quiet," was done anytime and anywhere she could. Sometimes in bed before sleep, sometimes in the morning shower, in the elevator on the way down to street level, in the back of the waiting car.

Several times a day, Oprah "checked in" this way. "I have to stay with the flow," she explains. "I have four Bibles and use them all.

"People talk about spirituality like it's a very complicated thing," Oprah says. "I don't think it is. I just try to listen to how I really feel. If something feels right, I do it. If it feels wrong, I don't. It's really very, very simple, but you've got to be willing to take your chances doing stuff that may look crazy to other people—or not doing something that looks right to others but just feels wrong to you."

The issue of blame was important to Oprah. To her, blame is the opposite of personal responsibility, which she sees as the first and most important step toward freedom. Blaming others for our fate or accepting blame from others for theirs keeps women from accepting responsibility for changing the things they can.

Oprah has never shied away from emotional issues. This was how startled audiences learned of her own rape at age nine and subsequent sexual abuse by relatives. Network dismay at these revelations was soothed by rocketing ratings.

As *Newsday*'s TV critic Marvin Kitman says, "She was the first one to really reveal herself; in doing that she changed the whole climate of TV talk shows. And she had plenty to confess."

When Oprah emerges from her dressing room, ready to begin the show, and is spotted by the crowd, a spontaneous chant often goes up: "Oprah! Oprah! O-prah!" There are photos to be autographed, hands to be shaken, crowds to be navigated with a mixture of acknowledgment and reserve, the tightrope of connection and distance that celebrities must balance upon.

THE REAL REASONS PEOPLE APPEAR ON THE SHOW

Why do so many people willingly bare their souls—openly discussing their perverse acts and shocking practices—on TV talk shows like Oprah's? The main reason may be that they are trying to rid themselves of shame and guilt.

According to psychiatrist Danilo Ponce, "The leading TV talk shows have become a kind of electronic confessional. They're similar to group therapy and Alcoholics Anonymous, where troubled people confess to others to overcome their problems."

Psychiatrist James Hodge agrees: "It's a new form of magical thinking—the idea that 'letting it all hang out' on TV will purge shame and guilt."

Among the secondary reasons these experts believe that we watch shows like "Oprah":

★ *The need for recognition*. "There are people so starved for attention they're willing to do anything to get it, even airing their dirty linen in public," said Dr. Ponce, a professor of psychiatry at the University of Hawaii Medical School.

★ *The need for understanding*. "Many child molesters, sexual deviants and rapists feel misunderstood," said Dr. Hodge, a professor of psychiatry at Northeastern Ohio University's College of Medicine. "Talk shows give them the opportunity to explain themselves."

★ *The need for acceptance*. When some disturbed people see the guests on talk shows being praised by the hosts, or applauded by the audiences, "they are encouraged to expose their own sleazy pasts to enjoy similar approval," Dr. Ponce explained.

★ *The need for sympathy*. Dr. Hodge notes that audiences are often very supportive of the guests. "Even when the guest has been guilty of a heinous crime," Hodge observes, "there is almost always at least one person who commends him for his openness and honesty and expresses sympathy for what he has suffered."

TALK SHOW HOSTS HELP MANY COPE WITH LIFE

Talk show hosts like Oprah have replaced the family in helping people solve problems.

Dr. Howard Garrell, a New York psychoanalyst who has done a three-year study of talk show viewers, has found that "for many people, Oprah and the others are the only family they have to rely on when facing everyday problems concerning love, marriage, stress, ill health, job, money and friends."

The prime reasons people have for replacing their real family with the electronic family: Most of us live a far distance from the people we should feel closest to—and the older generation is no longer equipped to help us solve today's problems.

"Many of the toughest personal difficulties people face today involve situations former generations haven't experienced, such as divorce, remarriage, stepparenting, surrogate childbearing, abortion, drug abuse and sex abuse," says Dr. Garrell.

"What does anyone's 80-year-old grandmother or 65-year-old uncle know about the stress of being a supermom, or husband-coached childbirth or talking to a teen about AIDS?"

Dr. Garrell says that "The world has changed so dramatically and rapidly that the older generation can no longer provide wisdom, comfort and help. The talk show hosts have stepped into that void.

"They offer helpful information, furnish data on subjects you might be embarrassed to discuss with someone you know, supply hope and direction—and are friendly and gracious regardless of how indiscreet you've been, your physical appearance or frame of mind, or how much you've contributed to your trouble."

What's more, avid talk show viewers are healthier, happier and better adjusted than nonviewers, said Dr. Garrell.

"They're better informed about health matters, complain less about loneliness and insecurity, feel more in control of their lives—and enjoy better relationships with their spouses and children."

WATCHING "OPRAH" CAN BE GOOD FOR YOU

Watching talk shows like "Oprah" can be good for YOUR mental health, according to Dr. Howard Glazer, assistant professor of psychology at Cornell University. "The shows deal with real people and their problems and the information you obtain can benefit your emotional state," says Dr. Glazer.

Dr. Glazer says such shows:

★ *Help put your own problems in better perspective.* "Many guests have major problems, much bigger than the ones we normally face," says Dr. Glazer. "When we hear these people talk, for instance, about a husband or wife with AIDS, your current fight with your spouse about the way to hang wallpaper pales in comparison."

★ *Give suggestions you can implement.* TV talk show guests sometimes have problems that are similar to the ones you face, and it's good to listen to them to see how they deal with the situation. For instance, a talk show may feature parents whose children are out of control. The parents recount what the kids have done and the solutions both successful and unsuccessfull they've tried.

"Your child may not be totally out of control but the case histories of the talk show guests may suggest constructive discipline techniques you could implement," says Dr. Glazer.

★ *Teach acceptance of others*. Many times TV talk shows present people that are a lot different from you, and listening to them can make you a more compassionate person. For example, you may feel that all prostitutes are despicable people, but you might find out that they are real women with very human fears and homes, said Dr. Glazer.

★ *Let you know you are not the only one with problems*. Perhaps you found out that your spouse had an affair. You're devastated, at the end of your rope. But when Oprah gives you a whole panel of people whose mates have had affairs, you learn you're not alone. That realization can help give you the strength to deal with the problem.

Others have resolved it—and there's no reason you can't, too!

TV TALK SHOWS CAN IMPROVE YOUR LIFE

One expert believes that just by watching programs like the "Oprah Winfrey Show" you can improve your life.

"Hosts like Oprah uncover the most fascinating qualities of ordinary people and experts alike," says psychiatrist Alfred Coodley. "It's not only great entertainment, it can make your life better."

That's because talk shows:

★ *Give you free advice on practical matters*. By tuning in, you get the best tips about nutrition, weight control, fashion, problem-solving and other vital topics.

★ *Improve family relationships*. A common subject on talk shows, for example, is extramarital affairs. As guests recount their experiences, you can learn what may draw a spouse into an affair—and how you can help prevent it.

★ *Help you understand human behavior*.

★ *Teach compassion*. Talk shows provide you with an emotional outlet. "If Oprah discusses spouse abuse and guests air their experiences, you can sympathize with the victims' pain, fear and shame. You become a more sensitive person," says Dr. Coodley.

★ *Overcome feelings of isolation*. "One time or another, most people feel isolated and alone," said the psychiatrist.

"Watching a talk show helps you feel connected to other people because guests reveal intimate things about themselves. Just feeling closer to other people can help you overcome a lonely time in your own life."

★ *You can also study talk show hosts' techniques and adapt them into your life*. Study how Oprah expresses true concern for people going through difficulties.

MOST FOLKS WOULD CONFESS TO OPRAH

If you were going to tell your innermost secrets to the world, which talk show host would you confess to?

That's what the *National Enquirer* asked fifty men and fifty women in five cities—and their choice was overwhelming: Oprah Winfrey.

The *Enquirer* asked people to select among Oprah, Phil Donahue, Sally Jessy Raphael, and Geraldo Rivera.

77

And an impressive fifty-four of the one hundred persons polled picked Oprah—exactly TWICE the twenty-seven who opted for Donahue!

Sally was third with fourteen votes—and Geraldo was the choice of just five persons.

Not surprisingly, the women that the *Enquirer* surveyed in the five cities (New York, Philadelphia, Orlando, San Francisco, and Washington, D.C.) were especially fond of Oprah. A solid sixty-eight percent said they'd choose her for their public revelations. Sally was second among women with sixteen percent, followed by Donahue with twelve percent and Geraldo with only four.

But men preferred Donahue to Oprah by a narrow margin—forty-two percent to forty. Just twelve percent chose Sally, and six percent favored Geraldo.

"I'd pick Oprah—she has the most heart," declared one polled Washingtonian.

A San Francisco student agreed: "Oprah is warm and easy to talk to. There's no brick wall between her and her guests."

NOT EVERYONE IS A FAN OF "OPRAH"

Not everyone is a fan. In an angry blast at talk shows in general, talk show legend Jack Paar blasted that today's hosts are a ratings-hungry pack of sleaze merchants, and charged they were polluting the airwaves with freaks, sex deviates, and other trash. "It reminds me very much of the circus days of years ago when for a dime you could go down to the sideshow and see the geeks," said Paar. "Oprah is a sideshow."

And then there was the husband who threatened to kill his estranged wife because she refused to watch "Oprah" with him. John Annis, of Petersborough, Ontario, called up his wife Hella, and eagerly told her to watch "The

Oprah Winfrey Show'' because the subject that day was ''forgiveness.'' When she said she wouldn't do it, he went completely berserk.

Annis stormed over to his wife's home and pounded on the door. She wouldn't let him in—so he crashed through the kitchen window, and then threatened to kill her. Hella kneed him in the groin, fled the house, and called police.

When cops finally cornered Annis he tried to drive off—with a policeman clinging to the hood of the car. Mr. Annis was given plenty of time to watch his favorite talk show. He was sentenced to six months in the slammer.

Chapter Five
Oprah Winfrey Arrives

Face it, when a man like Stedman—as good-looking as Stedman—starts dating a woman like me,
people are going to talk.
    —Oprah Winfrey on the man in her life, 1987

By 1987 "The Oprah Winfrey Show" was a certified mega-hit and Oprah was raking in big bucks because she had opted to take a hefty twenty-five percent of gross revenue rather than a star-size salary. The previous year Oprah had earned $7.5 million, and she would make much, much more this year because stations were paying up to four times more than they had in 1986. The little girl from Kosciusko had become the Queen Bee of Syndication.

That January, as Oprah marked her thirty-third birthday, she could honestly say, "It's a glorious time for me. I'm doing exactly what I wanted to be doing at age thirty-three. I feel I'm ripening, coming into my own. It's an exciting time, an exciting age."

She was living in a $800,000 apartment on the fifty-seventh floor of an exclusive high-rise with a glorious view of Lake Michigan and the Chicago skyline; she traveled around town in a chauffeur-driven Mercedes limousine, but she was still the little Baptist girl from Kosciusko.

"My ability to acquire things has changed," she said, "but *I* don't feel any different. So, I keep saying to myself, 'Well, I guess I'm not a star yet, because I don't feel like one.'"

Not that Oprah didn't enjoy all the privileges of her soaring income. Her personal indulgences included a wardrobe of fur coats. Her recently decorated, marble-floored apartment was accented with such high-tech touches as pedestal lamps that one visitor compared to fluorescent rocket ships. The custom-designed furniture was swathed in fabrics of either deep purple or cream.

That March Oprah returned to the Academy Awards to present the Oscar for Documentary Feature. The winner was a tie between a documentary on bandleader Artie Shaw and one on the homeless, *Down and Out in America*.

She was still concerned about her weight which was hovering around 180 pounds. "It *is* an obsession," she acknowledged. "It's all any overweight woman talks about. It just happens that I'm in the public eye so people think I talk about it more." She was planning to hire a trainer and a cook to help her get into shape.

And ABC was negotiating with Harpo Productions to develop a situation comedy to star Oprah. She would play a single talk show host living in Chicago, but in June plans were dropped after a disappointing pilot.

Oprah thoroughly enjoyed being a talk show giant, but she didn't want to look like one, so in March she hired Phil Damen (a nutritionist, cook, and exercise trainer) to help her lose some serious pounds. She desperately wanted to squeeze into a chic gown that had been designed for her by Bob Mackie for the Academy Awards where she was scheduled to be a presenter.

And Oprah was rapidly discovering that there could be a downside to stardom. In July she ducked into an airport ladies' room at the Los Angeles airport, with about ten female fans following her, and went into a stall. When she emerged, the women were right there and broke into a round of applause.

Oprah was more than a little embarrassed, but cheerfully signed autographs for all.

That June, Oprah swept the Daytime Emmys. Notably absent from the winners' circle was Phil Donahue whose show had dominated the category for more than a decade. It was as if their colleagues in the television industry were acknowledging that Oprah had taken the talk show format so brilliantly pioneered by Phil Donahue and enriched it, bringing it to a whole new level of entertainment, information, and service.

"The Oprah Winfrey Show" took all three top awards, for Outstanding Talk/Service Show, Outstanding Talk/Service Show Host, and Outstanding Directing of a Talk/Service Show to Jim McPharlin. The Outstanding Show award was shared by Executive producer Debra Di Maio, and producers Mary Kay Clinton, Christine Tardio, Dianne Hudson, and Ellen Rakietan.

Oprah was a hostess of the afternoon ceremony which was attended by over a thousand fans at the Sheraton Center in New York and aired by the ABC network, viewed by a record thirty-six percent of its daytime audience. Afterwards, Oprah and Stedman danced until dawn at Stringfellow's, a New York nightclub.

That July Oprah was so ecstatic about shedding nearly twenty pounds that she went on a shopping spree and bought $25,000 worth of dresses, skirts, blouses, etc., in her new size—fourteen.

"Now I've got to keep the weight off or I'll have a closetful of expensive clothes that won't fit," said Oprah.

In fact, she was so terrified of regaining the weight that she had tacked a photo of herself at her tubbiest to the door of her clothes closet.

OPRAH GOES TO FORSYTH COUNTY

That year, Oprah made news when she took her show to racially troubled Forsyth County, Georgia. No black person had lived in Forsyth County, population forty-two thousand, since 1912 when a white teenager was allegedly lynched by three black men who were subsequently lynched.

Oprah came, she explained, not to challenge or to confront, but to "explore people's feelings . . . to ask why."

Outside, longtime civil rights activist Rev. Hosea Williams led a small group of demonstrators protesting the show's all-white Forsyth audience. Williams publicly accused Oprah of having "turned all white."

Inside, Oprah listened as a guest in the audience explained to her the difference between "blacks" and "niggers." It seemed that "niggers" are blacks who make trouble.

And the audience at home saw and heard racial hatred, anguish, confusion, ignorance and one very brave black woman. Her composure was magnificent—even when a hate-monger asked his fellows: "How many of you who welcome blacks or niggers would want your son or daughter to marry one?" Her dignity was unassailable.

"SEE, DADDY, I AMOUNTED TO SOMETHING"

Oprah was finally able to pay back her parents for all that they had done for her. That fall, she insisted that her mother Vernita retire from her job as a hospital dietician, offering Vernita double her salary for the rest of her life. Oprah also bought Vernita a beautiful house in Milwaukee.

Vernon refused all gifts proffered by his daughter, saying all he wanted was a ticket to Mike Tyson's next fight. His celebrity daughter did more than that, she *took* Vernon to Las Vegas to see the championship match between Tyson and Tyrell Biggs.

Oprah was photographed looking proud and happy between the two most important men in her life: Vernon Winfrey and Stedman Graham.

The fight itself was a bit shocking for Oprah. She screamed when Tyson slugged Biggs so hard that his mouthpiece flew out of his mouth and landed in her lap. She shrieked until a bystander plucked it and tossed it back to Biggs's trainer.

Vernon Winfrey had not wanted his daughter to leave college in her senior year to take a job in Baltimore. He had encouraged her studies, and he wanted to see her finish college. He had been deeply disappointed when Oprah chose broadcasting over education and gave up her scholarship at Tennessee State University.

Somewhere deep inside her, Oprah always felt that she had let her father down.

And then that summer of 1987, as TSU's most famous alumna, Oprah was asked to give the commencement address.

Oprah agreed, but insisted that she finish her course credits first so that she could finally get her own degree.

On Commencement Day, she told the audience that her father had said she would never amount to anything until she got that degree. As soon as she got the diploma, she waved it in front of the crowd and said, "See, Daddy, I amounted to something."

Oprah also honored Vernon Winfrey in a more tangible way: by endowing ten scholarships at Tennessee State University in his name.

SPOTTED EATING HOT DOGS

The diet struggle continued, and Oprah complained that she couldn't have a pancake without it ending up in the tabloids. Sure enough, when she was spotted on a Los Angeles sidewalk, downing not one, not two, but three hot dogs dripping with mustard, onions, and sauerkraut, it made news.

STEDMAN

And Oprah was being seen more and more with Stedman Graham. At the Academy Awards in March, at the Daytime Emmys in June, at the NAACP Legal Defense and Educational Fund's National Equal Justice Award Dinner in New York in October, at the Twentieth Annual NAACP Image Awards and the Forty-Seventh Annual Golden Apple Awards, both in Los Angeles in December.

They looked to be very much in love, but Oprah knew about the whispers around them, mainly from people who didn't understand where she was coming from.

"Face it," she said, "when a man like Stedman—as good-looking as Stedman—starts dating a woman like me, people are going to talk."

Oprah insisted she was not talking about low self-worth, simply acknowledging reality. Stedman Graham was tall, dark, and movie-star handsome. (One might note that as a slim, elegant dark-skinned man, he resembled her adored father.) *Cosmopolitan* magazine described him "as rakish and debonair as Brenda Starr's Mystery Man."

Even longtime staff members—her family of choice—were wary of the relationship at first. "She was overweight and he was so attractive," producer Mary Kay Clinton acknowledged, "and we wanted to know: What's he after? What's he coming here for? Where did he come from?"

A former college athlete, a community leader on youth and drug issues, Stedman Graham was that rare combination: high-profile and closemouthed.

Oprah understood people's reaction to the sight of them together, and she tried to be philosophical about it. "People ask questions, and they are going to come up with their own answers."

Such as? she was asked.

"Money. They look at him and they look at me and they think, *Money. That's what he sees in her*—but they're wrong."

Sometimes trying to be philosophical didn't work, and Oprah's feelings got the best of her.

"They're way off! Way off! Stedman is the most independent, the most stubborn, the most proud . . . That man wouldn't take a nickel from me. Not that he needs to."

"A VERY DEAR FRIEND IS LIVING WITH AIDS"

That September, Oprah took the podium at a fundraiser for AIDS research in Chicago and told the audience: "A very dear friend of mine is living with AIDS." It would be a year until it was revealed that the "dear friend" was her longtime aide, Billy Rizzo.

Oprah was also quietly admitting to friends that she had "dropped a bundle" in the collapse of the stock market. She sold all her shares and joked that from now on she was through playing the market—she would stick to playing bingo.

HER GENEROSITY

But nothing gave Oprah greater pleasure that year than sharing her newfound fortune with her friends and co-workers. Before Christmas, she took three producers and her publicist to New York on a madcap trip that was half game/half shopping spree at some of the priciest stores in the world.

Christine Tardio, one of Oprah's producers, recalls the pleasure trip: "We go to Bergdorf's and she hands us each an envelope and in the envelope is a slip of paper and it says you have one hour to spend X amount of money. So we are frantically running around shopping and then she walks around and pays for everybody."

There was more the next day, when they went for boots and shoes at Maud Frizon, then on to a posh furrier where everyone got her choice of a mink or fox coats. "She was a little kid through the whole thing," Tardio recalled. "Oh! She's wonderful."

"I HAVE ARRIVED!"

By the end of 1987, "The Oprah Winfrey Show" was listed among the top five shows in syndication, with almost nine million households tuned in daily.

Oprah would never forget the moment when she realized she had really "arrived" as a star. It came during the 1987 Christmas holidays.

She had been invited to Aspen, Colorado, by Quincy Jones and suddenly found herself rubbing shoulders with the likes of Barbra Streisand, Jane Fonda, and Don Johnson.

She confesses that she was thrown for a loop, because she considered herself dull next to such glittering celebrities.

"I'm one of the most boring people you'd ever meet," she said. "This Aspen Christmas scene was unbelievable!

"You walk into a room and there's Barbra Streisand and Jane Fonda sitting on the floor. You try to be cool: 'Oh, hi, Barbra. Hi, Jane. Nice to see you.'

"One night, Don Johnson was having a party. So Quincy said, 'Look, babe, come to Don's house.'

"We get up to Don's house and I see people being turned back because their name isn't on the guest list. I say, 'God, if You love me, please let my name be on this list.'

"I get out of the car and a guy goes: 'Oh, hi, Miss Winfrey—go on in.' I think 'There is a God!' I didn't have to be embarrassed and turned away."

When handsome Don Johnson opened the door, Oprah turned to jelly.

"Don goes, 'Hey, Oprah. Here's a margarita.' Like he was expecting me or something.

"I go, 'Oh, God, I can't believe it. This is Don Johnson. I have arrived!' "

Chapter Six
Taking Control

If you have lived as a black person in America, you know all of those women, you just know them. They're your aunts, your mother, your cousins, your nieces.
—Oprah Winfrey, as she was about to coproduce and star in a TV miniseries based on the controversial novel, *The Women of Brewster Place*, 1988

In 1988, Oprah was jogging seven miles a day and earning an estimated hourly wage of $3,846 (the same as Phil Donahue).

Her spiritual side was as strong as ever. Oprah read a Bible verse every morning and believed that her life was directed by a kind of supernaturally inspired instinct. "I am guided by a higher calling," she said. "It's not so much a voice as it is a feeling. If it doesn't feel right to me, I don't do it."

Another way Oprah stated her philosophy: "It is easier to go with the river than to try to swim upstream. Anything negative that happens to me is because I have been fighting against the stream."

Oprah certainly looked like a star when she was in Aspen in January 1988 and stopped in at a bookstore party to help promote Donald Trump's new book, *The*

Art of the Deal. She was wrapped in a $200,000 sable coat, smiling broadly.

Sure, there were some awkward or strained moments, such as when Elizabeth Taylor appeared on the show to promote her new diet book. Many felt that Taylor gave Oprah a hard time in the interview, pressing her about her weight. But in spite of that, 1988 promised to be a year to stretch and grow and take on new challenges.

The biggest challenge awaiting Oprah may have been "The Women of Brewster Place," which she both co-executive produced and starred in. The four-hour ABC-TV miniseries, based on Gloria Naylor's best-selling novel, was the story of seven black women who shared the same tenement address in a northern city over several decades. (It would air in March 1989.)

"I read a lot," Oprah says, "and I try to read as many black authors as I can. I was reading *Brewster Place* while filming *The Color Purple,* and I decided then that I wanted it to be [a filmed project] that I could take part in.

"It's a great story," she told an interviewer. "It involves all these women and their spirit of survival and their attempt to maintain their dignity in a world that tries to strip them of it."

Perhaps, too, she had something to prove. "People said *The Color Purple* was a fluke for me," she told a journalist. "I had my own personal doubts. But in doing this movie, I discovered I really am an actress."

She also identified strongly with the women in the book. "If you have lived as a black person in America, you know all of those women, you just know them," she said. "They're your aunts, your mother, your cousins, your nieces."

Coincidentally, Reuben Cannon, the respected casting agent who is said to have had an important part in casting

Oprah for *The Color Purple* had also just read *The Women of Brewster Place*. "It became one of my favorite books," he recalls. "Then Carol [Isenberg, associate producer on *The Color Purple*] called me about *Brewster Place*, and the very next day, Oprah called and said, 'I hear something's going on with *Brewster Place*.' It was psychic energy. If Oprah didn't exist, I don't think this project would have happened."

Oprah landed the film rights, only to discover that none of the big three networks was interested in it. But Oprah believed in it. She saw it as a vehicle to tell simple, moving stories. She had to wait a few years until ABC came to her about other projects and she suggested *Brewster Place* instead.

"I'M INSULTED. I'M MORE CONSCIOUS OF MY LEGACY AS A BLACK PERSON THAN ANYBODY."

It was during a meeting with Brandon Stoddard, then president of ABC entertainment, that she pulled out a copy of *Brewster Place* and said, "This is what I want to do. I know you turned it down, Brandon, but obviously being the wise one that you are, you hadn't read it. I'll call you Tuesday," she told Stoddard. "I was relentless. I'd call and ask, 'Are you reading it? What page are you on?' "

At the center of "The Women of Brewster Place" is Mattie Michael, played by Oprah, a stout and stout-hearted woman who comes to Brewster Place, a big-city dead-end street, to start over. The rest of the cast was formidable: Jackée of television's "227"; Olivia Cole, who had won an Emmy for "Roots"; Mary Alice, who won a Tony for the Broadway play *Fences*; Robin Givens from "Head of the Class"; Lonette McKee; Paula Kelly, of "Night Court"; Phyllis Yvonne Stickney, of "Another World," and Cicely Tyson, who won an Emmy for "The Autobiography of Miss Jane Pittman," and Moses Gunn, William Allen Young and Paul Winfield. Between them, the distinguished cast had racked up thirteen Emmy, Tony, and Obie Awards and fourteen Oscar, Emmy, and Tony nominations. "This is the finest ensemble of actors I've ever been exposed to in my life," said Reuben Cannon, who became one of the film's producers.

Oprah confided to friends that she was so intimidated by Cicely Tyson that when Tyson showed up on the set on the very same day that Oprah was supposed to work, she prayed: "Lord, please let her leave soon." In fact, Oprah said that all the women became great friends. "That's why our scenes work so wonderfully, because we've become really bonded here." Oprah went on effusively: "Women have traditionally been viewed as being catty about each other, but there's none of that here. There's such a great spirit of . . . *womanness*."

The production began with a controversy. "Before we began shooting, we were approached by the NAACP to see the script. I do believe it's necessary not to be restricted in your work based on color. I believe as long as you tell the truth in your heart people have no right to criticize you."

It came down to an issue of control which has always been important to Oprah. "I just don't think you can allow yourself to be controlled," she said. "I'm insulted, too. I am more conscious of my legacy as a black person than anybody." Oprah insisted that "I have a responsibility, not only as a black woman, but as a human being to do good work. I am just as concerned about the images of black men as anybody, but there are black men who abuse their families, and there are white men who do it, too, and brown men. It's just a fact of life. I deal with it every day. So, I refuse to be controlled by other people's ideas and ideals of what I should do.''

And anyone who recalls her refusal to join in bloc voting at East Nashville High knows that Oprah will not bow to pressure from any race. "I believe that it is necessary to not be restricted in your work based on your color, and as long as you tell the truth in your work and your art, people have no right to tell you how to do it.''

Oprah insisted that the production was "very concerned about the image of black men and took great care to try to help understand why they were that way.''

Several months before filming began, Oprah had lost a lot of weight, but she took her role of Mattie so seriously that she was willing to regain ten pounds deliberately. "I feel more comfortable doing her weightier,'' she explained. "The more weight I lose, the sexier I feel, and Mattie is not a sexy woman.''

That May, while filming the miniseries, Oprah had a scene in which a rat invades her ghetto apartment and nibbles on her baby's bottle—and the star assured friends that she would overcome her fear of rodents and do the scene. But when the time came and Oprah spotted the huge rat on the set, she freaked out and yelled, "I can't do this . . . I just CAN'T!'' Producers got a stuffed rat for shots with Oprah and the real rat did his close-ups alone.

PSYCHIC PREDICTS: THE OPRAH DIET

In June 1988 Clarissa Bernhardt, a psychic famed for her incredibly accurate earthquake forecasts, saw big things in store for Oprah. Bernhardt predicted that Oprah would stun her fans by losing forty pounds in four months—and her "Oprah Diet" would become so popular she would announce plans to open a series of weight-loss clinics nationwide.

But by July 1988, Oprah didn't seem to care. She was up to around 190 pounds, and rumors abounded that she went wild on the set of the talk show when she couldn't find her favorite snack—potato chips, but not just any potato chips, Lay's potato chips.

Oprah halted taping and shouted to a crewman: "Get me my Lay's potato chips! I don't care what you have to do to get them—just get them *now* or I won't finish the show!" The man ran out and bought five fifteen-ounce bags. Oprah ate her fill and then continued taping, proving that you could always count on her when the chips were down.

HARPO TAKES CONTROL

This would also be the year when Oprah and business partner Jeffrey Jacobs fulfilled the second stage of the strategy they had laid out two years earlier, when Oprah was still only a local Chicago phenomenon and her station, WLS-TV, refused to give her an extra week off.

Oprah's first contract with Capital Cities/ABC and King World Productions, Inc., to syndicate "The Oprah Winfrey Show" had been considered extraordinarily generous to her, giving her twenty-five percent of total revenues after production and distribution costs. While this deal allowed Oprah to earn $2 million in 1986, $12 million in 1987, and $25 million in 1988, it still left most of the money in the hands of King World. Jeffrey Jacobs felt that Oprah was underpaid and urged her to seek a better deal.

With his help, Oprah began to practice the gentle art of leverage. She hinted she might give up the show when her contract expired in 1991. She asked for ownership, control of production, and a flexible schedule so she could devote more time to network specials, movies, and other projects. In exchange, she agreed to continue as host through 1993.

Oprah's company, Harpo Productions (Harpo is Oprah spelled backwards), gained ownership and control of "The Oprah Winfrey Show," and she secured the unprecedented guarantee that ABC would carry the talk show on its owned and operated stations for five additional years. Capital Cities/ABC, owner of WLS-TV, the station that produced the show in Chicago, agreed because the show's ratings were so strong on its owned and operated stations, and partly because "The Oprah Winfrey Show" was such a profitable lead-in to the local news at most of its stations.

She and Jeffrey Jacobs were not stopping there. Oprah also bought, for a rumored $10 million, an eighty-eight-square-foot studio which, when renovated, would provide facilities for producing motion pictures and television movies as well as her talk show.

According to Jeffrey Jacobs, Harpo's chief operation officer, Harpo Studios would be *"the* studio in between the coasts, the final piece in the puzzle" that would enable Oprah to do "whatever it is she wants to do, economically, and under her control."

That August, Oprah was saying that she wanted to cut down a bit. "I used to take every phone call from a guy who said he would jump off a building if I didn't talk to him. But I no longer feel compelled to aid every crazy. For two years I have done everything everyone asked me to do. I am now officially exhausted."

THE NEW OPRAH UNVEILED

Oprah remained unwilling to go public about what was obvious to careful Oprah-watchers: the woman was virtually melting away before their very eyes.

In November Oprah finally revealed the full details of her accomplishment. A triumphant Oprah, dragging a wagon loaded with sixty-seven pounds of lard to represent all the fat she had lost, even slipped into a pair of size ten Calvin Klein jeans on her show.

"This is how I lost 60 pounds on 400 calories a day and ended up with a great new body," Oprah confided to one insider. "It's like a dream come true."

Declared the star's closest friend and publicist, Christine Tardio, "Oprah says that losing all this weight is her single biggest accomplishment—even bigger than having her own show."

Tardio insisted that "from the first day she started her diet on July 6, Oprah never ate any solid food until October 17."

The diet that enabled Oprah to lose so much weight so quickly was a sixteen-week hospital and doctor-supervised fast program. It involved consuming five liquid protein drinks a day totaling four hundred calories. She followed it very strictly.

In addition to the liquid protein, Oprah was allowed to have half a lemon a day which she ate rind and all.

"Oprah's worst temptation is potatoes, in any form. Whether it's fried, chips or au gratin, she just loves potatoes," said Tardio. "For the first month, it was very difficult. There were cravings—just for a plain boiled chicken breast. Another time she craved a plain, crisp, crunchy salad with no dressing. But she never gave in."

Oprah ran or jogged every morning and night, mostly on a machine, for forty-five minutes.

Oprah confided to friends that she was determined to get even thinner and stay that way, for Stedman. Stedman had dated no one but tall, thin women before her, and their romance was something of an adjustment for him. It had taken him a long time to even tell her, because he knew how self-conscious she was about her weight.

Whenever the temptation to finally chuck her diet and indulge in some delicious food struck Oprah, Stedman was standing by to give her strength.

"Stedman has been very supportive of Oprah," said Tardio. "He makes sure that whenever she faces being tempted by food—at parties or public appearances, she is steered in the other direction. And he never tempts her by munching on snacks in front of her."

By the time she went public in mid-November, Oprah was down to a size ten and her goal was an eight. She wanted to lose another ten pounds for a little extra margin, with Thanksgiving and Christmas holidays coming up.

She was weaning herself back on solid food, eating things like steamed vegetables and a little meat, like chicken and turkey. She was on a program where she was eating one regular food meal a day. "But no sweets," said Tardio. "She's being very sensible about it. Slowly, over the next couple of weeks, she will integrate more solid food into her diet."

Famed diet expert Dr. Neil Solomon said that while Oprah's reported weight loss was possible, "It is certainly not a safe way to lose weight unless you are doing it under a doctor's supervision.

"In order for Oprah Winfrey to lose 60 pounds she had to eat 210,000 calories less than it would take to maintain her weight. This works out to eating about 1,900 fewer calories each day."

Although doctors say weight-loss programs such as Oprah's often result in side effects such as dizziness, light-headedness, weakness and fatigue, Oprah claimed that she suffered no such symptoms.

She dazzled the crowd at a Los Angeles testimonial dinner in her honor on October 22, 1988. She was presented with the National Conference of Christians and Jews Humanitarian Award, but her biggest prize of all was that she attended in a size ten dress. Just three months earlier, Oprah the former beauty queen had been wearing a size sixteen.

Even Vernon Winfrey was beside himself over his daughter's new look.

"I've fallen in love with Oprah all over again!" her father said. "Where did the rest of her go?"

"She told me, 'Dad, I took one look in the mirror and thought, Who's that—Diana Ross? I get tears in my eyes when I think of my transformation. I hope I'm an inspiration to overweight women everywhere.'

"Oprah's whole family is tickled pink with her new look," said Vernon.

Well, not exactly everyone, as Oprah soon discovered to her chagrin. An awful lot of folks preferred Oprah fat. She couldn't believe it! After all she had been through to lose sixty pounds, there were people saying that they preferred her plump.

"People have said they liked me the other way, but they're lying, they're lying," she insisted when she appeared on Johnny Carson's November 18 show.

The fall of 1988, Stedman presented Oprah with a $3,500 telescope for her new $2.9 million fifty-seventh floor apartment. But when Oprah realized that if she could see into other people's windows, they could see into hers, she rush-ordered $8,000 worth of draperies.

That fall, too, Oprah was among the ten most desirable celebrity spokesmen, according to a survey of Americans conducted for *Advertising Age*, the industry publication. Bill Cosby was #1, followed in descending order by Ronald Reagan, Bob Hope, Ed McMahon, Jerry Lewis, Johnny Carson, James Garner, Oprah, Lee Iacocca, and Paul Newman.

BEST FRIEND HIT WITH AIDS

In December 1988, Oprah was devastated by the news that a colleague she loved like a brother—and who had played a key role in her phenomenal rise to stardom—was dying of AIDS. Billy Rizzo had discovered eighteen months earlier that he had contracted the fatal virus.

Despite his affliction, Rizzo continued to work for Oprah and also courageously worked to help other people with AIDS.

"I love Billy like a brother," Oprah confided to a friend. "He's a wonderful, funny, talented guy and it's just heartbreaking to see him so ill."

That November, Rizzo believed himself so close to death that he phoned Oprah and other friends from his hospital bed to say goodbye.

Throughout his ordeal, Oprah loyally stood by her best friend and did everything possible to help Rizzo, who was a vice president of corporate relations at Harpo.

While Rizzo was in the hospital, Oprah checked on him every day.

Each night she prayed for him. If she didn't stop by to see him, she sent flowers or phoned him.

"Oprah also is taking care of him financially and seeing he doesn't want for anything," said a friend.

More than once, Oprah has said publicly that someone close to her was an AIDS victim—and insiders say she was talking about Rizzo.

Oprah attributed a lot of her success to Billy and felt lost and helpless knowing he was fighting a losing battle for his life.

When Oprah was starting out, it was Billy who set up her shows, booked guests, came up with ideas, and worked in the control room. "He was so energetic and creative that Oprah found him invaluable," said one friend.

Billy had been like a brother to her. She told one friend: "When things weren't going right for me, when my heart was sinking, I always had Billy to cheer me up. He'd always lend me his shoulder to cry on."

But now she was unable to help him. She told Billy: "I have all the money in the world and I can't help one of my dearest friends."

A NEW MISSION OF MERCY

Through Stedman Graham, Oprah had also taken on another charitable project, providing one meal a day for the population of one of the most bleak, poverty-stricken towns in South Africa.

On a business trip to South Africa, Stedman had visited Alexandra, a troubled black township where many desperately poor residents lived in tin shacks without water, electricity, sewage disposal, or food.

When he told Oprah about the tragic suffering he found there, she was deeply moved. She soon committed $50,000 a year to provide daily lunches and hundreds of loaves of bread to the elderly of Alexandra.

"I firmly believe that none of us in this world have made it until the least among us have made it," said Oprah.

Through her foundation, Oprah Winfrey Charitable Giving, she also helped support numerous United States charities. But Alexandra was perhaps the most vivid example of the good she did.

"We're feeding people who would starve without her," said Armstrong Williams, executive director of the foundation.

DISASTER IN THE KITCHEN

Oprah might have been the Queen Bee of Syndication, but she was a total disaster in the kitchen. That Christmas 1988, according to her half sister, Patricia Lee, "Oprah can't cook at all. She tried to cook Christmas dinner and she was on the phone to Mom and me asking how to make macaroni and cheese.

"We tried to tell her how," Patricia recalls. "But Oprah told us later she put in too much milk and wound up with macaroni-and-cheese soup!

"She also asked us how to make dressing. We said, 'Oprah, just go to the store and buy yourself a box of Stove Top Stuffing and call it a day!'

"It's kind of funny, Oprah not being able to cook and keep house," Patricia acknowledges. "But then again, she doesn't have to, because she's exactly what she said she would be—a star!"

Chapter Seven
Taking Chances

Consult the spirit within you first, and seek the truth. Get yourself straight first. Surround yourself with people who are smarter or as smart as you. And never give up power to another person.
—Oprah Winfrey in her speech to the American Women's Economic Development Corp. Conference, 1989

The dawn of 1989 found Oprah in her white-on-white apartment, a wraparound two-bedroom condominium so softly posh that it said "serene" before it said "money." She was deeply aware that, as she likes to say, "To those of us that much is given, much is expected," and she was determined to make herself worthy of all that had been given to her.

Outside the windows and far below, Lake Michigan stretched a celestial blue to the horizon. Here, above the brawling burly city of Chicago, the sound of traffic and of waves merged to produce a reassuring hum. So high up it was often wrapped in Chicago's lake-effect clouds, Oprah's home was literally "out of this world."

White marble tables seemed to float atop the pale carpeting. White couches banked against each other like plump clouds. The finest French crystal sculptures punctuated the living room. The only burst of color came from the masses of fresh flowers that were always present.

Nineteen eighty-nine opened with accolades from *Ms. Magazine* which saluted Oprah as one of their six "Women of the Year for 1988." According to *Ms.*, "the women have one overwhelming characteristic in common: grit. They are all fighters, all women determined to make a difference. They are part of an ever-growing circle of women from all over the planet who are working, each in her own way, to make this world more responsive to human needs." The other women honored included actress Anne Archer and anti-gun activist Sarah Brady.

Ms. saluted Oprah in particular "for showing women that we can climb as high as we want to go and inspiring us to take control of our resources and make them work for us and for a better world."

In an accompanying essay, the poet Maya Angelou eloquently saluted her friend: "Although she is only 34 years old, Oprah's road has been long and her path has been stony. . . . She was left in the care of her grandmother who believed in the laying on of hands, in all ways, in prayers, and that God answered prayers. She learned behavior from her grandmother that continues until today. She kneels nightly to thank God for His protection and forgiveness. She has a genuine fear of sin and sincerely delights in goodness.

"Unheralded success has not robbed her of wonder, nor have possessions made her a slave to property."

Oprah had come to look on her talk show as her ministry and felt strongly that she embodied a message: "You can be born poor and black and female and make it to the top." She felt that she had grown more in the past year than in the previous decade.

"This whole celebrity-fame thing is interesting," she said. "I'm the same person I always was. The only difference between being famous and not being famous is that people know who you are."

Those days, when Oprah sought advice, she turned to Bill Cosby, Sidney Poitier, Quincy Jones, or Maya Angelou.

Cosby had warned her: "No matter how rich you get—sign your own checks."

Cosby was also helping Oprah deal with the glare of publicity.

"At one time, I read everything anybody wrote, and I'd call to talk to critics when something hurt, to tell them I'm not a sleaze," Oprah admits. "But Bill Cosby told me there would come a time when it would not hurt, and then I would know that I was growing up. I'm at the point now where I feel like I'm not in it."

When Oprah found demands on her time and her new money overwhelming, the poet and author Maya Angelou told her: "Baby, all you *have* to do is stay black and die. . . . The work is the thing, and what matters at the end of the day is, were you sweet, were you kind, did you get the work done?"

Poitier was a great comfort when Oprah was wounded by criticism from the black community for many things, including her role in *The Color Purple* and her fondness for green contact lenses. "You are their hope," Poitier told her. He also warned her that she was "carrying the people's dreams" and that, emulated and idolized, she would also be resented and hated.

In her hallway she had proudly hung a framed letter from Winnie Mandela. "Oprah, you must keep alive!" it said. "Your mission is sacramental. A nation loves you."

"THE WOMEN OF BREWSTER PLACE"

When Oprah saw the final cut of "The Women of Brewster Place," she was thrilled. "I am very, very proud of it," she said. "It was an incredible experience. I haven't done a lot of acting and I really enjoyed it. I love women and working with these women was wonderful, because they're all so wonderful.

Oprah slipped away from Chicago to quietly celebrate her thirty-fifth birthday with Stedman in Deer Valley, Utah. At least, she expected it to be quiet, but when they arrived, they discovered her entire staff from the show was waiting to celebrate and ski with them!

There was another surprise when Oprah got back to her office on Monday: the Harpo staff surprised Oprah with a golden retriever puppy.

But there were some bad omens. As mentioned before, not everyone was thrilled with Oprah's huge weight loss. In fact, the *National Enquirer* announced the results of a reader telephone poll, and its readers at least preferred the old, chubby Oprah by a narrow margin. Fifty-one percent of those who called special telephone numbers claimed that their Oprah was the cuddly cutie with the ample curves, not the wasp-waisted woman she had become.

GOING PUBLIC WITH STEDMAN

More and more rumors swirled around Oprah and Stedman. Were they in love? Would they marry? Just who was this tall, handsome public relations executive who seemed to have swept Oprah off her feet and inspired her to slim down?

Stedman Graham, Jr., was born and raised in Whitesboro, New Jersey, one of six children of Stedman,

Sr., a construction worker, and Mary Graham, who worked nights at a special education state school while raising her children during the day.

Stedman had been divorced from Glenda Brown, his college sweetheart, for several years, and their daughter, Wendy, lived with her mother, a postal worker, near Dallas. Oprah had already met Stedman's family at a family reunion in North Carolina in June 1988.

Now Oprah was ready to go public to her fans, introducing Stedman on the show. Stedman had made a brief appearance when Barbara Walters interviewed Oprah in April 1988, but he was still a mystery man to most of her audience.

"So much that's been written about this relationship is untrue, and I thought it was time to clear the air," Oprah said. "I want people to meet Stedman for themselves and get a feel for what our relationship is all about. I also want people to get a sense of what it's like for him, or any private person to maintain a relationship with a person who's constantly in the public eye." Oprah credited Stedman with her weight loss.

Also on the show were Barbara Mandrell and her husband Ken Dudney; soap star Susan Lucci and her husband, Helmut Huber.

TAKING IT OFF WAS EASY . . . KEEPING IT OFF IS HARD

Just how long that weight loss was going to last was anyone's guess at this point. Oprah had regained ten pounds over the Christmas holidays, and despite fierce determination she had lost only half since then.

She was jogging seven miles a day, and watching what she ate, but she couldn't seem to enjoy a meal in public without making news. One morning in Los Angeles, after a six-mile jog with Stedman, the couple stopped at a restaurant. Oprah was dying for some pancakes with apple sauce, but begged Stedman to order them because she was afraid that some nearby diners like Tony Curtis might talk about her pig-out, and the gossip would end up in the tabloids. Stedman ordered the pancakes and they shared them. The story did end up in the tabloids, but Tony Curtis was not to blame.

In fact, Oprah was in an agonizing battle to keep her weight down. "Taking my weight off was a picnic compared to the agony of maintaining this weight loss," Oprah admitted to one friend. "I'm in the fight of my life!"

She was constantly tormented by hunger and so determined to keep her new slim figure that she relentlessly pushed herself every day through excruciatingly painful runs of up to eight miles, until she was on the brink of collapse.

Oprah was so obsessed with her unending weight struggle that she couldn't even escape in her sleep—because she dreamed about food.

"It's hell," she said. "Some days I want to buy a grocery store and eat everything in it!"

A friend added: "I've never seen Oprah so preoccupied with food. She agonizes every time she lifts a fork."

Oprah's will power weakened at one lunch when she ordered a rich chocolate pastry dripping with whipped cream.

"Oprah lifted a forkful, then suddenly stopped before she could get that little piece into her mouth," said a pal who was at her table. "Then she did something strange: She poured salt all over the pastry!"

Oprah told the fellow diner: "That looks crazy, but now I won't be able to eat that because it's ruined."

Friends said Oprah kept the pounds down by running at six o'clock every morning, bundled in a sweat suit, painfully huffing and puffing around a health club track until she was ready to drop.

"As she tries to force herself through one more lap, her sweat suit is soaked, she has sweat running down her forehead, and her face is actually contorted in pain," said one insider.

"At times it looks like she is ready to crumble. She'll kneel, take a couple of deep breaths, get up and go again."

What's more, on days when Oprah overate, she ran again at night. And friends said she was running so much she was even planning to compete in the Chicago marathon that October.

"I feel like all of America is waiting for me to gain weight," Oprah complained. "It puts terrible pressure on me."

During one lunch in Chicago, an entire restaurant fell silent when the waiter brought Oprah her meal.

"I couldn't believe it, everyone stopped talking to look at what I was eating!" Oprah complained. "My eyes welled up with tears and I thought 'Why doesn't everyone leave me alone?'

"But I said, loud enough for everyone to hear, 'It's broiled fish. O.K.?' I was so shaken, I could hardly swallow my lunch."

Oprah lost her willpower temporarily about a month earlier, when an eyewitness in a Los Angeles restaurant saw her eat an entire ten-inch pizza all by herself.

But she won another wrestling match with diet-busting temptation at a convention when she tried to avoid booths filled with mouth-watering goodies such as shrimp, brownies, cheese and chips.

"Oprah looked at the food in one booth, clasped her

hands tightly and walked away—right into another booth of food," said a witness. "Oprah told me, 'I can't stand it! It's agony to have to constantly monitor my eating. When I'm home alone, I want to run to the refrigerator and go wild.' "

The temptation is so overwhelming, Oprah even dreamed about food.

"She told me one night she dreamed she was chasing a hot dog through deserted city streets," said a friend.

Oprah confided, "The hot dog had arms and legs like the ones used in some ads. It kept dodging me and getting away, just like some crazy cartoon. Then I got this pesky hot dog cornered, grabbed it and was just about to bite it when I woke up. I was so disappointed!"

Sadly, Oprah's weight has gone up and down over the years, and she was fighting what experts said was likely to be a losing battle.

Research showed that near-starvation diets like the one Oprah was on train the body to burn fewer calories—and that continues even after the diet ends, according to Dr. Robert Stark, an expert on weight loss.

As a result, former dieters can gain weight by eating the same amount of food as those who haven't dieted.

Also, experts say severe diets don't develop healthy eating habits needed for long-term weight maintenance.

"Studies have shown that less than two percent of people who lose weight on this type of diet have been able to keep that weight off five years later," said Dr. Stark, who heads the American Society of Bariatric Physicians, a group of obesity experts.

"In many cases, dieters will be fatter than before!"

But Oprah vowed to beat the odds, partly because she wanted different acting roles from the frumpy matron she would be playing on her upcoming miniseries, "The Women of Brewster Place."

Oprah had been at least thirty pounds overweight when that was filmed, and she was determined never to look like that again.

"More than anything in my whole life I wanted to win the weight-loss battle," Oprah said at the time. "I want to show my audience and my friends that this is something anyone with the right motivation can accomplish!"

OPRAH'S DREAM HOUSE

Oprah also welcomed 1989 by acquiring her dream house: a sprawling million-dollar farm in Rolling Prairie, Indiana, a two-hour drive from her Chicago studio. Oprah paid $750,000 for the house and invested another $250,000 in improvements.

A pine tree-lined driveway led to the main house, a gray-stone building with the romantic turret which looked more like a French chateau than a Midwestern farmhouse. It had a dozen bedrooms, a baronial dining room, a screening room and TV theater, and an oak-paneled library where Oprah could display the valuable first editions of important American writers that she had begun to collect.

On the 160 acre grounds one could find a helicopter pad, several satellite dishes, a carriage house, and a two-car garage. There were a swimming pool, tennis courts, and riding stables. The driveway was lined with pine trees. This was all a far cry from the humble Mississippi farm where Oprah spent her early years.

Friends speculated that purchasing the farm was a signal that Oprah was ready to settle down with Stedman.

Surely if she *was* ready, Stedman would be the man. "He's the best man who's ever been in my life," Oprah said. "I have that love glow when I'm around him. You know the old cliché, 'A good man is hard to find'? Well, it's true. And the smarter you get, the harder they are to find. Stedman is right for me."

Neighbors reported sighting Oprah jogging in the area in a bright red track suit. "First she waved, then she stopped and introduced herself, and said she hoped we would be seeing a lot more of each other," one neighbor reported. "She said this was the place where she planned to put down some roots and get some of the good life away from the rat race."

OPRAH SELLS OUT!

In February, gossip columnist Liz Smith reported that a conference featuring Oprah as key speaker had sold out three weeks in advance. "If you don't think this woman has 'star appeal,' get this!" gushed Smith. "Who else would attract more than 6,000 women to travel across the United States to attend a meeting at which Oprah will be the keynote speaker?"

The conference of women entrepreneurs was held February 25 at the New York Hilton, sponsored by AWED, the American Woman's Economic Development Corporation. All 3,600 seats were sold out three weeks in advance. As Liz Smith enthused, "In Oprah Winfrey, they have the role model to end all role models!"

The audience fell in love with Oprah from the moment she bounded on to the stage in form-hugging black and peach.

A slim and trim-looking Oprah warmed up her listeners by letting them know that she thoroughly enjoyed her success:

"The life I lead is very exciting," she said. "Girl, it's fun. I have a good time, I phone for a limousine. I call room service, they ask you what temperature you would like your tea. Good life."

Then she moved into the truly inspiring body of her speech:

"One of the reasons I believe I have been able to achieve what I have is because I have sought truth in my life," she told the audience.

Sometimes Oprah used street talk to show how people explain their failures. The all-female audience loved it.

"If you are struggling and it doesn't seem to be coming together," Oprah went on, "you can't look outside of yourself for why it isn't working. . . . You just have to stop right where you are and look right inside yourself."

The afternoon took on the flavor of a revival meeting as the women greeted Oprah's words with shouts of "Amen, Sister! Amen!"

"What I know is that God, nature, the spirit, the universe, whatever title you wish to give Him—or Her—is always trying to help each one of us to be the best and do the best that we can."

Oprah recalled: "When I first approached the idea of owning the show myself, it was really scary for me because I've been accustomed to a slave mentality.

"I've been accustomed to thinking I can only do so much—and that maybe that was enough."

Oprah admitted that she had been fearful of what other people would think when she took control of her show, what other people would say, and whether she would be able to handle it.

"So I went within, as I always do, and asked the spirit: Is this the right thing for me to do?" she explained. "And the answer came back to me as a resounding yes!

"Then I asked the spirit, do you think I need a business course or something because my name ain't Iacocca?

"As I got very firm with myself, I then understood that the best way to run a business is to do it the way you run your life."

Oprah acknowledged that a lot of people came to her and said they wished they could have her life. She believed that they could: "What I want to tell you is that I believe all of us have the potential for greatness in our lives. Greatness does not necessarily mean being famous or being well known, but if you allow yourself to seek greatness in your life, you will be known for doing great things."

Oprah even outlined for the AWED audience her Ten Commandments for a successful life:

1. Don't live your life to please other people. "All that can do for you is bring you confusion," said Oprah. "I learned I had been living my life not only to please other people, but living my life by other people's standards."

2. Don't depend on externals to help you get ahead. "I learned that I could not look to my exterior self to do anything for me: If I was going to accomplish anything in life, it had to start from within."

3. Strive for the greatest possible harmony and compassion in your business and your life. "I've discovered if you treat people the way you wish to be treated at all times, you will get exactly what the universe has intended."

4. Get rid of all the backstabbers around you. "Believe me, when you are not there they are doing the same thing to you. Surround yourself with only people who are going to lift you higher."

5. Be nice, not catty. "If you find yourself always talking of somebody else, you have to cure that because feeling badly about how other women are doing has nothing to do with them—it has everything to do with you."

6. Get rid of your addictions. "You have to rid yourself of whatever is blocking truth in your life. Food was my drug, but for the problems in your life, including alcohol

122

and drugs, the cure is always the same. You start a minute at a time, an hour at a time, a day at a time, a week at a time."

7. *Surround yourself with people who are as good or better than you are.* "I want everybody, from my secretary to my accountant, to be as smart or smarter than I am. And you can't even begin to do that if you are having problems with yourself. So it all begins with getting yourself straight."

8. *If you're in it to make money, forget it.* "I am where I am not because money was ever, has ever, will ever be my motivation. If you want to accomplish the goals of your life, you have to begin with the spirit."

9. *Never give up your power to another person.* "There will be people who will try to tell you how to run your life, what to do, and so forth, that you don't need to start a business. But you already have all of the answers. Never allow another person to mean more to you in your life than you do."

10. *Don't give up.* "Always continue the climb. It is possible for you to do whatever you choose, if you first get to know who you are and are willing to work with a power that is greater than ourselves to do it."

Oprah even talked about her weight, insisting that she had not lost weight for Stedman.

"I was fat for a long time with Stedman," she said. "I decided to lose weight because for a long time I was tired of lying to myself. The weight was an untruth in my life. It served to block me, prohibit me from doing and feeling as good as I could. It stopped me doing things I felt I could do if I were a thinner person."

She urged her audience to be all that they could be.

"Whatever it is that is blocking the truth in your life, you have to rid yourself of blocks and barriers before you can go on. I have found that I can fly and that's because I got the weight, the garbage out of my wings, because for me, that was weighing me down.''

Chapter Eight
Coping With Success

I, like a lot of people here, spent a lot of time trying to be somebody I was not. I spent a lot of time trying to be Diana Ross.
— Oprah Winfrey in her commencement speech
at Morehouse College, 1989

Although Oprah often went to Bill Cosby for advice, there were times when she chose to ignore it. For example, he had warned her about the pitfalls of owning a restaurant, but in February she went ahead and opened The Eccentric, at 159 Erie Street, in the River North section of Chicago. Her partners in the 450 seat venture were Rich Melman whose Lettuce Entertain You Corporation had already given the world Ed Debevic's, Ambria, Un Gran Cafe, Shaw's Crab House and more than a dozen other trendy Chicago dining spots; Kevin Brown, the manager, and Michael Kornick, the chef. Oprah was totally involved. She even refilled the toilet paper in the bathrooms.

"I have to check the bathrooms every half hour; they're very strict about that," Oprah told visitors at the opening festivities. "Besides peeling the potatoes, I do get to make the Perrier sodas—my favorite. But I won't be answering phones, because I can't tell you how to get here."

Some visitors compared the eclectic decor of the Eccentric to a French brasserie, including the awning outside which read: "Food Art Reality Hope Life Literature Liberté." There was an English bar, an all-American dance floor, an Italianate art gallery-coffee bar, an enormous main dining room and an informal café. The kitchen was behind theatrical dark red curtains.

The walls of the Eccentric were covered with art, most of it by Chicago artists, and Melman announced plans for other artists to paint "live" in one corner of the room. He even hoped to have poetry readings eventually. A sign on one pillar read: "Stay Real/Never Dull/No Rules."

"You've heard of restaurants as theatre? This is restaurant as multi-media event," raved Colman Andrews in the *Los Angeles Times*.

Oprah was often on the scene, sipping cranberry juice while greeting patrons. The house specialties included Oprah's mashed potatoes, hand-mashed spuds with horseradish, and Oprah had been spotted in the kitchen, peeling and mashing her own potatoes to get them just right. There was also Oprah's Pasta, which came with a sauce of chilis, tomatoes, and garlic on fusilli, topped with dried ricotta cheese.

Oprah was enjoying her good fortune. That spring she had just bought her first horse, a thoroughbred which she planned to stable at her new farm in Rolling Prairie.

But it took time to get used to all that spending money. Once, Oprah went shopping for silverware with a friend and fretted over the choices, until she realized that she could buy any pattern she wanted.

"We stopped dead in the street, and I said, 'I can get both!' We started jumping up and down and screaming," Oprah remembered.

"THE WOMEN OF BREWSTER PLACE" MAKES HISTORY

When the miniseries aired in March, it drew an eye-popping thirty-seven share, making "The Women of Brewster Place" the highest rated miniseries for the 1988–89 season. *The New York Times* praised it as "remarkably affecting television," and called it "good old-fashioned melodrama," and especially lauded Oprah's "first-rate performance."

The Times had one complaint: "Just about nothing is heard for men who, almost without exception, are dismissed as irresponsible, even vicious louts. The film could be subtitled, without too much exaggeration: 'Revenge of the Black Female.' "

The New York Daily News observed that "those upset by the negative portrayal of black men in *The Color Purple* may be equally disturbed by 'Brewster Place'."

Oprah bristled at such criticism. "The book is not untruthful about the portrayal of men," she told *The News*. "If it's not exploitative but it's truthful, that's what's important to me. For anyone to put me in that defensive mode makes me ill."

Soon there was talk of a sequel. An ABC network executive said, "We're looking for a way to bring the show back as a mini—or series. We've begun discussions with Oprah." The only problem, he explained, was that Oprah was "much thinner and her character would have to adapt."

In fact, Oprah was not pleased with her appearance in the miniseries. She was barely recognizable in a gray wig and dowdy green and yellow housedress. She claimed that she had deliberately gained weight for the role of the stocky Mattie, but by the time the miniseries aired she had slimmed down to a size ten.

"I can't believe I was that big, really," she told interviewers. "I looked at all the pictures of me that were taken only a few months ago, and I just can't believe it. I do believe in padding now."

OPRAH VS. LIZ

That March, Oprah shared prime space on national newsstands with Elizabeth Taylor. Slim and glamorous, Oprah graced the cover of *Us* magazine while a heavily painted Taylor, looking tired and rather matronly, appeared on the cover of *People*.

How ironic! A little more than a year ago, Taylor had been promoting her diet book on Oprah's show. Then Oprah had been sixty pounds heavier, and Taylor thirty pounds thinner. Looking back on their last encounter, it was clear that Oprah was entitled to the last laugh. But that was just not Oprah's style. Never had been, never would be.

Instead, Oprah celebrated her new cover girl status by going shopping for a new home and purchased a high-rise Water Tower condo on East Lake Shore Drive. The apartment took up an entire floor, overlooking the Oak Street Beach and further fueled rumors that she planned to wed Stedman.

UNFORGETTABLE OPRAH

That same month, Oprah was officially dubbed an "unforgettable woman," one of a select number of celebrated women featured in a series of ads for Revlon cosmetics. Oprah said she hoped the designation would inspire young blacks.

"As a child, it never occurred to me I might be considered beautiful, because none of the models looked like me," she said. "If just one little black girl sees the photo and thinks she's beautiful because she sees a part of herself in me, I will be grateful.''

The photograph by Richard Avedon, dean of fashion photographers, was a montage of sophisticated images of the newly slim, cat suit-clad Oprah. It first appeared in the glossy fashion magazine *W*, followed by a dozen other high-fashion and upscale publications. Oprah donated her $100,000 modeling fee to Chicago's inner-city schools.

ANOTHER AIDS TRAGEDY STRIKES OPRAH

It was also in March that another AIDS tragedy struck Oprah close to home. Her estranged half brother, Jeffrey Lee, twenty-eight, revealed that he was dying of AIDS. Even more tragic, Jeffrey claimed that his big sister had turned her back on him.

Oprah and Jeffrey shared the same mother, Vernita Lee, but not the same father. He openly admitted that he was gay and declared: ''I have AIDS and Oprah knows it, but she's not sympathetic. She's made it clear that AIDS or not, I'm on my own.''

Jeffrey Lee complained bitterly that Oprah's attitude was that it was his own fault and it served him right. He claimed that ''Oprah believes that every gay is going to get AIDS eventually.''

Young Jeffrey claimed that he had not spoken to his sister since November. ''At the end of last year, I was in the hospital and felt really dreadful,'' he said. ''I thought I was going to die. Oprah never came to see me. And I don't get any money at all from her.''

Sources close to Oprah defended her, insisting that although she hated her brother's life-style, she helped him out financially in the past and had paid his rent for months. And while she no longer gave him money directly, she had increased the payments she made to her mother Vernita and had let her know the money could be used to help Jeffrey.

"I don't think homosexuality as such offends Oprah," Jeffrey said. "What really upset her was my lifestyle—partying, funning around, not holding down a job.

"Oprah told me, 'You need to get God in your life. You really need Jesus.' "

Jeffrey, who found out he had AIDS about eight months earlier, claimed Oprah was "unsympathetic" when he discussed it with her in November.

"She just said, 'Oh, God, I'm sorry.'

"She told me that she hoped I'd be able to deal with it, to accept the fact that there's no cure yet, to accept the inevitable. She was sorry . . . but not very sympathetic," he said.

"It wasn't a surprise to Oprah because of my gay lifestyle. Although she did not use these words, it was a kind of 'Serves you right, you brought it on yourself' attitude."

That attitude toward him is "ironic" considering her well-publicized support for her staffer and close friend Billy Rizzo, who also has AIDS, said Jeffrey.

"I know that she's close to Billy. People say she's helping him every bit of the way, but I'm not bitter about it."

Oprah had never been close to Jeffrey. When she left her mother's home in Milwaukee at thirteen, Jeffrey was only six.

Despite that, she had always been supportive of him.

"She used to always help me out financially," he acknowledged. "If I needed $500 or $2,000 she'd just give it to me. But we had a big row. This was before the AIDS thing. She didn't like the way I was living." In fact, it was understood that Oprah had paid Jeffrey's rent on a very nice apartment in Chicago.

"I don't get any money at all from Oprah now. My

mom gets a monthly check and my mom helps me. If any of the money Oprah sends Mom reaches me, I'm unaware of it," said Jeffrey, obviously bitter at being cut off. "I consider whatever money comes from Mom is from Mom and not from Oprah."

Some say Oprah paid Jeffrey's rent through last June, but then she refused to pay it any longer and instead raised her payments to her mother.

But according to Jeffrey's landlord, Vernita Lee had failed to pay the rent and then gave him a $1,400 check that bounced. In December, the landlord finally kicked Jeffrey out, and sued Vernita for the money.

When Oprah found out about the bounced rent check, she told one insider, "My mother is getting dunning notices from this landlord and never once tells me what's going on. What am I going to do with these people? I'm heartsick."

Oprah's public relations representative, Christine Tardio, defended her boss and said that "Oprah tripled the monthly allowance she was giving her mother and told her that if she wanted to pay Jeffrey's rent then it would be up to her mother. It was understood that her mother could use the money for herself or to support Jeffrey."

"I'm not going to get any more involved in Jeffrey's financial situation," Oprah reportedly told one friend. "He should be taking care of himself. I'm torn over these financial situations that both he and my mother are involved in, but it's not my responsibility to be bailing them out each time they get into a jam."

Oprah realized that her actions might seem harsh to outsiders. "It may make me seem like a hard person. They can say I'm ignoring my family and all, but you've got to look at the total picture," she insisted. "All the years that I went without a family, and now they want me to be part of a family I don't even know."

Jeffrey added: "I really don't have any animosity to Oprah. Let's face it, I basically screwed myself up by being irresponsible.

"I know Oprah has millions and could make things a lot easier for me . . . take some of the anxiety out of my life.

"But I'm not bitter. I love her very much and I always will."

LETTERMAN SNUBS OPRAH

That April there were rumors that David Letterman had infuriated Oprah. David—who had been dubbed "The Host Stars Love to Hate" by such celebrities as Cher and Shirley MacLaine for his smart-alecky ways—was always outrageous, but with Oprah he seemed driven to outdo himself.

Here's what happened: Oprah, on a Caribbean vacation, sat down in the dining room of the swank Tiawana Beach Hotel on Saint Barthélemy Island in the French West Indies with Stedman, who spotted Letterman lunching.

Oprah said "Hi!"—but David barely grunted, so Oprah shrugged and ordered lunch. A while later, a waiter handed Oprah a slip of paper from Dave. Oprah looked up just in time to see the grinning Letterman wave and leave, then looked down in shock . . . at Letterman's lunch check! Outraged, Oprah hollered for the hotel owner, who ended up stuck with David's bill.

There were still more hassles with Letterman in May when the "Late Night with David Letterman" show visited Chicago. The story around Chicago's Loop was that Letterman's nightly wisecracks about Oprah had reduced her to tears. Certainly, when Oprah visited the show the atmosphere was strained.

Letterman has always seemed obsessed with the money

Oprah is making. Months later, when he signed his own historic deal with the CBS network, he commented that he wasn't getting *that* much of a raise from what he was getting at NBC, because "Oprah's got *all* the money."

THE WEIGHT BATTLE IS ON AGAIN

Oprah's battle with her weight was on again, and she and Stedman checked into an exclusive health spa to drop the thirty pounds she had gained on her Caribbean vacation.

This time, she and Stedman secretly headed for the Golden Door Spa in Escondido, California, twenty miles north of San Diego. The $3,500 a week private health facility was situated in the rolling hills of the San Diego mountains, among avocado and kiwi fruit trees.

Oprah and Stedman checked in on March 12, 1989, cutting out two days before their scheduled week-long stay was complete to appear on Johnny Carson's show.

The Golden Door was serenely beautiful, designed to resemble a Japanese inn and to give visitors peace of mind. The staff glided around quietly in white kimonos and sneakers.

Every room had a private garden and a wardrobe was waiting: warm-up suits, shorts, gloves, and a scarf for early morning walks. Stedman, who did not have a weight problem, worked out. Oprah was on a nine hundred-calories-a-day diet. She missed the 6:00 A.M. wake-up call several mornings, but by midday she was into the routine, which began with a four-mile run, then moved on to meditation and aerobics.

After lunch, there were swimming and beauty treatments, massages and facials. After dinner, which was a small piece of chicken or fish, there were fruit juice cocktails before bed.

On March 17, Oprah left the facility to get to Burbank where she was scheduled to appear on "The Tonight Show with Johnny Carson." She confessed to Carson that she finished up her vacation with a trip to the spa.

That April Oprah swamped all rivals in the *National Enquirer*'s Reader Phone-In Poll. The weekly tabloid had asked readers to call special 900 numbers to vote for the talk show host they liked best: "The one who keeps you riveted to the tube with hard-hitting questions on controversial topics, sparking sizzling conversations with fascinating guests."

Results were announced on April 4, and Oprah swamped her five opponents, pulling 44.4 percent of the vote or almost double the eighteen percent of second-place finisher Geraldo Rivera.

Sally Jessy Raphael was third with fifteen percent.

Phil Donahue, so long regarded as the top dog of the talk show hosts, placed a distant fourth with a mere 11.4 percent of the total.

Motormouth Mort Downey, Jr., was fifth, getting 7.3 percent, and, in last place, was Larry King, who received just 3.9 percent.

MORE PSYCHIC PREDICTIONS AND AN HONORARY DEGREE

There was more good news from psychics: in May, Miami psychic Micki Dahne, who accurately predicted the Canary Islands jumbo jet collision that killed more than five hundred people, announced that Oprah would get married in a spectacular ceremony right on her talk show, and it would be one of the most watched events in TV history.

Oprah received an honorary degree from Morehouse

College, the distinguished all-male institution in Atlanta, on May 21.

"The world awaits what you have to give," she said after receiving her honorary Doctor of Humane Letters degree. "The pressure is on." Oprah announced that she was donating $1 million to establish the Oprah Winfrey Endowment Scholarship Fund at the school.

Oprah also told the crowd: "I, like a lot of people here, spent a lot of time trying to be somebody I was not. I spent a lot of time trying to be Diana Ross."

A few weeks later, Oprah ruffled some other feathers, in Detroit, when she did not show up at an NAACP gala there. One guest complained, "They gave us a cock-and-bull story about bad weather, but how could the weather be that bad in Chicago during the summer?"

All was forgiven when they learned that three people were nearly electrocuted by lightning from the same storm that grounded Oprah. And Spike Lee and Danny Glover were no-shows, too.

"LOOK AT ALL THOSE ZEROES"

That spring, Oprah made a surprise visit to a San Francisco skid-row church for Easter services, stunning the 250 worshipers, many of whom were recovering crack-cocaine users and alcoholics. After the service, Pastor Cecil Williams told Oprah that he had been so flustered by her appearance that he had forgotten to take up a collection. Oprah whipped out her checkbook and dashed off a check. Rev. Williams stuck it in his desk without a glance, then took Oprah to meet hundreds of poor folks and addicts, who had gathered for the church's free breakfast program.

"Oprah was wonderful," said Rev. Williams. "She

walked among the people, kissing them and shaking hands.''

When she left, the pastor examined the check and gasped: "Lord, look at all those zeroes.''

Oprah had donated $10,000, creating her own Easter miracle.

A few months later, Oprah followed up with a check for $5,000, to pay for a Mother's Day feast of ham and chicken for needy women and their babies.

"JUST BETWEEN FRIENDS"

That June, Oprah got to explore another subject that has always fascinated her with a prime time special, ''Just Between Friends,'' a collection of interviews with long-time friends. The idea came to her when she visited an elementary school and was reminded of the friendships formed at that age.

The show was a friendship sampler of sorts, featuring interviews with a highly diverse group of best friends. Most notable among them, Oprah and her longtime best friend, Gayle King Bumpus, discussed their relationship.

They talked about how they hang on the phone for hours, telling each other everything, and would never, ever have a bust-up over anything. *Unless* one of them found out that the other had ''slept with my man.''

Bumpus revealed that she even flew to Chicago every six weeks or so, mainly to see Oprah.

''Gayle helps keep me grounded and centered,'' Oprah told Kay Gardella of *The New York Daily News*. ''She adds balance to my life. We've been friends since 1976 and have a relationship like none other. We're like blood sisters.''

The camera also recorded an assortment of friends, old and new, rich and famous, not rich and not famous. They included: The Roches, sisters who formed a singing trio; Nathan Goldberg and Vincent Ricciotti, New York cabdrivers who have lunched together virtually every day for seventeen years; Caleb Gerard and Imelda Balacuit, college-age platonic friends; a group of Iowa women who had been friends for forty years, and Sara Fisk and Rachel Tadeo, two seven-year-olds who were interviewed while playing dress-up in their parents' clothes.

The most compelling segment was the improbable relationship between white American tennis great Stan Smith and the black South African author Mark Mathabane.

Mathabane, once a promising tennis player, approached Smith during a tournament in South Africa, and Smith invited him to play. From this chance encounter, rather unlikely under apartheid, sprang a friend-and-mentor relationship.

Mathabane recalled how Smith got him a tennis scholarship. When he gave up the sport to focus on his studies, Smith continued to support him.

Most notable among these profiles were probably Earvin "Magic" Johnson and Isiah Thomas. "It's true, genuine love," said Thomas.

The message from all the interviews was the same: friendship is important.

As for the talk show, Oprah assured Gardella that "We'll do fun things and have on lots of celebrities. But things I'll never do is invite skinheads on the program, members of the KKK, or do a show on devil worshipers or sadomasochism."

She defended talk shows like the one on which she interviewed six women who claimed that they were raped by their gynecologist against accusations of "trash TV": "People wondered how I could ask them such questions," Oprah said, "but 75 women filed suit against this man. It happened."

Actually, Oprah was about to experience some of the most serious fallout yet from one of her more controversial shows.

In early May, on a show devoted to Mexican Satanic Cult Murders, Oprah introduced her audience to "Rachel," who claimed to have multiple personality disorder and to have participated in human sacrifice rituals and cannibalism as a child.

Rachel claimed that since 1700 her family had engaged in such activities and assured the audience that other Jewish families across the country ritualistically abused and sacrificed children.

To many in the audience, it seemed that Oprah never effectively challenged the woman's wacky claims.

The next day, all hell broke loose. A spokesman for the Anti-Defamation League called the program "potentially devastating." The director of the Religious Action Center of Reform Judaism in Washington expressed "grave concern about the lack of judgment and the insensitive manipulation" of the unfortunate Rachel.

The president of People for the American Way said: "I think what happens here demonstrates how . . . freedom has to be married to responsibility."

Oprah met with Jewish community leaders on May 9. Three days later, a joint statement was issued, in which Oprah said, "We recognize that the "Oprah Winfrey Show" on May 1 could have contributed to the perpetuation of historical misconceptions and canards about Jews, and we regret that any harm may have been done . . .''

On behalf of community leaders, Barry Morrison of the Anti-Defamation League said: "We are satisfied that Oprah Winfrey and her staff did not intend to offend anyone and that Oprah was genuinely sorry for any offense or misunderstanding.''

THE STEDMAN RUMOR

There was one cloud on the romantic horizon that year: An ugly rumor about Stedman began to circulate in Chicago in May and soon spread to other media centers.

The nasty story will not be repeated here except to say it arose from wild and false rumors that Stedman was gay. It reached the point where it was mentioned on ''Entertainment Tonight'' on May 19.

The next day, an outraged Oprah told her TV audience: ''It is a vicious, malicious lie and no part of it, absolutely no part of it, is true. . . . I have chosen to speak up because this rumor has become widespread and so vulgar that I just wanted to go on record and let you know that it is not true. . . .''

But Oprah was still devastated by the smear campaign two days later when she telephoned her father in Nashville.

''She was very upset about the whole situation with Stedman,'' said Vernon Winfrey. ''Oprah was frustrated and in tears over all the lies and rumors. All the fuss has really gotten to Oprah.''

In a frank interview with Laura B. Randolph in *Ebony* magazine, Oprah blamed herself for the rumors.

''I believe in my heart that had I not been an overweight woman that rumor would never have occurred,'' she told Randolph. ''If I were lean and pretty, nobody would ever say that. What people were really saying is why would a straight, good-looking guy be with her?''

Far from driving Oprah and Stedman apart, the sheer viciousness and ugliness of the rumors only brought them closer. Oprah was deeply impressed by Stedman's strength. She learned from him, Oprah says. "He was so brave, and I have never loved him more."

A VISIT TO THE WHITE HOUSE

On June 27, Oprah and Stedman were guests at the State Dinner at the White House for Australian Prime Minister Bob Hawke. The guest list included cable king Ted Turner, ABC News president Roone Arledge, Hollywood producer Jerry Weintraub, actor Joel Gray, golfer Greg Norman, comic Garry Shandling, and the President's brother, Republican fund-raiser Jonathan Bush.

AN EMMY UPSET

Just days later, Oprah and Stedman attended the Daytime Emmy Awards at the Waldorf-Astoria Hotel in New York where there was a startling upset. The award for Outstanding Talk/Service Show Host went to Sally Jessy Raphael!

Accepting her first Emmy, a gleeful Sally Jessy noted that she had been in television for thirty-three years and credited the sudden "nationwide explosion in talk" with making her a star.

A shaken Oprah may have been consoled a little by the fact that her program still took honors for Outstanding Talk/Service Show and for Outstanding Director of a Talk/Service Show which went to Jim McPharlin. It's worth noting that as Supervising Producer, a new title for her, Oprah shared the Outstanding Talk/Service Show honors with Debra Di Maio, her executive producer, and Ellen Rakietan, Dianne Hudson, Mary Kay Clinton, Angela Thame and Alice McGee, her producers.

OPRAH MUST USE TOUGH LOVE

That summer, Oprah was also forced to use some tough love on her own sister, Patricia Lee. Out of the blue, Patricia's daughter, Chrishaunda, called her in Chicago. "Please, Oprah," she said. "Help Mom. She needs you. We need you!"

Oprah had no idea anything was wrong with her half sister who lived in Milwaukee with her daughters, Alicia, sixteen, and Chrishaunda, fourteen. Oprah sent a monthly allowance of $1,200 to provide for the girls, and she would visit and talk with them by phone when she could.

Chrishaunda told Oprah that Patricia was staying out two or three days at a time doing drugs. Chrishaunda and Alicia were left at home alone at night. There was no food in the house. They didn't have money for school supplies. The situation broke Oprah's heart.

Deeply concerned, Oprah called Patricia. She demanded to know what was going on and offered her help. But Patricia refused to admit she had a problem.

Oprah told a friend: "There was nothing I could do unless she admitted she had a problem. All my resources were no good unless Patricia admitted that she needed help."

Oprah told her sister, "You've betrayed my trust. Your allowance is cut off. You have to recognize that you have a problem!"

Although she was cutting her sister off, Oprah was not about to abandon her innocent nieces. Oprah had her mother Vernita take the girls in to care for them properly at her suburban Milwaukee home, and Oprah herself went clothes shopping with them.

"WHAT IS EXPECTED OF ME? WHAT DO I OWE PEOPLE?"

That summer the diet was not going well. In mid-July, Oprah was spotted in Gertie's Chesapeake Café in Berkeley, California, chowing down on crabcakes with gusto. She then started on her companion's chicken and shrimp gumbo and apparently liked it so much she ordered a huge helping for herself. Her handsome dinner companion was not Stedman Graham, however. He was Guy Johnson, the tall, thirtyish son of her friend and mentor, the poet Maya Angelou.

But Oprah's weight problems and the pressures of constant dieting may explain an incident that occurred in July as well. Oprah kept 450 top high-school students dazzled during a fifteen-minute speech in San Francisco, but she turned into a tiger lady when one student approached her for some career advice after the program. "I don't give free advice!" she snapped. With that the boy flipped to Oprah's picture in his program, ripped it out, and hurled it to the floor. Stunned, Oprah turned on her heels and flounced off.

There was another incident in an airport that July, that Oprah shared with Eric Sherman in *Ladies' Home Journal*:

"I was sitting reading a paper, waiting for the plane, when this woman who recognized me came up and stood up and stood with her face so close to me, I could have kissed her on the lips—all I had to do was pucker!"

According to Oprah, she spoke to the rather aggressive woman for a few minutes and then went back to reading her newspaper. Almost immediately, the woman's friend appeared to scold Oprah for being rude.

At first, Oprah was devastated. "I prayed on it," she told Sherman. "What is expected of me? What do I owe people? I realized I had to come to terms with this celebritydom. I realized I can't walk around feeling miserable because I didn't embrace everybody in the airport.

"So I don't hug people anymore," Oprah said. "It's always made me feel uncomfortable. That's growth. But it took a woman in an airport to make me feel really, really, really bad all the way to Miami to see it."

There was an edge to her remarks that August when she appeared at a black theatre festival in Winston-Salem, North Carolina, joking that folks had shown up to see if she had "gained the weight back."

Oprah told those gathered that black theatre had been instrumental in her rise to television stardom. She mentioned watching Ruby Dee perform in *A Raisin in the Sun* on her family's small black and white television set when she was growing up on her grandmother's Mississippi farm. That production and her participation in the black church had inspired her to build a career she knew would one day involve acting, she said.

"I let that vision carry me," she said. "If there had not been black theater, there would not be an 'Oprah Winfrey Show.' "

In September, Oprah joined Norman Lear and the cast of "A Different World" at the Bel-Air Hotel in Los Angeles to host a fund-raising brunch for the Los Angeles Rape Treatment Center. They raised $300,000, and Oprah said that Lear's TV work over the years had helped bring rape "out of the closet."

Still, there were so many demands on Oprah's time that she was forced to give up her work with the Kidadah project, although she stayed in close touch with the progress of the Little Sisters of Cabrini Green.

TV GUIDE FIASCO

Maybe she didn't let her weight bother her publicly, but Oprah could not help being humiliated by a fiasco involving a cover story in *TV Guide* the largest selling magazine in America. It should have been a fabulous moment: Oprah the subject of a cover story: "Oprah! The Richest Woman on TV?" and featuring a glamorous and surprisingly slim Oprah on the cover, sitting on a pile of money. There was only one problem: It was soon revealed that although the smiling face was Oprah's, the body was Ann-Margret's!

True, Oprah had packed on ten pounds and shot up a dress size since ending her widely publicized diet, but thanks to Ann-Margret's body, she looked absolutely ravishing on the August 26 cover.

TV Guide never told its readers that it was a phony cover. The extremely lifelike picture had been copied by artist Chris Notarile from a stunning ten-year-old photo of Ann-Margret in a gown by famed Hollywood designer, Bob Mackie.

"Perhaps Oprah just wasn't slinky enough for *TV Guide* anymore," said an insider.

Although Notarile refused to discuss the instructions he had been given by *TV Guide* editors when he fashioned the new-and-improved Oprah, he admitted, "I was attempting to draw a glamorous Oprah. It's like Frankenstein: You create something new by putting it together from old things. I know the picture looks real—it's supposed to."

But Ann-Margret, who found out about the cover from Bob Mackie, thought the artist and *TV Guide* had gone too far. "She was stunned," Mackie said. "They didn't change a thing in the picture except the skin tone and they drew in the pile of cash Oprah—or should I say

Ann-Margret—is sitting on. From the neck down, both pictures are exactly the same, including the sparkles off the beads on the dress I made.

"That's even Ann's ring Oprah's wearing!"

Ann-Margret did say, "When I first saw the cover, I was very angry at Oprah. I thought this was a very cheap stunt and she shouldn't use my looks to improve on her own. But after a while I calmed down when I [understood] that Oprah had been used by *TV Guide* just as I had."

The magazine had never told Oprah of its plans to give her a new body, according to Oprah's spokeswoman, Chris Tardio. And one of Oprah's closest friends said, "Oprah was shocked when she saw *TV Guide*. She feels hurt, angry and absolutely mortified by the whole thing.

"She told me, 'This is the most embarrassing thing I can imagine. Just about everybody in the whole country will see that picture. I thought I looked pretty decent, but I guess the real me isn't good enough for *TV Guide*. The whole thing stinks.' "

The talk show queen also told an insider, "Under different circumstances, I would probably be delighted to switch bodies with Ann-Margret, but not to sell magazines. This cover is exploitive of women and personally humiliating to me.

"They wouldn't picture Phil Donahue on the body of Arnold Schwarzenegger. Just like him, I deserve to be treated with dignity."

Chapter Nine
Oprah's Spiritual
Coming of Age

Sometimes I look at Stedman and I just can't stand it. I go, "Oh, my heart be still."
—Oprah Winfrey on the man in her life, 1989

By late 1989, Oprah was so deeply involved with Stedman Graham that she had even reluctantly taken up one of his favorite pastimes. She had started taking golf lessons so she could join him on the course. "I really hate golf," she confessed, "but I'll chase those little white balls around because it's what he likes."

In August there were rumors that she had finally made her wedding plans—and that she would tie the knot with Stedman at Christmas the following year.

Stedman had agreed to move to Chicago from North Carolina early in September to be with Oprah because she was unhappy with their long-distance romance. And she was insisting on an old-fashioned long engagement, so for fifteen months he would be showering her with flowers and romantic love notes.

During this period, which Oprah was calling a "trial marriage," they would live in separate homes. Oprah and

Stedman both felt that living together before marriage was morally wrong and set a bad example.

The lovebirds drew up a blueprint for their future during a five-hour meeting in a locked and moving limousine—because Oprah wanted to make sure Stedman couldn't walk out if he didn't like what she was saying!

Oprah had insisted that they find a place where the two of them had to stay put, even if it meant they had to handcuff themselves together.

Finally, she said, "I want to rent a limo and lock the doors." Stedman simply smiled and agreed.

Their romance had already logged three years, and Oprah wanted desperately to marry and have children. But Stedman, who had been married and divorced once before, had always sidestepped setting a wedding date. And over the months Oprah had grown more and more frustrated.

Finally Oprah told a friend: "We've just never hashed out where our lives were going. Then one morning while I was running I realized our relationship had no direction and that I wanted more.

"I couldn't stand it any longer. I called Stedman and told him we needed to sort this thing out right away. I said, 'Steddy, I want to come to North Carolina and nail you down for life.' "

Oprah was terrified that Stedman would refuse to talk things out, but to her surprise, he readily agreed.

She flew to North Carolina. Instead of taking Oprah to his home, Stedman rented a suite for her at the Stouffer Winston Plaza Hotel in nearby Winston-Salem, so they could be alone.

But the two decided they couldn't do any serious negotiations in the suite.

Even though the discussions sometimes got heated, they never raised their voices. If Stedman got mad he just walked away, and if Oprah got mad she went into another room.

They were afraid that with all the crucial decisions they had to make, they wouldn't get anything done if either of them was able to leave the room.

So they rented a limo and told the chauffeur to lock the doors until they got things settled!

Oprah and Stedman got into the limo at noon the day after Oprah's arrival and told the driver to give them a long, slow tour of Winston-Salem while they talked.

As the drive began, Oprah and Stedman held hands. Oprah whispered: "Dear God, help us find our path. Help us build upon our love."

Then Oprah began telling Stedman: "I want you in Chicago—right now! When I need a hug, I want to be able to run to your arms, not dial your area code."

After a long discussion, Stedman finally agreed to move to Chicago around Labor Day. Oprah offered him a job with her production company, Harpo, Inc., but he bristled at that suggestion.

"I'm my own man," he told her. "I want to be your spouse, not your employee. Case closed!"

Although marriage had long been on their minds, both were old-fashioned, and Stedman had never formally proposed to Oprah the traditional way, on his knee with a ring in one hand and a bouquet of flowers in the other.

But he had assured Oprah that he would do it right after moving to Chicago, where he planned to open a branch of his public relations firm.

Reportedly, Oprah and Stedman agreed to have two children before Oprah turned forty. She wanted a daughter, and he wanted a son.

To her surprise, Stedman told Oprah he wanted to sign a prenuptial agreement, for her sake, to make sure she kept the fortune she had worked so hard to build.

"I don't want 'his' and 'hers' checking accounts," Oprah said.

But Stedman insisted, telling her: "There's going to be a prenuptial and that's all there is to it! We're getting married—you aren't adopting me!"

That evening, the sweethearts sealed their agreement with a romantic dinner and toast "to our five year plan."

Oprah later told a friend: "I'm thrilled. That really was a day that changed my life forever."

"I WANT TO RAISE A CHILD WHO UNDERSTANDS HE OR SHE IS CREATED FROM GOODNESS AND POWER IN THE LIGHT OF GOD AND CAN DO ANYTHING HE SETS HIS MIND TO"

Oprah told other friends that she was thinking seriously about having a child. "It has to do with sharing all I know now with someone from the time that person was born. It has to do with contribution and extension and growth," she explained. "I relish the thought of trying to raise a child. I'm curious to see what it would be like to raise a child, teaching him responsibility, a sense of caring, but also independence."

Oprah went on: "So I want to raise a child who understands he or she is created from goodness and power in the light of God and can do anything he sets his mind to.

"Some days I really want a girl because you can dress her up and she'd be so cute—she'd be like me. Then I think I'd want to have a boy because I'd like to name him Canaan. Canaan Graham is such a strong name."

There was no doubt she had Stedman for the father. "He'll be a wonderful father. He really gives me a glow. Sometimes I look at Stedman and I just can't stand it. I go, 'Oh, my heart be still.' "

But there was the problem of a long-distance romance: "With Stedman based in North Carolina and me in Chicago, we only have weekends together," Oprah complained. "All that's going to change next year when Stedman moves to Chicago."

But, it seems, Stedman had already sat down with Oprah and told her frankly that if she wanted a relationship, she would have to start working on one.

"OPRAH WINFREY KILLED MY SON!"

Oprah was also discovering the dark side of fame, especially when her show was blamed for the deaths of two viewers.

That was the charge of top medical experts who said that her show focused on an extremely dangerous sexual practice, and a man and teenage boy who watched the episode were killed while imitating what had been described.

And the outraged father of one victim said flatly that his son's death was Oprah's fault.

"Oprah Winfrey killed my son!" a bitter Robert Holm charged.

Dr. Park Dietz, a former professor at the University of Virginia and America's leading authority on the practice, said that he warned the "Oprah" staff: Don't run that episode—because people will die.

But they ran it anyway.

"It's irresponsible," stormed Dr. Boyd Stephens, chief medical examiner for the city and county of San Francisco. "It's like teaching people how to make explosives out of household chemicals!"

Holm, the grieving father of thirty-eight-year-old victim John Holm, said he had even hired a lawyer and was considering suing Oprah.

"Her show led to John's death—and I will never forgive her for that," Holm said. "I just don't understand how Oprah could do such a callous, destructive thing."

The episode, which aired May 11, 1988, concerned autoerotic asphyxiation, a deadly perverse and sexual practice that accidentally kills as many as one thousand Americans a year.

Oprah agonized over airing the episode, she admitted in an interview in the 1989 issue of *Cosmopolitan* magazine. She said that at first she told her staff: "No way. What if somebody tries it? I don't want to be responsible."

But after meditating, "It began to seem right for her to go ahead with the show," the magazine reported.

Just a few hours after the episode aired nationwide, Robert Holm found his son dead.

"John was a wonderful boy," said Robert, sixty-eight, of Thousand Oaks, California. "He was very healthy, loved the outdoors and had never engaged in any weird stuff until he watched that show."

Robert Holm told interviewers that he last saw his son alive at about four o'clock in the afternoon. John said he was about to watch "The Oprah Winfrey Show" at 4:00 P.M.

"I had to go do some errands and then go to an Elks meeting. I came back late. John wasn't in the house. The television was still set on Channel 7, the channel he'd watched 'Oprah' on.

"The garage lights were on, but the door was locked from the inside. I banged on the door, but there was no answer. I had to break in. That's when I found his body. It was horrible.

"I thought John killed himself. But when the rescue squad came, one of the workers said he knew how my son had died because he'd seen the 'Oprah' show that afternoon.

"I blame the 'Oprah' show for my boy's death. I lost

156

my son and my best friend in the world. I'm absolutely devastated—and I've hired a lawyer to look into the possibility of suing Oprah for what she's done."

In fact, the show's producer was warned that the episode probably would result in lawsuits, revealed Dr. Dietz, the coauthor of a book on the practice.

"The producer called me before the show aired—and I told her I wanted nothing to do with it," said Dr. Dietz, who taught law, behavioral medicine, and psychiatry at the University of Virginia School of Medicine.

"I argued that television is not a suitable medium for discussing this subject because the risk of people imitating it is too high.

"On May 10, the day before the 'Oprah' show was to be done, I had a heated discussion with the producer. I told her that if the show were aired, it would foreseeably result in one or more deaths.

"She seemed insensitive to the prospect of her show killing human beings.

"I told her: 'If you do that show tomorrow, I expect that someday I'll be an expert witness in a lawsuit against Oprah and "Oprah" [the show] for reckless and negligent conduct—and I will tell the jury about this call.'

"She told me: 'We're going to do it anyway.' "

Dr. Dietz, a forensic psychiatrist in Newport Beach, California, said that after the episode aired he learned of John Holm's death and also the death of a teenage boy who accidentally died while trying the practice after watching the show.

"I heard about the teenage boy's case from an FBI contact of mine at the FBI Academy in Quantico, Virginia," he disclosed.

Dr. Dietz said that based on the known facts, he had concluded that the "Oprah" episode was the "primary cause of death" of John Holm.

This past May, the *Journal of Forensic Sciences* published a letter to the editor from Dr. Dietz in which he detailed his warning to the producer and indicated that other viewers also might have tragically died as a result of the episode.

"The case [of John Holm] . . . brings the death toll to two from this show, and still counting," the expert said in his letter.

A direct link between Holm's death and the "Oprah" episode was confirmed by Dr. Ronald O'Halloran, assistant medical examiner for Ventura County, California, who investigated the case and coauthored a report on it for the *Journal of Forensic Sciences* last November.

"John Holm tried it [the technique] and died after watching the 'Oprah' show," Dr. O'Halloran flatly declared.

When asked to comment on the experts' charges that Oprah's show led to the deaths of two viewers, "Oprah" spokeswoman Chris Tardio stated: "We were incredibly responsible in doing that show."

But Dr. Stephens charged that the only reason Oprah aired the episode about the sexual practice was "to make the show more sensational."

Said the medical examiner: "I wouldn't watch the 'Oprah' show if you tied me to a chair in front of the television.

"The 'Oprah' show should be banned!"

"BREWSTER PLACE" GOES TO SERIES

Although "The Women of Brewster Place" had been nominated for a prime time Emmy for Outstanding Mini-series, and Paula Kelly had been nominated for Outstanding Supporting Actress, when it was time to announce the awards on September 17 in Los Angeles, they were shut out in a swell of support for the two blockbusters that season: "Lonesome Dove" and "The Winds of War." The latter won for miniseries, and Colleen Dewhurst, a sentimental favorite, nudged out Kelly for Supporting Actress.

The disappointing showing in the Emmy Awards did not deter enthusiasm for Oprah's next project. That November, Oprah was so hot that the ABC network announced that in addition to her syndicated talk show she would also star in the network's "Brewster Place," a weekly half-hour drama spun off the miniseries. The network had ordered thirteen half-hour episodes, scheduled to begin production in January for an April debut. The series would be shot in Oprah's new Chicago studio, allowing her to handle both shows simultaneously.

Oprah would reprise her role as Mattie Michael, and it would be set mainly in the late 1960s, sparing Oprah the aging makeup that she had to experience for the miniseries.

A SISTER'S PROBLEMS

Oprah's half sister, Patricia Lee, meanwhile had reportedly become so desperate for drug money that she was selling off her furniture and jewelry to buy drugs. Her daughters were living with Vernita, and Patricia's situation was breaking their hearts.

Finally, in October, about four months after Oprah cut her off, Patricia hit rock bottom. With no money to pay her rent, she was facing eviction.

"Patricia had enough," said a friend. "She called Oprah in tears, crying out for help. And Oprah told me 'That was her most important step—to admit there was a problem.' "

Oprah arranged for counseling and got Patricia into a

treatment center to deal with her drug problem. While Patricia was struggling with her drug demons, Oprah took special interest in her daughters.

Many times during her travels, she would get off an airplane and run to a pay phone to call and see how they were doing.

Even Stedman, who had his own teenage daughter, would often jump on the phone and encourage them.

Oprah even visited Patricia in treatment. She told a friend: "She's still my sister. I can't abandon her. I cut off the money—not my love."

Patricia told her sister: "I'm so grateful to you. You've helped me save my life. You were there for me when I needed you. I love you. I couldn't have done it without you."

When Patricia completed her rehabilitation treatment, she moved in with her mother and daughters, knowing she had Oprah's complete love and support.

"OPRAH IS VERY AMBITIOUS"

In spite of her many interests, Oprah remained committed first and foremost to "The Oprah Winfrey Show," the source of her wealth and power. Lest anyone think otherwise, King World Productions assured stock analysts in December 1989 that there was no threat that Oprah might be leaving in the near future.

King World, best-known as distributor of "Wheel of Fortune" and "Jeopardy!," had come a long way to appear at the annual Paine Webber, Inc., Media Outlook Conference.

A few years earlier, King World would not have been considered a big enough player to merit an invitation to a five-day gathering that included such old-line companies as Dow Jones & Co., Dun & Bradstreet Corp., Time Warner, Inc., New York Times Co., and Tribune Co.

By 1989, King World's three mega-hits, "Wheel," "Jeopardy," and "Oprah" produced more than $1.5 billion in revenue, accounting for eighty-eight percent of the firm's $396 million in revenue in fiscal 1988. Net profit was $76 million.

But analysts wondered openly: Suppose Oprah were to leave for other endeavors, such as her acting career?

"Oprah is very ambitious," a King World executive acknowledged. "She wants to act in movies and TV shows." But, he also noted, there were not many parts for black women, and Oprah's only real avenue was to produce shows herself.

To produce these shows, she would need a lot of money and the best way to get that money was to stick to her day job, for which she was contractually obligated to King World through 1993. It was a mutually beneficial arrangement.

Oprah was always looking for ways to keep the talk show fresh. That October she brought the show to New York for a week, then moved to the West Coast and various locations at Universal Studios. It was the first time she had done the show from either city.

While in New York, she would appear at the Westbury Music Fair for a benefit to raise money for the Madison Square Boys & Girls Club and the Urban Women's Shelter in Harlem. The 2,900-seat theater sold out in two days.

Oprah confessed to gossip columnist Liz Smith that she was tired. "I've been traveling recently and went through five time zones in five days. I was in London, France, L.A., Atlanta, Columbus and Chicago. But I can't wait to get to New York."

One of the shows that Oprah would be taping in new York was a reunion of the *Steel Magnolias* cast. ("Don't ask me how we managed to get them all back together at once in one place.") She was also doing a show on "New York's Classic Women" that would feature Ivana Trump, Lauren Hutton, Adrienne Vittadini, and Beverly Johnson; another show would feature Bill Cosby who would talk frankly about his daughter's recent problems with drugs.

Smith asked Oprah how she could possibly keep up the pace and she laughed: "I want to seize the time while it is here, and I love what I'm doing."

OPRAH WOWS WESTBURY

Oprah's fans greeted her with a standing ovation at the Westbury Music Fair the night of October 26, although no one was clear about exactly what she was going to do. The first hour was a carefully wrought, consummate blend of stand-up comedy, penetrating poetry (including some by Maya Angelou), dazzling monologues, and just plain down-home chat.

Whether recalling her childhood or recreating moments in the lives of significant black historical figures like Sojourner Truth, she kept the crowd spellbound.

This was followed by a question and answer hour that drew relatively few questions. The audience was more interested in paying homage to Oprah, telling her, for instance, how they had lost weight or straightened out their lives, thanks to her inspiration. She handled it all with grace and charm, reflecting a sincere interest in everyone.

One critic, at least, was swept away. "Should she ever harness her popularity and translate her doctrines into a political program," raved Bob Harrington of the *New*

York Post, "America might just get its first woman and first black president in one fashionably dressed package."

OPRAH AND ROSEANNE JOIN FORCES

Although Oprah was usually able to rise above lurid tabloid tales about herself, occasionally one would get to her, especially if it touched on her professionalism or sincerity. Naturally, she was outraged at tabloid stories that had her and Roseanne Barr warring over Roseanne's weight. She joined forces with Roseanne, herself a frequent target of the tabloids, and the two stars went back on the air for a united, no-holds-barred counterassault.

"There wasn't one single thing they said that was true," insisted Oprah of an article that had her and Roseanne locked in a "furious feud" following the recent taping of an "Oprah Winfrey Show" and quoted Oprah as telling Roseanne, "Girl, I'm going to level with you. You'd look and feel better if you'd just lose a good 40 pounds."

"The truth is, I never saw Roseanne after the show— and, for the record, I never sent her Optifast in the mail, as the story maintained. I did send her six bottles of Cristal champagne and six dozen roses as thanks for doing the show—and received a lovely note from her in return."

"I COME HERE CELEBRATING EVERY AFRICAN, EVERY COLORED, BLACK, NEGRO AMERICAN EVERYWHERE .... I COME CELEBRATING THE JOURNEY ..."

That December, Oprah toured the awards circuit from Washington to Los Angeles. On December 3, she charmed the one thousand guests who filled the Washington Hilton's Crystal Ballroom for the Forty-fourth National Convention of the National Council of Negro Women. In black pants and gold top, escorted by Stedman, Oprah took her responsibilities as Mistress of Ceremonies most seriously.

"I come here tonight celebrating not only the finalists and the honorees and the rest of us gathered here in this room," Oprah began, "but I come here celebrating every African, every colored, black, Negro American everywhere that ever cooked a meal, ever raised a child, ever worked in the fields, ever went to school, ever sang in a choir, ever loved a man or loved a woman, every cornrowed, every Afroed, every wig-wearing, pigtailed, weave-wearing one of us."

She paused for breath and to acknowledge the hearty applause and laughter that greeted her words.

"I come celebrating the journey, I come celebrating the little passage, the movement of our women people. I include everybody because I believe that it is everybody's contribution that has allowed us to stand, that has allowed me to stand on solid rock here tonight at the Hilton Hotel."

Dorothy Height, president of the National Council of Negro Women, lauded Oprah as "so valuable because she has risen to the heights but her feet are still on the ground."

Later that month, Oprah was in Los Angeles for the Twenty-second Annual NAACP Image Awards where she was named Entertainer of the Year and won three other Image Awards, presented to performers and shows that present fair images of blacks in the media. Oprah wore a necklace worth a half-million dollars and was also honored for her work on "The Women of Brewster Place" and for the "Prime Time Oprah."

"I'LL NEVER TALK ABOUT MY DIET AGAIN"

Sadly, it looked as if Oprah was losing her weight battle after all. She had conquered poverty and sexual abuse, but she was helpless in the battle against her weight. She confessed she had regained seventeen of the sixty-seven pounds she had lost in 1988, and was vowing that she would never discuss her weight publicly again.

But it was Oprah herself who had turned her diet into the most talked-about weight loss in history.

On November 15, exactly one year after Oprah reached her lowest weight (120 pounds), she devoted "The Oprah Winfrey Show" to a discussion of her constant struggle to keep from regaining the weight.

"I promise, after this show, I am never going to talk about this diet again," declared Oprah. "And if a reporter asks me about it, I'm going to start humming. I'm not saying another word about it."

In addition to her low-fat, low-sugar diet, Oprah said she exercised every day on a Stairmaster machine that simulated climbing stairs. Two or three days a week, she also worked with weights, and she did aerobics six days a week.

"Nothing feels better than finishing—nothing," she said.

Oprah added that the support of her fans and friends helped her keep on her weight-loss program—except for one good friend, Bill Cosby.

"I went over to Mr. Cosby's house to have some sweet potato pie. He then said: 'This really isn't the best sweet potato pie. I have some really good sweet potato pie.' And he sent three sweet potato pies to my hotel, which I continued to eat for the rest of the week. . . . You know what happens once you get off course."

Oprah read a few letters from fans who gave her encouragement—or who were inspired by her slim-down success.

One came from thirteen-year-old Veronica, who wrote:

"I just wanted to tell you that I've started another diet today because of you and I'm going to stick to this one because I'm tired of people making jokes and talking about me."

Oprah later told a close friend that "the absolute hardest part of dieting is doing it in the public eye.

"Whenever I order something fattening to eat in a restaurant they call the newspapers. It seems like they get the story before I have the meal delivered to my table!

"One day I ordered apple pancakes in a restaurant and read about it in two newspapers the next day!

"My biggest problem is that I love to eat—and no diet or exercise can take away the craving I have for fried foods and salty dishes.

"This is the hardest thing I've ever done in my life," Oprah admitted to her friend. "Anyone who says it's easy is lying. There is no easy way to keep off the excess pounds.

"I hate exercising. It's torture for me. It's horrible, but what can I do? I have to continue. There are just too many people counting on me.

"It's a fight that goes on every minute of the day . . . I guess, for the rest of my life. But I'm not going back to my old fat self!"

A DEATHBED RECONCILIATION

As the year drew to an end, Oprah experienced a deathbed reconciliation of sorts with her brother Jeffrey Lee.

"My sister Oprah has forgiven me for all my mistakes," Jeffrey told a friend shortly before he died that December 22 at the age of twenty-nine. "I was a thorn in her side, but I always loved her—and she always loved me."

Oprah and Jeffrey had not talked for over a year because they disagreed about his wild life-style. Jeffrey confessed that he stole from Oprah to feed a cocaine addiction and deeply disappointed her when he told her he was a homosexual. But she never stopped loving him.

"I turned my back on Oprah, but she never gave up on me—and now it's time to set the record straight," said Jeffrey.

"I want people to know that Oprah has a heart of gold and she helped me to the end. She paid my medical expenses through our mother. Without her financial support I couldn't have lived this long or as comfortably.

"But I was selfish and took advantage of her goodness," said the contrite little brother. "Over the years I let her down by partying, drinking and using drugs."

Jeffrey sincerely regretted the pain he had caused her. "I ripped her off to buy cocaine and misused the help she gave me. I'm sad about that now. I wish I had been stronger."

Jeffrey was relieved that Oprah continued to care deeply for him. "Despite all the wrongs I committed, my mother told me that Oprah didn't bear a grudge against me. She never stopped loving me and remembered me all the time in her prayers. She forgave me totally for all the times I had hurt and upset her."

As Jeffrey spoke in Milwaukee, his weakened body was ravaged by pain. His lips were covered with a white fungus, one of many infections that ravage AIDS victims. He paused to wipe his mouth with a tissue, then continued:

"Oprah disapproved of my life-style and believes that homosexuality is wrong, but while hating the sin, she loves the sinner. That's why she has friends who are gays. She loves and helps them, although she cannot condone their lives.

"But I hurt inside because I know homosexuals don't go to heaven. Oprah and I agree on that."

Like Oprah, Jeffrey believed in God, but feared God might not forgive him his sins—real and imagined. "I think she will go to heaven—she is such a good honest person—and it would give me great comfort to believe it would be possible for us to meet in heaven."

Sadly, young Jeffrey Lee had come to believe that it might not happen.

"Now that the end is getting close, I want Oprah to know that throughout our troubles, although I let her down time after time, I still loved her and was proud of her," said Jeffrey, struggling for his dying breath.

"And I want Oprah to remember me with love, not pity."

Sadly, the little brother Oprah used to look after when she lived in Milwaukee, the little brother who played outside on the porch while inside the house she played "the Horse" with her parade of older men, the little brother who spilled the beans and told their mother about the thug who invaded their home and nearly killed her over money he insisted Oprah owed him, that little brother was gone, a tragic victim of a dread disease that had claimed so many. And there was nothing Oprah could do about it, except intensify her fund-raising efforts to find a cure and a treatment for the great scourge of the era.

"OPRAH WILL NEVER HAVE CHILDREN"

It seemed that Oprah's family would never stop causing her heartache. Right about the time that her younger brother died, Oprah's mother gave a strange interview in which she made a startling prediction: "Oprah will never have children. I just don't see her with kids of her own."

Vernita Lee had given birth to Oprah, her first child, out of wedlock when she was nineteen years old, and she never quite understood her gifted daughter.

"Oprah is very driven," she told an interviewer. "She's been striving to 'be somebody' since she was a young girl. Her career is the most important thing in her life, not kids.

"It's not that she doesn't love kids—she loves them dearly. She just doesn't have the patience to deal with their exuberance," confided the fifty-four-year-old Vernita.

Vernita already had two teenage granddaughters from her daughter Patricia and acknowledged that Oprah made a real effort to be with them, taking them shopping and buying them wonderful new school clothes. Oprah had even taken the girls out to California and to her farm in Indiana.

"But after a while you can see the look on her face," said Vernita. "She just runs out of patience. Oprah will say, 'O.K. take them, I've had enough.' That's fine for nieces, but you can't do that with your own children."

Vernita was aware that in interviews Oprah had said that she would like at least two children, but she was skeptical.

"As a grandmother and mother, I pray that it's true. But as Oprah's mom, I don't think she'll ever have kids."

Even though friends were predicting that Oprah would marry longtime boyfriend Stedman Graham at Christmas next year, Vernita said her daughter was just too busy to have children.

"Oprah keeps such a busy pace, I don't see how she'd

find time for kids. Some days she gets only four or five hours sleep. She's up at 6 A.M. and out the door to run. Then she's back to get showered and ready for work.''

Vernita was also awed by her daughter's tremendous responsibilities. ''She has the talk show to do every day,'' said Vernita. ''She bought a studio, so now she has that to run. She gets requests to speak and she has a foundation that donates money to worthy causes. She's just not ready to give all that up.''

Ironically, Vernita thought that among Oprah's many talents was her potential to be a great mom.

And she thought Stedman would be a perfect father for the children.

''I spent the Fourth of July weekend with Oprah and Stedman on her farm in Indiana,'' Vernita revealed. ''We had such a good time, I told Oprah that I want Stedman for a son-in-law.''

Oprah told her mother: ''Not yet, Mama, not just yet.''

And then, her mother said, Oprah winked.

''ONE OF THE THINGS PEOPLE DON'T KNOW ABOUT ME IS I'M REALLY VERY FUNNY''

As usual, Oprah dealt with her grief over the death of her little brother by immersing herself in her work. Her empire was rapidly expanding. She was building her new Chicago studio and had several productions in development. The ''Brewster Place'' series was a major priority.

''But the most important project of my life will be Toni Morrison's Pulitzer Prize-winning novel, *Beloved*,'' she said at the time, ''though I really can't think of it until my studio is built. I have to find a writer who can take the book and turn it into a screenplay without losing the essence of what the author conveys.'' The book focused on the problems of post-Civil War blacks who had to wrestle with their slave past.

Oprah had also optioned *Kaffir Boy*, Mark Mathabane's autobiographical novel about a black South African who comes to America, and she had Alex Haley at work on a script for her called *Madame C.J. Walker*, about the first black woman to build a cosmetics empire.

"Yes, most of the things I have bought so far have been black written projects," she acknowledged. "I don't want to do exclusively black work. What I'm looking to do is work that means something.

"I need at least two other projects that are very different," Oprah said. "I'd like to play a more contemporary role, something sexy—with my clothes on—something fun. One of the things people don't know about me is I'm really very funny."

The idea of playing a romantic heroine may have been what attracted Oprah to *Cold Sassy Tree*, but that project got away from her. Oprah made a bid for the rights to Olive Ann Burns's book, but Turner Network Television got the project for Faye Dunaway. "I went right after it," Oprah acknowledged. "But they already had the rights. I was told after the writers' strike that it might be available. But it wasn't. It was my favorite book last summer.

"You can sit around and wait for others to do it for you," she told journalists, "but that way you get offered schlock scripts. When I find good work, I try to purchase it and see that it gets done. I don't have to be in all of them. I'm just interested in seeing good work come to the screen."

Chapter Ten
Oprah's Most Unforgettable Guests

It's interesting to me that I'm called a "talk-show host" because I understand in my heart that there is something deeper, stronger, and more important going on with the people who are affected by the show.

> —Oprah Winfrey answering critics who call shows like hers exploitative

Although Oprah has been hosting her talk show for almost ten years, she shows no signs of growing tired of her role. She strives to keep it fresh and with a broad range of topics and locations, from rioters in Los Angeles, to hurricane-devastated Charleston, South Carolina, to an interview with Robert James Waller, the author of the best-selling romantic novel *The Bridges of Madison County*, beside one of the covered bridges of Wisconsin that he has made famous.

Here is a "talk soup" of some of the more memorable moments of recent "Oprah Winfrey Show"'s:

THE FEUDING SISTERS

When Oprah flew in guests for an April 1993 show on feuding sisters, she got more than she bargained for—identical twins Marie and Anita got into a fistfight at their hotel, and security had to be called. Marie punched Anita in the face so hard Anita says she couldn't eat breakfast the next morning. As Oprah listened, the sisters tried to explain.

ANITA: "I was having a phone conversation with a boyfriend back home about my insecurities being on television.

"Marie and my mother overheard my conversation about 'Oh, I'm not sure if I want to go.' They both jump on me, 'We did this and we've done that . . .'

"I jump up and tell my mother . . . 'Look, if there's any money involved, I'd be more than happy to pay.' Next thing I know, Marie gives me a slug to my jaw when I'm not looking."

Marie said she hit her sister to protect their mom. She accused Anita of being drunk at the time. But Anita denied this.

THE DISAPPEARING MILLIONAIRE

Millionaire businessman Domer Ringuette, fifty-three, disappeared without a trace in the middle of his campaign to become town alderman—only to turn up six months later as a poker dealer in Las Vegas.

The only clue he left behind was a call to his daughter in Texas telling her if anyone contacted her looking for him not to worry. Domer, of Chicopee, Massachusetts, revealed to Oprah in April 1993, why he decided to walk away from his former life.

DOMER: "Well, I've always wanted to be a poker dealer since I was sixteen. And I've mentioned it through the course of my life that I planned on doing it in the future. Well, finally one day I decided, 'Here I am 53, if I don't do it now, I'm never going to do it.' So I did it."

OPRAH: "So you always wanted to be a poker dealer, but you ended up being a real estate owner and the publisher of a newspaper . . . And that's not what you wanted to do?"

DOMER: "They don't have poker in Massachusetts, so I couldn't be a poker dealer in Massachusetts."

THE PRIEST WHO FAKED HIS OWN DEATH

After her father's funeral in 1969, Patricia Moody discovered her dad had died once before—he was a Catholic priest who faked his death so he could marry Patricia's mom Catherine! In August 1993, as Oprah listened, mother and daughter revealed Father Raymond (John) Carrigan's incredible secret.

CATHERINE: "He wanted to leave the priesthood to marry me. But in those days, a priest did not do that."

OPRAH: "So he faked his own death?"

CATHERINE: "Yes, he went fishing in Oregon, pushed the boat out and they hunted all over for his body."

Father Carrigan started using the name John, moved to California, and opened a stationery store. He kept the secret for more than fifteen years until he was killed in a car accident. Patricia was shocked to discover that her father had been a priest and that she had relatives on his side.

PATRICIA: "The day that he really died it was on the front page of the newspaper and his family saw it. I was about fourteen and they showed up at the door. I was just devastated."

MULTIPLE PERSONALITIES LINKED TO CHILD ABUSE

More and more people are being diagnosed with multiple personality disorder (MPD)—the bizarre illness that was vividly portrayed in the television movie "Sybil." Oprah blamed the rise on an increase in the number of child abuse cases.

In May 1992, one woman, Lisa, who had been adopted, confided to Oprah how she first developed fourteen different personalities to cope with the torment of child sexual abuse she suffered from a male baby-sitter.

LISA: "I was about 12. I started feeling like I had to hide . . . then it started getting really chaotic at home and because I was so depressed and miserable about being adopted and sexually abused.

"I started to feel like I was different people or different moods. One minute, I was happy, I was ecstatic . . . the next minute I wanted to die.

"You know, I didn't know who I was."

THE $30,000-A-MONTH SHOPAHOLIC

Plumbing business owner Charles Muntwyler's savings were going down the drain—because his shopaholic wife Susan spent up to $30,000 a month packing her Imelda Marcos-style closet with clothes and shoes!

In June 1992 Oprah sent her cameraman to the Muntwyler house and Charles took them on a tour of his wife's bulging closets.

CHARLES: "As you can see, this is a very moderate house. My wife wants a big expensive house. . . . Let me show you where the money goes. . . . This is our basement, also known as Sue's closet. As you can see, everything from fur coats to Bloomingdale's leather and $1,000 dresses.

"She can't wear the same dress twice to any party. God forbid somebody sees her with the same outfit twice.

"A hundred and eight pairs of shoes last time I counted them."

After the filming of her closet, Susan promised to stick to a $4,500-a-month budget. But she did buy just one more pair of shoes . . . when she and Charles appeared on Oprah's show.

"MY HUBBY RAPED ME—AND GOT AWAY WITH IT"

Trish Crawford said her husband taped her eyes and mouth shut, tied her up, and then raped her while recording the attack on videotape—yet a jury found him not guilty!

Trish, who was divorcing her husband, recounted her ordeal to Oprah in July 1992.

TRISH: "He grabbed me, he carried me to the extra bedroom where he already had ropes tied to the bed.

"He had this whole thing premeditated. He tied me. He continually hit me.

"He threatened me with a knife. He threatened to hurt my children. They were in the next room.

"He hit my hand, which was tied, with a hammer, put me through 3½ hours of torture."

Her husband testified they were just playing a sex game.

TRISH: "He turned to the jury. He said, 'I did not rape my wife. How can a man rape his own wife?' "

OPRAH: "And the jury took how long to come up with the not guilty verdict?"

TRISH: "About 46 minutes."

SHE FOILED HER MOM'S MURDER PLOT

Jennifer blew the whistle on her mom—to keep her from getting away with murder! Jennifer's mother and her mom's fiancé Michael were planning to kill Michael's ex-wife and asked Jennifer for help. But she went to the cops instead.

Jennifer, who wore a wire to record Michael for police, shared the diabolical murder plot with Oprah in August 1992.

JENNIFER: "My mother said she was going to send a gun to my house and I was to pick (Michael) up at the airport and then he was going to drop me off . . . and then kill her and then come back and get me and then go back to the airport."

Police nabbed Michael after he landed and picked up the gun. He and Jennifer's mom were arrested in January 1992.

OPRAH: "How does your mom feel about you now?"

JENNIFER: "I don't know. I haven't talked to her . . . I disowned her."

"I'M A VIRGIN MOM WITH TWO KIDS"

Mom Julie Halligan had given birth to two children, but when she appeared on "The Oprah Winfrey Show" in February 1993, she was still a virgin.

Julie, who was thirty-five and single, explained to Oprah why she decided to have daughters Whitnee, four, and Ashley, two, without having sex.

JULIE: "I have always believed that your wedding night should be special and you wear a white gown for a reason . . . plus I haven't met anyone.

180

"And I feel like you need to be in love and at least love that person to go to bed with them.

"I have never found anyone like that. I do date, but I haven't found anyone I'm truly in love with, and I'm not going to bed with just anybody.

"So I went to a clinic and looked into artificial insemination and then had Whitnee.

"And I wanted to have another one by the time I was 35 if I hadn't gotten married. And I was 33 when I had Ashley.

"I'd love to be married, but it's not my first goal in life. I wanted children really bad. And I have my children.

"If I get married fine. If not, it's not the end of the world for me."

OPRAH: "Good for you. Good for you."

THE GUEST WHO WASN'T

Sometimes even Oprah's compassion and patience run out as they did in September 1990, when Oprah was said to have raised holy hell and cancelled an appearance by Vicki Long, the Atlanta woman who claimed she had slept with an archbishop, because Ms. Long ran up $7,000 in hotel bills in four days and charged them to Oprah.

Vicki, who had practiced the laying on of hands with the archbishop, a priest, and a nun, had been booked into the Chicago hotel where Oprah's guests usually stayed, but insisted on moving to the posh Four Seasons.

"Vicki proceeded to run up an outrageous hotel bill—on Oprah," said a source close to the show. "Oprah was furious over demands for personal security . . . and thinly veiled demands for money." Oprah told the source:

181

"That girl's looking at me as the next gravy train." Oprah ordered Vicki and her entourage to hit the road.

WHEN BABY-SITTER MARRIES "DADDY"

What happens when Dad divorces Mom and marries the baby-sitter? Oprah found out in January 1992 when she listened to a bitter brother and sister, Jack and Elizabeth. They relived the shocking moment their father told them that their baby-sitter—who had been with the family since she was a teenager—was becoming their stepmom.

ELIZABETH: "I was approximately [in] fifth grade . . . and the best is . . . he told us in a restaurant!"

JACK: "On my younger brother's birthday."

ELIZABETH: "On his birthday—that he was marrying P.J., as we always called her."

JACK: "The baby-sitter."

ELIZABETH: "I stood up and I go, 'You're marrying P.J., the baby-sitter?' . . . I'm like, 'You've got to be joking.' "

P.J., now thirty-five, has since become president of their father's company and has had three children with Jack and Elizabeth's dad.

CHER: "THE YOUNGER MAN I WANTED TO MARRY—AND LOST"

Although Cher could have almost any man she wants, she lost the one she wanted the most—her bagel baker boyfriend Rob Camilletti. She revealed this in an eye-opening interview with Oprah in January 1991.

"I did really want to marry Robert," Cher admitted as she talked publicly for the first time about her breakup with her former live-in love who was only twenty-two when they met. "He gave me a real feeling of being taken care of and we had the best time. I never felt that way about anybody. It was just a great relationship.''

Cher also told Oprah that the romance changed her outlook about aging, making her realize you're only as young as you feel.

''Forty was my favorite year,'' she confided to Oprah. ''But on my 40th birthday I got a call from the director of *Witches of Eastwick* and he said, 'You can't play the part you want because you're not sexy enough.' ''

Cher landed another role in the movie, but spent her birthday down in the dumps.

''I'm sitting there and my children and my friend are bringing in a cake, singing 'Happy Birthday'—and tears are streaming down my face because he's telling me I'm not young and sexy enough,'' she said.

''Then I met Robert. We had the best time! Of the two of us, he always said I was the much younger.''

Although Cher flaunts her sexuality and dresses like a red-hot teen, she assured Oprah that behind closed doors, she and Rob were just like an old married couple.

''We went to the movies and we played cards,'' Cher recalled. ''We watched *The Godfather* epic every night before we went to bed.''

Because Rob was eighteen years her junior, the romance bolstered Cher's reputation for cradle robbing. Her other young men have included rocker Richie Sambora and actor Val Kilmer, but she insisted to Oprah that ''I'm not looking for my age range. I like street men . . . I don't like smooth men. I'm sure they're nice, but I want someone fiery.''

She also revealed to Oprah that despite her reputation as someone who flitted from man to man, she really wanted marriage, but didn't know if it was in the cards.

''It's something I think about all the time and I'd really love to do it,'' Cher said. ''It would have been a mistake with Robert. But we have a great friendship—better than my friendship with anybody."

WHY WARREN BEATTY WANTED TO BE A DADDY

Ladies' man Warren Beatty told Oprah that he had given up dating steamy sex sirens for diapering a wet infant during his January 1992 appearance on her talk show.

The star, looking forward to the imminent birth of his daughter with actress Annette Bening, confided to Oprah his reasons for wanting to become a father at fifty-four.

OPRAH: "You want to change diapers?"

WARREN: "Yeah."

OPRAH: "Go to PTA meetings?"

WARREN: "I don't know. I'm not throwing my hat in the air about the diapers, but I . . . yeah, I do."

OPRAH: "You want to impart your value system or your morals?"

WARREN: ". . . I think I would like to teach a child that it's O.K. to be happy."

OPRAH: "Good."

WARREN: "That's about the main thing. And to be honest. And if I can do that I think I would have done the job pretty well and then maybe I could learn from her."

THE SECRET WEAKNESS OF SLY STALLONE

His Rocky character can take a punch without blinking, but Sylvester Stallone's own ego bruises easily! He confessed to Oprah in March 1992 that he hates being criticized by fans and reviewers.

OPRAH: "But does it hurt your feelings?"

STALLONE: "Hey, no one likes to be [told]: 'His career is more mysterious than crib death.' Everyone wants affirmation—especially performers. . . . Yet it's really amazing how fragile someone's ego is. You can get thousands of accolades . . . and one person writes you a letter and says, 'You are really horrible. You are the worst.' And you're like: 'Who was that? Find him. I don't care where.'

"That's the frailty of the performing psyche."

LOVE-HUNGRY LANDLORD WANTED MORE THAN RENT

Twenty-two women charged that their landlord didn't just collect rent—he tried to collect sex from them, too. They angrily accused the manager of their San Francisco apartment complex of grabbing their private parts, letting himself into their homes while they slept or showered, and even raping two tenants.

One of the women, Elena, revealed to Oprah in April 1992 that her sexual abuse at his hands started from day one.

ELENA: "When I went to pay him my first month's rent, he scooted his chair up in front of me and ran his hand up the inside of my leg . . . and said, 'Baby, I'll take anything you've got.' This was in front of my 8-year-old daughter, who was terrified because I just let someone touch me where I had told her to let no one touch her."

OPRAH: "What did you do?"

ELENA: "I left as quickly as possible."

The women said the manager threatened his female tenants with eviction if they said anything, but they formed a group and complained to authorities. The abuse stopped when landlord Skinner was arrested and charged with two counts of rape. He denies any sexual harassment and has pleaded not guilty to the rape charges.

OPRAH WORKS OUT WITH SCHWARZENEGGER

Muscleman Arnold Schwarzenegger promised to put Oprah Winfrey through a grueling workout . . . by directing her in a movie. He revealed his plans for her during an interview on her show in May 1992.

ARNOLD: "I would be so tough on you. I would do things 50 times over and over just to teach you a lesson that you can't get everything you want . . . But how much greater can I make you? I mean, you're a great actress."

OPRAH: "I would be willing to let you try. I really would."

ARNOLD: "O.K. That's a deal."

"MY HUSBAND IS SO CHEAP . . ."

On a June 1993 show, Susie told Oprah her husband is so cheap that when her doctor recommended she get a dishwasher he bought her a $1.99 sponge!

SUSIE: "One time I cut my hand really bad and my husband had taken me to the doctor and I had some stitches put in. And the doctor said, 'Listen, I don't want you to wash dishes for a while, not until those stitches come out.'

"My husband had heard this. So he takes me home and he drops me off and he disappears for an hour.

"And he comes back and he says, 'Susie, have I got a dishwasher for you.' Well, I had tears in my eyes. You have to remember he never buys me anything.

"So he said, 'Close your eyes.' So I closed my eyes.

And he opens up this bag and he's got a sponge on a stick for $1.99. And that's not all. He gave me a pair of rubber gloves.''

"AFTER NINE YEARS, I FOUND OUT MY SON ISN'T MINE"

When Howard Plunkett filed for divorce, he discovered that the nine-year-old son he loved with all his might was another man's child. Howard shared his heartbreak with Oprah in June 1993.

OPRAH: "His wife Liz admits to having a one-night affair years ago but says she always believed it really was his child and is just as shocked as he is."

HOWARD: "I remember the day I got the news he wasn't my son. I was devastated. All I could do was cry."

OPRAH: "What happened?"

HOWARD: "I filed for divorce and [Liz] said she wasn't going to let me see him because I'm not on the birth certificate. And I said, 'Well, I'll get on it then.' So I had a DNA run."

Liz left Howard off the birth certificate because her divorce from her first husband had not become final when Jason was born.

The DNA test proved Howard was not the father.

Howard and Liz were hoping to tell Jason the truth, and both now wanted him to maintain his relationship with Howard.

"FAMILY PHOTO FOILED MY TWO-TIMING LOVER"

Kathy Reagan thought she and her live-in fiancé had a picture-perfect relationship—until she showed up at his law office unexpectedly and spotted a photo of him, his secretary, and her children. Kathy revealed to Oprah in May 1993 that the photo was all the evidence she needed to convict her lawyer of misconduct.

KATHY: "We started making wedding plans. He's a lawyer and he had a secretary for five years.

"Little things started popping up. I'd walk into the office and there'd be a miniature golf scorecard with her name and his above her desk.

"One day I walked into his office unknown and there's an 8 by 10 picture of him and her and her kids on his desk. My picture was nowhere to be found.

"He, sort of, 'Well, she's just a friend and I take good care of her kids'—giving me all these lines."

Kathy called off the wedding and kicked her fiancé out.

"I WAS A TARGET AT A SHOOTING CONTEST"

TV newscaster Tim made news when he went to cover a skeet-shooting contest and got blasted by shotgun fire! The anchor at WBKO in Bowling Green, Kentucky, relived his harrowing misadventure for Oprah in April 1993:

TIM: "It was a state competition. There was probably a couple of hundred people there. So I said, 'How do I go to the nearest site so I could [film]?'

"So the guy just said, 'Go down this trail.'

"When I got down, my instincts said, 'I think they're shooting in my direction!'

"But I couldn't see them, I was in a real wooded area. I was trying to find out what direction they were shooting.

"About that time, I got shot. It was just boom, boom, boom, constant shooting. So my first instinct was just yelling.

"I said, 'Hey, stop, I'm up here!' "

OPRAH: "Why didn't you hit the ground?"

TIM: "I did. Buckshot was in my tennis shoes all the way up to my shoulder . . . 57 pellets. They pulled out 37 at the hospital. I guess 20 didn't actually stick.

"My nickname was 'Buckshot' for a couple of weeks."

A WOMAN SAVED HIS LIFE AFTER HE WAS RAPED BY THREE MEN

Michael was so ashamed after three men raped him that he considered killing himself—but his wife's love saved his life. Michael shared his dramatic story with Oprah in April 1993:

MICHAEL: "I was walking down the street and these men were checking out their van. As I was walking by, one of them grabbed me from behind and threw me in the van. And they tied me up at knife point and then later it became a gun.

"Each one raped me. It went on from 11 at night until 3 in the morning. And then they took me to a bridge and threw me off."

OPRAH: "They left you for dead?"

MICHAEL: "Yes."

After the rape, he was traumatized for years.

MICHAEL: "I thought maybe there was something that these men were attracted to. Maybe they thought I was gay.

"I thought maybe I had to prove myself, so I tried to sleep with as many women as possible . . . I still didn't feel any better about myself.

"I went celibate for five years, until I met my wife. And she's the only thing that saved me because I thought of killing myself so many times."

"WHY I FORGIVE MY DAUGHTER'S KILLER"

"My daughter's fiancé shot her to death. But I forgive him—because he loved her!"

Compassionate mother Becky Hamilton made that startling revelation to Oprah with her daughter Dana's fiancé Ron at her side on a March 1993 show.

Dana was killed in January 1991 when Ron's hunting rifle accidentally discharged inside their home.

Dana's fourteen-year-old sister had died in a car accident a year earlier, and the family was just getting over her death—when tragedy struck again.

OPRAH: "Dana had met Ron and was starting to feel better about herself? And life was getting a little better, correct?"

BECKY: "Right. Dana was just getting her life back together. And this man, I have to thank. If it hadn't been for him, for the first time in years, Dana was happy. And it was because of him.

"And I could never, ever in my heart hold anything against him because the last few months of her life, she was the happiest she had ever been. And it was because she had found him to love and he loved her. And he said from the first time he ever laid eyes on her, he knew that he loved her."

"A PSYCHIC VOICE SAVED MY LIFE"

"A voice from heaven saved my life!"

Jeanne Sternecker made that astounding claim to Oprah on a March 1993 show. She stated that a psychic premonition saved her from being crushed to death when two walkways at a Kansas City, Missouri, hotel collapsed in 1981 and killed 111 people.

JEANNE: "A voice said 'Jeanne' and I jumped up. And I could not see who called me. And I looked up and that's when I saw the support pull through the ceiling and some plaster start falling. Then I heard the command 'Run!'

"My husband stood up to see what in the world was wrong with me. And I said, 'Please run. Oh, my God, *run!*' And it seemed like I couldn't get the crowd to move. We only got about five feet before it fell. I had been sitting under the second and fourth walkways."

OPRAH: "So it would have fallen on you."

JEANNE: "Yes."

OPRAH: "So you think it was the voice of God?"

JEANNE: "Either that or one of His helpers."

THE "OTHER WOMAN" WAS A MAN!

What's worse than your husband having an affair with a woman named Jackie? . . . Having an affair with a man named Jackie! Jackie, a homosexual who dates married men, revealed to Oprah on a March 1993 show just what happened when a suspicious wife stormed into his love nest and learned "the other woman" was a man.

OPRAH: "How long had you been dating her husband?"

JACKIE: "About three years. He got me an apartment. I would see him maybe an hour a night, a couple on Saturday."

OPRAH: "She realized that there was another relationship going on?"

JACKIE: "She assumed it was a woman because he called me Jackie. And one day she came to my house. . . . At that time I had a full beard. She said, 'I want to see your sister or your mother. I know she's seeing my husband . . . I had a detective find this apartment. I know this Jackie lives here and I want to see her now.'

"I said, 'I hate to be the one to tell you this, but I'm the only Jackie living her.' She fainted right on my doorstep."

"MY GRUBBY LOOK DRIVES WOMEN WILD"

Joe Lando, the rugged cowboy who costars with Jane Seymour on TV's "Dr. Quinn, Medicine Woman," claims the secret of his success with women is his bad grooming habits! Joe revealed on a March 1993 show that his dirty, unshaven face and uncombed long hair drive women wild!

OPRAH: "Do you think your hair is sexy?"

JOE: "They pay me now not to cut it, so . . ."

OPRAH: "So it's working for you, is it not?"

JOE: "Yes, it's paying off."

OPRAH: "Did you start out with the intention that, 'Well, I think this is going to be a sexy kind of thing?' "

JOE: "Absolutely not. I didn't think about that. I thought that I looked at what this person did, the character I play . . . I don't think he would be so preoccupied with his hair. I don't have to shave, I don't comb my hair. I actually get dirty every day for the part."

OPRAH: "It's working."

JOE: "Yeah, it's working. I think he doesn't look quite dirty enough, yet, but we're working on it."

SUCCESSFUL DENTIST FREELOADS OFF HIS MOM

"My son is a leech!"

That's the angry complaint of mom Sondra Boston,

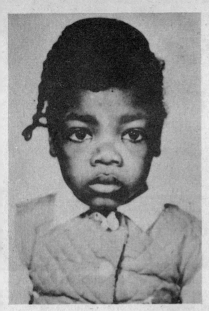

Oprah Winfrey, age 4,
in Mississippi.
© *Jim Leggett*

Oprah the
young newscaster,
Nashville, 1976.
Jim Leggett

Oprah relaxing in her office at WLS-TV, Chicago, 1986. She was about to make her movie debut in *The Color Purple* and *The Oprah Winfrey Show* was about to go national. *Charlie Knoblock/AP/Wide World Photos*

Oprah's outspoken half-sister Patricia Lee.
© *Ray Fairall Photoreporters*

Oprah's father
Vernon Winfrey.
Jim Leggett

The mansion Oprah bought for her father in Nashville.
Steve Lowry/Nashville Banner

Oprah taping her show at the Improvisation Club in Los Angeles with the stars of "Comic Relief '87". From left: Robin Williams, Billy Crystal, Dudley Moore and John Larroquette. *Lennox McLendon/AP/Wide World Photos*

One of the first photos of Oprah with her new beau, Stedman Graham, 1987. © *1987 Scott Downie/Celebrity Photo*

Oprah in a
Bob Mackie dress,
on the arm of
Stedman
Graham, at the
Academy Awards
in 1987.
*Ralph Dominguez/
Globe Photos, Inc.*

Oprah with mentor
Quincy Jones.
*John Barrett/
Globe Photos, Inc.*

Oprah celebrates her 67 lb. weight loss and shows off her new size 10 figure on her show, 1988. *AP/Wide World Photos*

Oprah nose-to-nose with Jesse Jackson, July 1988.
AP/Wide World Photos

Oprah with
Rosa Parks, the
legendary civil
rights activist,
1989.
© 1989 Scott Downie/
Celebrity Photo

Oprah receives the "Broadcaster of the Year" award from Bill Greenwald, president of the International Radio & Television Society, 1988. The award honors outstanding media figures who have enhanced the communications industry. *Wide World Photos, Inc.*

Oprah with her People's Choice Award, 1988. *AP/Wide World Photos*

Oprah,
dad Vernon, 1988.
© Bob V. Noble/
Globe Photos, Inc.

Oprah at the opening of her Chicago restaurant, the
Eccentric, 1989. *Globe Photos, Inc.*

The slim Oprah
of 1988.
Globe Photos, Inc.

Oprah at the
NATPA Convention,
New Orleans, 1991.
© 1991 John Barrett/
Globe Photos, Inc.

Harpo Studios, Oprah's $20 million production complex, takes up almost an entire city block on Chicago's West Side. *Bruce Powell*

Oprah with her talk show audience. She makes a point of shaking hands with every guest after the show. *Globe Photos, Inc.*

Oprah laughs it up with Bob Hope on her show, May 1990.
Wide World Photos, Inc.

Los Angeles mayor Tom Bradley plants a kiss on Oprah, as Benjamin Hooks, executive director of the NAACP, and Stedman Graham look on at the 81st Annual NAACP convention in Los Angeles, July 1990.
Alan Greth/AP/Wide World Photos

Oprah at her most glamorous at the Grammy Legends Tribute, 1990.
© 1990 Michael Ferguson/ Globe Photos, Inc.

Oprah with Faye Dunaway at the opening night party for *From the Mississippi Delta* in New York, November, 1991. *Mark Lennihan/AP/Wide World Photos*

Oprah at the
18th Daytime Emmys,
1991.
© 1991 Adam Scull/
Globe Photos, Inc.

Oprah at the
19th Daytime Emmys,
1992.
© 1992 Adam Scull/
Globe Photos, Inc.

Oprah at the
20th Daytime Emmys,
1993.
© 1993 Jonathan L. Green/
Globe Photos, Inc.

Oprah speaks at the Inauguration of President William Jefferson Clinton, January, 1993. © 1993 John Barrett/ Globe Photos, Inc.

Oprah at the 1993 presidential inauguration, with, from left: Jack Nicholson, James Earl Jones, Edward James Olmos. © 1993 John Barrett/Globe Photos, Inc.

Oprah with Paul Simon and Quincy Jones, 1993. © Michael Ferguson/ Globe Photos, Inc.

Oprah promoting her autobiography at the American Booksellers Association Convention in May, 1993. Weeks later, she changed her mind and withdrew the manuscript. © 1992 James Smeal/Ron Galella Ltd.

whose son Lorenzo is a successful thirty-year-old dentist who just bought a brand-new car and goes on expensive vacations. But he refuses to move out of his mother's house or even help pay the rent!

Lorenzo revealed to Oprah in February 1993 why he doesn't want to fly the coop.

LORENZO: "I've been in school all my life. That's all I've ever known. And when I graduated, I was so burned out. . . . My mother invited me home."

OPRAH (to Sondra): "Did you mean for him to stay there forever, though?"

SONDRA: "I thought within six months that he'd be ready to go out there and get something. It's now going into over a year and he's talking about 'in the next year or two.' "

LORENZO: "What fool in their right mind would want to leave . . . ?"

OPRAH: "So you're going to stay at home indefinitely?"

LORENZO: "I enjoy being there with my mother. If my mother doesn't want me in that house, buddy, believe me, she would have the door chained and the locks changed and everything else."

ROBIN WILLIAMS: "WHAT MAKES ME TICK"

What's wacky Robin Williams really like?

The comic got serious for a moment when he revealed to Oprah in January 1993 that he's most like the sensitive English professor he played in the hit movie *Dead Poets' Society*.

ROBIN: "I think [the philosophy of] *Dead Poets' Society* would probably be what I believe the most. I believe creativity is a force. I believe it's something that by cultivating that, you really find something wonderful. That is my philosophy.

"More than just living for the moment, I think it's being able to find that which you truly love. The passion of that will carry you through. It doesn't matter what it is, whether it's telemarketing, business, math or art."

GREAT-GRANNY GIVES HOMELESS HER HOUSE

When Ken and Maria Wagner and their four children lost their house to Hurricane Andrew, widow Claire McNamara gave them hers! The kindhearted great-grandmother was so moved when she saw the family's plight on TV that she turned over her two-bedroom, two-bath house in Miami to the family for as long as they needed it. Then Claire, who had lived in the house for twenty-seven years, moved in with her granddaughter in Connecticut.

Ken revealed on a January 1993 "Oprah Winfrey Show" how he reacted to Claire's incredible offer.

KEN: "We were completely floored. You don't run across people like Claire. They're few and far between. . . . We were surprised at first and we didn't believe it. Claire gave us the boost we needed to get our lives started again. And we're very thankful for that."

The family has since gotten back on its feet and is planning on moving to Cocoa Beach, Florida.

"I LEFT MY WIFE AND WENT HOME TO MOM"

Married man Mike Kotlowski is so afraid of commitment that he stayed with his widowed mother after he was married—and at one point even put his wife Mara and their two-year-old child into a homeless shelter. In January 1993 Oprah listened as Mike explained their bizarre relationship.

OPRAH: "Mike once drove Mara and their child to a homeless shelter and then drove himself back to his mother's . . . What is it? A fear of being with your family or what?"

MIKE: "Letting my mother have too much control over me . . . I was afraid of losing my home with my mother and being the type of person that she is, I gave her too much control."

Mara and her son Mikey, now three, live in their home now. Mike took a step toward breaking his mother's hold over him by preparing for it on Oprah's show. And he revealed that he is planning to move out of his mother's house and rejoin his wife and child.

MARLA WON'T MISS THE DONALD'S MONEY

Donald Trump's fortune and all it could buy weren't very impressive to Marla Maples, she told Oprah during a November 1992 appearance on the show, the day before Donald announced he'd broken off their engagement.

MARLA: "Meeting Donald—I mean, he was another man. You meet lots of rich people in your life, you meet lots of poor people . . ."

OPRAH: "If I say, 'How has being with Donald changed your life?,' most people would probably assume that it means you can buy more dresses or shoes or whatever."

MARLA: "I hate shopping, number one. I wish I liked it. I could have a lot of fun!"

BARRY MANILOW: "MY NIGHTMARES ABOUT THE NAZIS"

Pop star Barry Manilow felt so guilty about his success that the Jewish singer started having nightmares about Nazi World War II concentration camps! On an October 1992 show, Barry revealed to Oprah why the nightmares began and then finally stopped.

BARRY: "I guess it was guilt coming at me for all of my success. Yeah, I did have a period where I was having dreams of concentration camps . . . Terrible—the worst nightmares I've ever had. And thank goodness they've gone."

OPRAH: "Because don't you recognize by now, of course, that you deserve the success?"

BARRY: "Now I do. But I went through a long period, Oprah, of not believing that I did . . . I think we all have to change . . ."

OPRAH: "And believe that God created us to have an abundant life and to have pleasure."

RAPIST TORMENTS VICTIM—FROM BEHIND BARS

Carie thought her nightmare ended when the man who raped her was sent to prison—but she says he terrorized her with phone calls from behind bars.

Oprah listened to Carie's story on a September 1992 show, then asked her why, since her tormentor Christopher had to phone collect from jail, she accepted the calls.

CARIE: "My brother was serving some time for some unpaid tickets and Christopher somehow knew about it and was using my brother's name.

"And then he's say, 'Hello Carie,' and I immediately knew who it was. He'd say, 'Don't tell your family.' "

OPRAH: "But wait a minute, Carie. I'm not here to put you on trial, but listen, if he calls—you're being harassed—and they say, 'Collect call from Chris whatever his last name is. How does he have an opportunity to say 'Hello'?''

CARIE: "Well the first couple times, I guess it was fear."

OPRAH: "So you listened out of fear?"

CARIE: "Yeah."

But Christopher called into the show from jail and strongly denied ever harassing Carie.

COMA MOM'S STRANGE AWAKENING

Debi Caruth was in a car accident that put her into a three-day coma—and when she woke up, she discovered she no longer loved her husband Keith or her son Joey from her first marriage! Debi, who was in the crash five months after marrying Keith in 1990, revealed to Oprah in August 1992 how her family became complete strangers to her—and she couldn't even grasp the concept of marriage.

OPRAH: "You didn't understand marriage?"

DEBI: "No, I still don't understand marriage."

OPRAH: "You don't understand the kind of husband and wife thing, what that means?"

DEBI: "No, I have a real hard time. I have this piece of paper that says on March 27, 1990, I married this man, but . . ."

KEITH: "That's where it ends."

DEBI: "That piece of paper says I'm married to this man, this is my husband and people have taught me that when you're married to a man that you live with this man, you sleep with this man, you take care of this man, this man takes care of you, you have this household

197

you take care of, and I'm like, 'Wait a minute.' I don't know.''

Debi and Keith are seeing a psychologist once a week, and she is learning how to live and care for her son.

JILTED WIFE FIGHTS FIRE WITH FIRE

When Cookie's husband flaunted his girlfriend in front of her, Cookie got mad . . . then she got even.

The jilted woman told Oprah on an August 1992 show how she took out her anger on her husband's favorite things: his TVs and his wardrobe.

OPRAH: ''You went and took the clothes out, put them in a pile and burned them up?''

COOKIE: ''Lamp oil to make it go faster and make sure it burns fast and hard. . . . Just hangers were left. The sad part is I left one pair of underwear and a sock behind, overlooked it.

OPRAH: ''When did you take the hammer to the TV sets?''

COOKIE: ''Probably about two hours later, after I burned his clothes. . . . You know where you plug them in the back? Well, I just took a hammer and smashed the plug in.''

Cookie and her husband are in the process of divorcing.

KING OF CADS BARES HIS SOUL

Rhodah DelValle found out that the man she was dating was married, and then to make matters worse . . . she was pregnant by him! Oprah Winfrey asked Rhodah's married boyfriend Bobby why he would cheat on his wife, lie to Rhodah, and then get her pregnant.

OPRAH: ''What was your reason?''

BOBBY: ''I don't know.''

OPRAH: "You don't know?"

BOBBY: "I was going through a little turmoil at the time."

OPRAH: "But why not just be up front from the beginning?"

BOBBY: "I guess it's somewhat of an ego trip.

"Yeah, or too many Budweisers—one of the two."

MOM PAYS PRICE FOR SPOILED SON

While Joyce was away, her grown son James sold everything of value in her house—because the spoiled son says she "owed" it to him! In June 1992 Joyce told Oprah that she's always been generous to a fault with her children, but it's gotten out of hand. James told his mother: "That's the price you pay for having children."

JAMES: "I feel that I'm owed what they saved for me all those years while I was growing up . . ."

OPRAH: "What about taking care of you all those years and looking after you when you were ill?"

JAMES: "Well, that was all fine and good, but I feel that I'm still owed the money."

THE GIRL WHO LOVED DADDY TOO MUCH . . .

Being daddy's little girl can destroy your marriage! That was the warning from Beth and Jonny to Oprah's female viewers. The divorced couple confessed that the deathblow to their marriage came when Beth said she didn't want to spend eternity by her husband's side.

BETH: "I'm so emotionally tied to my dad. . . . Me and Jonny were talking about death one time and he said he wanted me to be buried with him. I said, 'No way. I'm going to be buried with my dad.' "

JONNY: "And I said, 'Fine. I'll be cremated.'"

OPRAH: "Wow! And so now you are not together? You're divorced?"

JONNY: "Right."

OPRAH: "After one year."

"MY HUSBAND LEFT ME—FOR ANOTHER MAN"

Diane's husband Norman left her after thirteen years of marriage and two children—for a married man!

Diane revealed to Oprah in March 1993 that she had a nervous breakdown and tried to kill herself when she finally found out her husband was a homosexual.

Oprah confronted Diane's husband and asked him why he had never told her.

NORMAN: "Well, 15 years ago in a small town in New England, you just didn't. . . . If you were gay you hid it."

OPRAH: "We want to know why you didn't tell Diane."

NORMAN: "Because I knew she was going to use this against me and she did."

Norman explained that when they first separated Diane filed for divorce citing "irreconcilable differences." But after she found out he was living with another man, she changed it to "adultery."

TRAPPED AT HOME—BECAUSE SHE FEELS SO UGLY

Beauty is in the eye of the beholder, but ugly is all in Janet Vickers's mind. For twenty-five years this normal-looking woman has been a recluse because she feels she's too ugly to leave home!

Janet confessed to Oprah in January 1992 why she thinks she's so unattractive.

JANET: "It's obvious, I'm just ugly."

OPRAH: "And what do you think is ugly about you?"

JANET: "Oh, everything. My nose. My mouth. I have skinny legs and a big body. Flat butt."

OPRAH (kidding): "Lots of people have a flat butt. I envy them. That's one thing I can't say, Janet. My butt is not flat."

GUESTS WHO HOAXED THE SHOW

No show is immune from hoaxers, and "The Oprah Winfrey Show" is no exception. What is it about the show that inspires otherwise respectable people to make wildly false claims just so they can get on television? For some it is publicity; for some it is a twisted need to expose the weaknesses of a superstar; for some it is simply that they will do anything to meet Oprah.

Here is a rogue's gallery of some of Oprah's most memorable hoaxers:

Con man Joe Baca bragged that he went on "The Oprah Winfrey Show" in September 1992 pretending to be married to a bigamist—and the show fell for it hook, line, and sinker. Baca claims that no one even asked him for identification.

It all began for Baca when he was watching the show and an 800 number flashed on the screen with the message: "Are you married to a bigamist? If so, call us."

"I'm not even married, but I'm a practical joker, so I called the number as a gag," Baca recalls. "I'm also a big Oprah fan and hoped this might lead to a chance to meet her."

Baca gave the woman who answered the phone a false name, Ray Carlson. He told her he had been married eight years and had two children, but that he had found out a few months ago that his wife Vivian was leading a double life . . . with a husband and child in another state!

"The next day, a producer named Chris McWatt called and said he loved my story," says Baca. "He asked if my wife would appear on the show with me. I told him I'd get back to him.

"After telling a woman friend in another state about the gag, I gave Chris her number. Then he called her, she played along with the joke, but refused to go on the show."

That didn't stop producer McWatt from inviting "Ray Carlson" on to the show. On August 23, 1992, Baca was whisked from Fort Collins, Colorado, to Chicago.

"I had planned to confess the scheme to Oprah when I met her before the show," Baca claims. "Yet I doubted I would even get that far. Just to be in her studio audience you have to show picture ID. But incredibly, no one asked me for identification!"

Instead of meeting Oprah backstage, Baca was greeted by a woman who told him that a producer wanted to talk to him.

"I was certain the jig was up," Baca says. "Sweat poured down my brow."

But when the producer came into the room where Baca was waiting, he said, "Ray, we love your story so much we're going to put you on first!"

"My jaw dropped," Baca recalls. " 'Are these people crazy?' I asked myself."

Within minutes, Baca was onstage with two women who said they'd been married to the same man.

After Oprah introduced him, he told his tale and said his wife, Vivian, was a sales manager who traveled a lot. He added that he had never suspected anything until he got a phone call from a woman who said Vivian should "call Margaret. It's urgent. The baby is sick.

"I talked about confronting my wife—and about how she had even deceived me during pregnancy," Baca said.

Oprah demanded, "Well, what are you, blind or something? I mean if your wife got pregnant and there was another baby someplace, you would know about it."

"Of course I would!" Baca admits. "The scam is over," he told himself.

But Baca came up with a lame excuse. He said his wife had told him she'd had a miscarriage while on a business trip.

At one point, Oprah said, "Something's funny here." As soon as they cut to a commercial, she hustled off for a talk with Chris. "I figured by now she had to know I was a fraud," says Baca.

"But when the taping resumed, Oprah said my story sounded so unbelievable she had made sure the producer had checked it with my relatives.

"That was baloney. No one even asked for the phone number of a relative. When Oprah went to the other guests, I knew I had succeeded.

"Within hours I was headed home, still shocked that I had gotten so far with a joke! And on September 7, my segment aired across the country."

AN APOLOGY

When Oprah learned she had been duped by Joe Baca, she admitted it to her viewers and publicly apologized.

"This past Labor Day, we did a show that a lot of you saw about men who discovered their wives were married to more than one man," Oprah said in a special taped segment. "There was a man on that show who said that after eight years of marriage he found out that he had been deceived by his wife. We later found out that we were the ones who were deceived."

Oprah also said she'd been fooled only once before in more than ten years as a talk show host. That was in 1987, when a woman posed as a wife who'd been wed fourteen years and hated sex.

"We always check several sources to verify our guests' stories, but this time we missed," Oprah said in her statement, which was taped for airing on September 16, 1992. "I am sorry and thought you should know what happened."

Baca continued to get more mileage out of the hoax, however, when he appeared on "The Jenny Jones Show" in November and was interviewed by Jacquin Stitt—best known as the winner of the *Ladies' Home Journal* Oprah look-alike contest. Besides bearing a remarkable resemblance to Oprah, Jacquin also turned out to be a man.

ANOTHER PHONY GUEST CONS OPRAH TWICE!

Housewife Michelle Unger claims that she has conned "The Oprah Winfrey Show" not once, but twice!

"First, I appeared on "Oprah" and spun a fictional tale about sleeping with my husband's boss," says Michelle. "Then I went back on the show two years later and lied that my husband quit having sex with me after watching the birth of our child."

Incredibly, Oprah's staff did not bother to check out either story before Michelle appeared on the show. Oprah only learned that she had been conned when one of Michelle's pals tipped her off after her second appearance was taped.

"Oprah found out at least two weeks before the segment aired this past May 11. I thought, 'Well, the game is up. They'll yank the show.'

"Oprah had plenty of time to pull the episode. But to my surprise she did n't. Instead, she ran it anyway!"

Oprah ran a disclaimer—which warned viewers that the segment might contain lies—before the show. But even the disclaimer misled viewers, says Michelle, who claims the star "lied three times" during the statement.

Michelle, twenty-four, says she was stunned that Oprah and her staff never caught on to her scam in advance of taping even though she met Oprah and her aides face-to-face at each appearance, and dealt with the same producer both times; used her real first name but a different last name during her appearances, and gave the same phone number and same Michigan address.

Michelle, who attends Wayne State University, appeared on the second show with a college pal, Guy Diehr, posing as her husband.

After the show was shot, Michelle says, "Oprah" staffers got wind of her most recent scam.

"At that point, I was asked to send in a copy of my marriage license as verification," she says. "I told an 'Oprah' producer, Alice McGee, that my 'husband' and I had only a common-law marriage, no wedding ceremony. Then I asked her if I could just send her a wedding picture, and she said, 'Yes!'

"So the next day I put on a wedding dress at a store, and Guy and I had a 'wedding photo' snapped by the clerk. We sent the fake picture to Oprah—who spliced it into our appearance on her show."

Michelle's misadventures started in April 1991 when she was watching TV at her Utica, Michigan, home. She heard Oprah say at the end of the show: "If you've had an affair with your spouse's boss, call 1-800-HI-OPRAH."

Said Michelle: "Well, I was curious. So I called—and to my shock, I reached an 'Oprah' producer, Alice McGee."

Michelle told Alice that she had slept with her husband's boss and that her husband had gotten fired because of it.

"That was a total lie," Michelle admits. "I never gave Alice any real details. But 20 minutes after I hung up, she called back and said they wanted me on the show!"

Two days later Michelle was flown to Chicago. Though not paid for her show appearance, she says she was provided with a limousine and nice hotel suite and was "treated like a queen."

She wore a black wig on the show to alter her appearance.

"After I got back home, Alice McGee called and asked for some verification of my story," Michelle recalls. "So I referred her to a pal, who verified it. Alice never knew I'd already tipped off my pal!"

On May 9, 1991, Michelle's story aired on "The Oprah Winfrey Show."

Michelle kept quiet about her deception. Then in March 1993, she saw Oprah on TV issuing a call for women whose sex life was affected after their husbands watched them give birth.

"I just couldn't believe it. It was as if Oprah was inviting me to do it all over again!" she says.

"So I called, and to my surprise I reached Alice McGee again. I told her my husband hadn't touched me since he watched me give birth three years ago. Alice said, 'I love it!' "

Michelle says she ran into a problem when Alice told her they also wanted her husband on the show—because her real husband was totally against it.

"But I phoned my college friend Guy Diehr, and he played my husband.

"After our appearance, Oprah's people told us it was such a great show that they wanted to hold it for sweeps week (when ratings are measured)."

After Michelle's hoax was discovered, Oprah taped a disclaimer, that said, in part: ". . . I want you to be aware of something we just learned here on the 'Oprah' show today. There are some doubts about whether two of the guests (Michelle and Guy) you're about to see told the truth.

"Before we booked them, every effort was made to verify their story. We looked at what they told us were their wedding photos.

"We talked with six people who all swore their story was true . . ."

But Michelle retorted: "Oprah lied to her viewers in her disclaimer. She said they'd just become aware of the hoax that day—when in fact her staff had been calling me for weeks.

"And they didn't look at our 'wedding photo' or try to verify my story before we were booked—they did it afterward. They also never talked to six people. They talked to only three—*after* the show was taped.

"I've long suspected that some of the people on talk shows make up their bizarre tales," says Michelle. "Now I'm convinced of it."

Chapter Eleven
Bold New Ventures

Everybody's desire for me to have a wedding has nothing to do with my knowing I'm ready to be a wife. That's a whole different responsibility that I can't handle right now.

> —Oprah Winfrey answering the constant question, 1990

The dawn of 1990 found Oprah firmly ensconced in her Water Tower Place aerie. The recently redecorated apartment was just the right setting for a mega-star with its marble floors, crystal chandeliers, low marble tables and Art Deco wall sconces, its marble Jacuzzi with the gold swan fixtures, and the plush white sofas in her state-of-the-art media room.

The year opened with an alarming prediction from a famed New York psychic. Shawn Robbins, who has amazed experts with her incredibly accurate economic forecasts, predicted that Oprah and Arsenio Hall would tumble into a steamy romance and team up on screen as a singer-and-comedy duo in a remake of one of the old Bob Hope-Bing Crosby "Road" movies.

On a more serious level, there was a shocking blast from fellow talk show host, Geraldo Rivera, who ripped into Oprah and their talk show colleagues.

"I'm sick of trash TV!" Rivera raged. "Shows like Oprah and Donahue and even my own have gone over the line and we've all got to stop piping sleazy, perverted material into America's homes!

"I'm the first to say, 'I'm stopping it!' Now it's time for the others to follow. Oprah, enough of the sleaze!"

The spectacle of the rambunctious Rivera rebuking his colleagues for their lack of taste and social responsibility must have seemed truly hilarious to some, but Oprah has always been sensitive to criticism. His charges must have wounded her deeply.

"Somebody's got to stand up and say 'Enough,'" stormed Rivera. "Well, I'm the guy who's taking the first step. I'm through with schlock TV. From now on, I'm going to concentrate on vital public issues."

The outspoken Geraldo went on to declare: "Daytime talk shows have covered such shocking topics as sex with animals, sex-change operations, lesbian marriages, incest and worse. And it seems that with each passing week, the topics get more and more bizarre."

Geraldo acknowledged that he had been a part of that.

"I can look back at shows I've done, and while many were excellent I have to admit I went overboard a number of times. In November of last year alone, I did shows on sex-crazed women, battered lesbians and a topless donut shop.

"But I'm judged far more harshly than the others on daytime TV.

"Their shows are just as outrageous as mine, at times more so. But I'm the one who's been taking all the heat."

He insisted Oprah and others covered the same subject matter he did, but they never got anywhere near the criticism he did.

"Oprah did a show on which a perverted sex practice was described, and medical experts later said two viewers

212

died while they were trying the practice what they'd seen on 'Oprah.' Despite that, almost nobody got on her case.

"If I had done that show, it would have been international news," Rivera charged. "My God! I probably would have been slapped in prison!"

As usual, Oprah publicly ignored the criticism and concentrated on celebrating her thirty-sixth birthday. Oprah recalled what Whoopi Goldberg had told her on the set of *The Color Purple*: "It—and I mean It with a capital I—doesn't even start to happen until you're 36."

"I took Whoopi at her word," Oprah says. "And so far, for me, this is the most exciting birthday I've ever had." She considered the past twelve months her Wonder Year—her spiritual coming of age.

Oprah had racked up a year of enormous accomplishments: Her restaurant, the Eccentric, had become a Chicago institution overnight; her talk show was now seen by twenty million people worldwide. She was the first black individual and only the third woman to own a TV and film production complex, Harpo Studios, where her talk show and her new series would be filmed. She was following in the footsteps of Mary Pickford and Lucille Ball.

Her birthday gifts from Stedman Graham included a beautifully restored classic 1957 black Mercedes coupe.

Even her skiing had improved. Those who saw her on the slopes that winter noted that she had picked up the sport quickly and, having started out on the beginner slopes, by season's end she was delighted to be "up in the greens." Now she was up to the blue intermediate runs.

"Oprah's a really good athlete with good balance," said an instructor. "She can ski just about anything."

It would not be long before Oprah would be able to join Stedman on the black-diamond expert runs. But that was not her motivation. Said Oprah: "Skiing is the next best thing to having wings."

"I FEEL BLESSED TO BE AROUND HER"

The good times with Stedman were about to get better. After three years of dating, Stedman was moving to Chicago. They both had had enough of a relationship on the run. Stedman's public relations company was based in North Carolina and traveled all over the world, including to South Africa.

"He was in different cities all the time," Oprah complained, but she was always on the run, too. "I'd tell him, I'll meet you at the American Airlines counter."

So, Stedman was scheduled to move into Oprah's condo in Water Tower Place. He intended to open a branch of The Graham Williams Group in the "Windy City."

Whatever adjustments needed to be made, Stedman seemed more than willing to make them. "Oprah is worth whatever I go through," he said at the time. "I feel blessed to be around her. My life has changed because of the relationship. We've felt each other grow; we've had good times and down times. We have a very good relationship. We enjoy each other and care about each other. That's what's important."

The couple was soon seen running together and working out at the East Bank Club with their personal trainers or at services at the Trinity United Church of Christ on the South Side where Oprah was a longtime member.

"It gets better the more time we spend together," Oprah told a friend. "We get excited going to the grocery store."

"Stedman is ideal for me," Oprah said. "I can't imag-

214

ine or think of—nor have I ever seen or experienced—anybody who would be more ideal for me.''

But as for marriage, Oprah was vague: ''Everybody's desire for me to have a wedding has nothing to do with my knowing I'm ready to be a wife. That's a whole different responsibility that I can't handle right now.''

Even sister Patricia Lee approved of Oprah's beau.

''She and Stedman are perfect for each other,'' she said that March. ''That girl is crazy in love with Stedman.''

But Patricia revealed that they were a real-life Odd Couple: ''Though Oprah and Stedman are in love, they're opposites,'' she said. ''They're like Felix and Oscar on 'The Odd Couple.' Stedman is neat and likes to clean and cook, while Oprah is a slob who hates housework of any kind.''

In fact, Patricia said, ''She's always been sloppy. When she was young, she left books and clothes and stuff all over the house. Mom was always after her to help by washing dishes or something, but Oprah almost never did.

''Oprah is lazy. She just leaves her clothes where they drop on the floor,'' said Patricia. ''One time she walked into her studio wearing a new $50,000 fur coat, took it off—and just let it drop! Luckily, she's wealthy enough to hire somebody to pick up after her!''

Little sister Patricia also revealed another of Oprah's flaws: She bites her nails!

''Oprah is also a very nervous person who has bitten her fingernails to the quick since she was a child,'' said Patricia. ''If it weren't for her manicurist she'd have stubs!

''The only thing that stops Oprah from biting her nails now is the false tips she wears.''

"I JUST WANTED TO DO GOOD WORK, SO I CREATED AN ENVIRONMENT FOR THAT"

In March a garish neon sign proclaiming "Harpo Studios" went on, and the new venture officially opened when "Brewster Place," the series, began taping at Oprah's new production facility. As owner of her own film studio, Oprah was now officially a mogul.

The $20 million facility on Chicago's near West Side was the very model of a modern high-tech film and video facility, from the marble staircase in the foyer to the workout equipment in the employee fitness center. Yet, Oprah acknowledged that "It's hard to put into my mind that this all belongs to me."

Mondays and Tuesdays, Oprah would tape two episodes a day of her talk show. Wednesday morning she would tape the fifth episode. From 2:00 P.M. Wednesday until end-of-shooting Friday she would be filming "Brewster Place."

In the new series, Oprah would return to the role of Mattie Michael, but her character was now running a restaurant on Brewster Place. The network ordered thirteen episodes, and King Phoenix Entertainment was producing the series in association with Harpo.

The cast and crew of "Brewster Place" came to 148, and they planned to complete one episode every five days, eventually they expected to cut back to one every four days. It was a killer schedule, even for a star who claimed she only needed four hours of sleep a night.

"We've been practicing how I can do this," Oprah told the reporters and critics invited to tour the new studios. "We've fine tuned things with our Oprah Show producers. And in the acting, I'm really a very quick study."

Oprah explained how she prepared for a role: "What

I do for all my characters is develop a little history book for them. So for me, it's almost like channeling; you just let the character take over.''

Nevertheless, some of the very emotional scenes did affect her deeply. "There have been some nights that it was hard to drive home,'' she acknowledged.

But she assured those on the tour that the talk show, which had been taping at Harpo since January, remained her top priority. After all, it had made her one of the ten richest entertainers in America, according to *Forbes* magazine.

"That talk show is the foundation on which all the rest of this was built," Oprah said. "I'll not let it slide or ever lose control of it. I love doing that show. It lets people know they're not alone and it lets me be myself. It's the easiest thing I do all day. It's certainly easier than acting.''

Oprah insisted that she wasn't concerned at all about "Brewster Place" 's fate in the ratings. "I don't think about things like that,'' she said. "I think about living in the moment. Right now I'm thinking about the next scene we have to shoot.''

Oprah revealed that she had started building the Harpo Studios even before there was a network commitment for the "Brewster Place" series. "I said I was going to do this series when I did the miniseries,'' Oprah said. "But when I said that, I was the only one saying it.''

In fact, according to Chicago journalist Mark Caro, neither Oprah nor Jeffrey Jacobs, her business advisor, had any idea that she would have a weekly series to shoot there when the studio opened. "But with 220 talk shows to tape each season, they knew that Winfrey's acting opportunities would be greater if the distance from television to film studio were across the hall rather than across the country,'' wrote Caro.

"It gives Oprah a chance to act,'' said Jacobs. "We control the schedule.''

217

Oprah acknowledged that there had been times when even she was not so sure the series would ever get made. Then producer Reuben Cannon sent her to the movies to see *Field of Dreams,* Oprah recalled. "And I did, and he said, 'Well, did you get the message? If you build it, they will come.'"

Oprah built Harpo Studios, and the series came.

"We invested $20 million into the structure after we bought it when it was the Fred Niles Studio," Jeffrey Jacobs told George Christy of *The Hollywood Reporter.* He said they had hired top architects and technicians to design the studio and create work areas for filmmakers' staffs.

"One complaint we had from writers is that they rarely had any light in their offices, so we opened up the walls," Jacobs said. "We have a screening room with THX audio (complete with a popcorn machine and candy counter), and if a firm wants to broadcast from the studio, we have the equipment to satellite it around the world."

Oprah's show could be done completely in-house: commercials, promotions, bumpers, and roll-ins.

"I don't want to sound like I'm patting myself on the back, but I think I have managed to handle all this very well because I have insisted on having control," Oprah told the visitors. "Yes, I do have people to organize my life, but nobody organizes it without me knowing what I'm doing."

She and Jeffrey Jacobs had chosen everything from the carpets to the popcorn machine in the screening room. "It's no fun if somebody else does it," Oprah said. "I picked every piece of tile, every doorknob, every gidget, every gadget, every carpet sample."

Harpo Studios soon became a tourist attraction.

Occupying a full city block, 100,000 square feet, the studio stood out in the West Side Chicago neighborhood best known for its fruit and vegetable markets.

"We created this so that I would be able to do what I've told you before that I want to do," Oprah told her opening-day visitors. "I just want to do good work, so I have created an environment for that."

Oprah had personally chosen every piece of furniture as carefully as she chose her colleagues. "You have to surround yourself with people you trust, and people that are good. But they also have to be people who will tell the emperor you have no clothes."

Harpo's staff of fifty had its own fitness center; a company chef prepared breakfast and lunch in their café.

Oprah's office was a retreat: the walls were covered in mauve and green tapestry; side chairs deep green and silver. Oprah's gleaming mahogany desk was immaculate.

There were many framed photographs of friends and Stedman.

Oprah also praised Jeffrey Jacobs for freeing her from her "slave mentality," telling her visitors that:

"He allowed me to see that not even the sky was the limit," she told their visitors. "I believe you could be anything within limits, and now I tend to believe you can be anything and you can really do anything."

CONTROVERSIES SURROUND HARPO STUDIOS

Almost immediately, Harpo Studios aroused controversy. It began with the discovery that Harpo did not quite take up an entire city block. The building covered most of a block, except for an area occupied by fishmonger José Velez's El Rey Seafood Market and another store.

Velez told the media that Oprah's lawyers had tried to get his lease so they could have his store bulldozed and build a parking lot.

"Oprah's always talking about how proud she is of the

little people who work hard to get ahead in life, because she used to be one of those people," said an angry Velez, an immigrant from Ecuador.

"Well, I worked hard for my business and now she wants to use it for parking cars.

"I put my life savings in this," he added. "I began with nothing and worked hard. I have a family to feed. If I had to close down I would become a bum in the streets, because I would have nothing. My children and family would go hungry.

"Maybe she wants the whole block for herself," Velez fumed.

Oprah even offered to pay $500 more rent than Velez, but now the landlord finally told Oprah and her lawyers to take a hike and was letting Velez renew his lease.

"It's a miracle," said the satisfied fish supplier. "This time the little guy wins."

The next image problem came with accusations that Harpo Studios, where "Brewster Place" was being shot, was not a "union shop." A story in the *Chicago Tribune* soon corrected that misapprehension, stating that there most definitely was an all-union crew employed on "Brewster Place."

It was true, however, that "The Oprah Winfrey Show" used a free-lance crew. Jeffrey Jacobs explained to the *Tribune* that "Harpo Studios is just a building. If somebody wants to rent space, we don't ask if they're using a union crew."

Another source pointed out that by using nonunion crews, Oprah was providing more opportunities for minorities who represented just a small percentage of NABET (National Association of Broadcast Employees and Technicians) and IATSE (International Alliance of Theatrical Stage Employees).

Even after putting in fourteen-hour days at the studio,

Oprah would often return home to her condo and spend another hour on the phone with Jeffrey Jacobs. Sundays would be reserved for Stedman. As Oprah told friends: "Sunday's going to be a big personal day—we're going to do it, have to do it, on that day."

"Her involvement as star and as executive producer will be constant," said series producer Reuben Cannon. "She's not just the star of our series; she's the franchise."

The title change was significant, Cannon went on: "Some of the criticism we took on the miniseries was because the story was told from a particular point of view, that of the women of Brewster Place. The black male roles were either absent or they were not positive."

Cannon was optimistic about the future of the series: "I trust we will not receive that criticism in the series because we have wonderful black role models." There would also be black writers creating the scripts. There would even be a script by Oprah's friend and mentor, Maya Angelou.

The series was set in 1967, with Oprah slightly younger, in her mid-40s. Oprah's character, Mattie Michael, has lost her job as a hairdresser and bought a restaurant, "La Scala," with her friend Etta Mae (Brenda Pressley). Olivia Cole reprised her role as Miss Sophie, the officious and opinionated owner of the neighborhood grocery. From the original cast of the miniseries, only Oprah and Olivia Cole returned to the new show.

Oprah was unswayed by those who doubted that it would make a series. "I have no fears about this," she said. "What most people in television don't realize is that you don't have to fake real life. You don't have to have canned laughter or canned situations."

Chapter Twelve
Upsets and Setbacks

Real marriage is the sacrificing of your ego, not for the other person, but for the relationship. That's how you become one, because the relationship becomes the number-one priority. I am really not in that place.

> —Oprah Winfrey's answer to the Marriage Question, 1990

Even before "Brewster Place" aired, it was being touted as a hit, based on Oprah's enormous popularity as a talk show host, and the fact that it promised to be a lighter version of the miniseries. But Oprah was also worried that she might have taken on more than she could handle. She confided to a friend that "it's going to be hard, and it will take a lot of time. I don't know how I will do it—but you do what you gotta do."

Unlike the miniseries, which was true to the novel on which it was based, "Brewster Place" would be much more a creation of Oprah Winfrey's. "We didn't try to change the movie because that's what Gloria Naylor wrote," she explained. "Now we have the opportunity to use what she wrote as just the root of all the other things that can happen."

It was very important to Oprah to bring serious black characters to television. She said that "Most people out there have no contact with black people ever. Their only images are the ones portrayed on television. . . . There's a whole reality outside of what most people know, where the black community functions on its own, where people own businesses, where people care about their property and their children and pay their taxes. The point of having your own company is that you can show that.''

The character of Mattie was equally important. ''She had the 'Nobody Knows the Trouble I've Seen' syndrome,'' Oprah said, referring to the old Negro spiritual. ''I've known women like Mattie all my life. I sort of carry them around with me. But they're not fun to play and they're not interesting.'' Oprah worked to give Mattie a sense of humor and a broader range. With that in mind, Mattie and her best friend, Etta Mae, became co-owners of the restaurant. And nosy Miss Sophie's grocery store closely resembled the Nashville market once owned by Vernon Winfrey.

''This is only the fourth time I've acted,'' Oprah acknowledged. ''I guess I'm a natural, but I'm very short on technique. I actually live the moment, almost like channeling the character. But once I release it, it's released. By the end of the day, when it's time for the closeup, I'm just emotionally whipped. Unless I can actually feel the pain, I think I didn't do it right. But you can't feel it for 12 takes.''

Oprah, who had never studied acting, explained her personal method: ''You cheat your ego. You know, in normal life you get up in the morning, you tell yourself who you are. You're ugly. You're smart. You're powerless. And then you go out and behave as if that's what you are. When you're acting a part, you just tell yourself something else.''

Oprah had another secret for getting into character that she confided to an interviewer: ''I deliberately put on fat cotton underpants when I play [Mattie]. It makes me feel like her.''

But over all, in spite of the demanding schedule, Oprah loved acting. ''Playing Mattie is a vacation from all the stuff that Oprah Winfrey has to deal with,'' she said. ''Mattie's not in the *Enquirer*. Mattie doesn't have 200 checks on her desk to sign. She's not running a studio. She doesn't have the whole celebrity deal.''

On days they shot on location, folks from the neighborhood crowded around the set and approached Oprah between takes like an old family friend, giving her advice on her weight and her hair. She handled it all with warmth and humor.

'' 'Brewster Place' is as important as anything I've ever done,'' Oprah said. ''I'd say I'm not putting my career on the line, but I'm certainly putting a lot of my professional expertise on the line. Because I'm not only an actress doing it, but I've said to the network, 'I *guarantee* you that this is going to work.' ''

That April, Oprah generously underwrote the costs of a lavish wedding for her longtime executive producer Debra Di Maio, even flying the fifty guests first-class to Florence, Italy, for the ceremony. Sadly, she had to work on ''Brewster Place'' and her own charter flight was cancelled; another plane was disabled, so she missed the wedding.

Oprah did make it to Atlanta later that month to be honored by the Southern Christian Leadership Conference Women's Organizational Moment for Equality Now, for her achievements in business and entertainment.

"THE OPRAH WINFREY SHOW" GOES INTERNATIONAL

Oprah's talk show had begun to go international: It aired once a week in Japan, using Japanese voice-overs. "Oprah is clearly a worldwide TV personality as she speaks to common human interests around the globe," said Fred Cohen, president of King World International, which sold the show to Japan. It was also seen in New Zealand, the United Kingdom, the Netherlands, Thailand, Canada, Saudi Arabia, and Bermuda.

That July, "The Oprah Winfrey Show" became the first regularly scheduled talk show to crack the Soviet bloc. Polish TV had acquired fifty-two episodes of the show which would air weekly with a Polish voice-over on Sunday nights, one of the most widely viewed time slots on Polish TV.

Oprah taped promotional spots for the new venture in which she said: *"Dzien Dobry* (good day), my show is from the second-largest Polish community in the world, Chicago. I am excited to be on my favorite Polish channel, two. *Dziekuje* (thank you)."

Announcing the deal, Tomasz Kaczek, deputy director of Channel Two, said, "We have chosen Oprah because after 40 years of Communism . . . we feel that we can all learn to speak more openly by the example of Oprah Winfrey."

"IT'S TOUGH TO HAVE A RELATIONSHIP WITH SOMEONE LIKE ME"

As always, Stedman was there with quiet support and a shoulder for Oprah to lean on. Sometimes she had to wonder how he put up with her. "It's tough to have a relationship with someone like me," Oprah acknowledged. "And the older I get, the tougher I am. . . . Because I control so many things in my life, I have to work at not being controlling when I'm spending time with Stedman."

Sometimes things got really wild, like when they were driving, and Oprah insisted she knew the fastest way. Once, Oprah was so insistent that Stedman finally gave in and took her "shortcut," even though he knew the street was blocked.

"When I realized that I had been a real jerk and that he had allowed me to be a jerk, I said, 'Why didn't you just tell me that you knew the street was blocked?' "

According to Oprah, he responded: " 'It's easier for me to just drive down the street and turn around than to try to explain that to you, because you would be convinced that it wasn't blocked.' "

"That's when I realized, God, I'm really bad," Oprah recalled. "But I'm working on it. Now I get in the car and start humming just to keep myself from saying 'Go that way!' "

And Stedman was respectful about the other important man in her life: Vernon Winfrey. That spring, when Oprah and Stedman paid a surprise visit to her father in Nashville, she told a friend: "We slept in separate bedrooms. I would absolutely not even try it. I wouldn't even dare try it! Are you kidding? We had bedrooms at opposite ends of the hall. 'Yup, Dad, I'm down here,' " she said.

But even though Oprah called Stedman "the best catch there is," she was growing testy at the constant question: Why aren't you two married?

"We're not married because I'm not ready to be married," she told one interviewer, a bit impatiently. How many times had she been asked that question? "We're not married because I'm not ready to be married. Real marriage is the sacrificing of your ego, not for the other person, but for the relationship. That's how you become one, because the relationship becomes the number-one priority. I am really not at that place."

As for the children she used to talk about, Oprah was vague. "I certainly have no business having children at this time," she admitted. "Time is running out, I know, but I'm going to give myself a few years. Got too many other things going. I believe you *can* have it all. You just can't have it all at one time."

Oprah also claimed that she had come to terms with her weight. "The weight is still a struggle for me," she said, "but I'm handling it. It is an illusion to think that going on a diet and dropping the weight can resolve whatever the weight problem is. Because it's more than just food. Holding on to the weight was, for me, a way of protecting myself. Covering myself. Weight has its purpose in my life. I haven't figured out what it is. When I do, I will have climbed another step. Won't that be wonderful! And I get a little closer every day to understanding it."

But meanwhile, Oprah would no longer allow her weight to determine her life. She now refused to weigh herself, and she would not let the constant press scrutiny get to her.

This was obvious that February when it was rumored that Oprah, returning from a ski weekend in Vail, Colorado, got an attack of the hungries as her chartered jet warmed up on the runway. She ordered the pilot to hold it, then had a car take her a quarter mile back to the terminal where she charged into a snack bar and ordered four giant hot dogs slathered with the works, plus large fries, then gobbled them down as she raced back to her jet.

A rueful Oprah must have been thinking about stories

like that when she told a reporter that she had developed a great respect for fish.

Fish, Oprah?

Yes, she explained. "Because I live my life in a fishbowl. I know how it is, guys. I won't even look in fishbowls anymore. I think, 'They must get sick of people walking by looking at them.'"

She confessed that she had no elaborate master plan for her future. "I am a live-for-the-moment, do-the-best-you-can-do-this-day kind of person," she said. "I never think of what's going to happen a year from now, two years from now, five years from now. I don't know. I really only worry about today."

Her generosity expanded. There was a generous $500,000 contribution to Chicago's Academy for the Performing Arts; $1 million to Morehouse; $250,000 to Tennessee State University; and $200,000 to Chicago's Corporate Community School.

OPRAH'S LOVE CRISIS

Oprah's grueling eighteen-hour-a-day work schedule was starting to strain her relationship with Stedman, and he had reportedly vowed to walk out on her if she did not spend more time with him.

Stedman had moved to Chicago six months earlier to spend more time with Oprah. At first they saw each other several times a week and nearly every weekend.

But recently Oprah had been working around the clock, juggling her talk show, her prime-time series, her studio, and her production company.

Her hectic schedule left her only enough time to see Stedman twice a month. Fed up, he put his foot down in early May and shook Oprah with a bombshell ultimatum: Love me or I'm leaving.

231

Oprah confided to a family friend: ''He told me: 'Either you make a commitment to me and our relationship now—or I'm leaving!''

A stunned Oprah, who once said she was opposed to living together before marriage, proposed that they move in together, and Stedman quickly agreed, although he would keep his own apartment.

Oprah was already remodeling her twenty-five-room apartment to the tune of $4 million. Their posh new home would reportedly have an exercise room, a master bedroom they would share, plus a private bedroom, bathroom and study for each of them.

''It's hard for us to find time for ourselves, but the new home should help,'' Stedman told a friend. ''This is a difficult time for us. Oprah's schedule is a back-breaker.''

Since ''Brewster Place'' had begun filming in mid-March, Oprah was up every morning at 6:00 A.M., and she never got to bed before midnight.

''Oprah is in the studio by 7:45,'' said an insider. ''On Monday and Tuesday mornings, she tapes two talk shows. Then she spends half an hour taping promos for the five shows she'll do during the week.''

Monday and Tuesday afternoons Oprah devoted to rehearsing for upcoming talk shows, meeting with department heads, and even personally signing weekly paychecks for her eighty employees.

She headed for home between 7:00 P.M. and 8:00 P.M. and spent evenings reading ''Brewster Place'' scripts and talking on the phone to her business partners.

Incredibly, Wednesdays were even more hectic.

After taping another talk show on Wednesday morning, Oprah headed for the ''Brewster Place'' makeup studio at 11:30 A.M. She rehearsed with other cast members until 3:30 P.M., then filming would begin and it usually continued until about 11:30 P.M.

"Thursdays, Fridays and Saturdays are devoted to the filming of 'Brewster Place,' " said the insider. "The taping runs from 8 A.M. until 11 P.M. or 11:30 P.M. Even if her character Mattie Michael isn't on stage, Oprah is on the set all the time since she's an executive producer.

"On Sundays Oprah is up at 6 to read the papers, then she devotes the rest of the day to preparing for another week—reading books and screenplays, boning up on upcoming talk show guests and tending to business matters."

What made Oprah run?

The insider pointed to Oprah's dirt-poor roots, and speculated that she had come to equate money and hard work with security.

"She makes $40 million a year and she's worth $250 million, yet she won't let up. She's determined to be not just the richest woman in show business, but the richest person in show business."

But that ambition was taking its toll. She rarely had time to exercise these days and had slowly gained back twenty-five pounds.

Also, the usually cheerful Oprah had become irritable and short-tempered.

Stedman remained silent as Oprah sank deeper into her obsession with her work, but finally he could take no more. According to the family insider, he told Oprah:

"I know you're trying to make a success of your new show, but there has to be time for me. I need you—all of you."

Oprah told the family insider: "I'd always been opposed to living with a man, but I realized how much I wanted to be with Stedman.

"I didn't want to just squeeze him in now and then any more than he wanted to hang around like a poor puppy dog, waiting for a moment alone with me."

The lovebirds planned to move into their new home in a few months, and Stedman was convinced it would save their relationship.

He told his close friend: "She's hot right now—and she belongs to her 20 million fans. The stress of her success could wreck a lot of relationships, but my love for Oprah will survive that."

"I HAVE TO TAKE MY HAT OFF TO WINFREY"

When "Brewster Place" premiered that May 1, some critics welcomed the new show. Dorothy Gilliam of *The Washington Post* had dismissed the miniseries as a "stereotype ridden polemic against black men," but in her review of the first episode she said, "I have to take my hat off to Winfrey. She has redeemed herself in fine fashion, especially in her treatment of black men."

Gilliam lauded everything about the series and noted that it was totally controlled by Oprah. "With her wealth and power," Gilliam effused, "Winfrey could have continued to be one of those black people who forgot where she came from, denied her own roots. With this version of 'Brewster Place,' however, Winfrey has demonstrated a willingness to take risks and a socio-historical understanding of herself and the world."

Others saw "Brewster Place" as tame but pleasant, and Jay Sharbutt of the Associated Press said it resembled "a black urban counterpart of Hamner's 'The Waltons,' with its emphasis on decency and optimism, and even occasional narration by the lead character."

Kay Gardella of *The New York Daily News* also found the new show bland and tepid. And she, apparently, was in the majority. After only four episodes had aired it was clear that the show was not going to make it. It was soon cancelled—the biggest setback of Oprah's career to date.

There were several factors besides low ratings involved in the decision. For one thing, it was expensive to film because it was a period piece and called for special sets. Each episode was estimated to cost between half- and three-quarters of a million dollars to produce, which didn't include the cost of the three sound stages Oprah had built especially for the show, or the cost of shooting on location or the salaries of the crew.

No one criticized the quality of "Brewster Place," but there were unfortunate realities of the TV market place that had to be faced. One high-ranking advertising executive assured this author that "Brewster Place" might have done very well on PBS, but it lacked broad appeal. As a half-hour dramatic series, it was difficult to schedule. The subject matter was considered "too mature for a half-hour program." The executive suggested that if Oprah had been willing to do a show in a Roseanne-type format, or even "Alice," she would have been unbeatable. Her professionalism, talent, and high standards remained unquestioned.

Although Oprah was deeply wounded by the cancellation of "Brewster Place," she could cope. She had her talk show; she had Stedman; she had a raft of other projects in development.

The ABC network was still fully committed to Oprah. In May it was announced that Harpo Productions would produce four movies for the network under a new production deal with Capital Cities/ABC. Oprah would star in two of the movies. The agreement also called for prime-time TV pilots and a series commitment. The ABC movies would be syndicated by King World.

AN EMMY UPSET

That summer, as Oprah prepared to host the Seven-teenth Annual Daytime Emmy Awards in New York City, she glanced in her mirror and hated the way she looked. Her weight was up to 160 pounds, and she could barely fit into a size fourteen. Depressed and discouraged over her ballooning figure, she still performed her host duties professionally, even when it became clear that "The Oprah Winfrey Show" had been completely shut out of the awards.

As host, Oprah explained that the Daytime Emmy Awards was "the show with more tears than a soap, more prizes than a game show, more thanks than a prayer meeting and more people with more things to say about other people than even 'The Oprah Winfrey Show.' " It was a rare instance of Oprah poking fun at her show.

The winner of last year's statuette for Best Talk/Service Show Host, Sally Jessy Raphael saw her program take the top prize in its category, while she lost the hosting trophy to first-time Emmy winner Joan Rivers, who broke down and sobbed as she accepted it. Everyone knew about her disastrous late night talk show which had been brutally cancelled by Fox, followed by the suicide of her husband.

Joan was kind of the comeback kid for that year. As she said in her acceptance speech: "Two years ago, I couldn't get a job in this business. My income dropped to one-sixteenth of what it was before I was fired and people said I would never work again and my husband, as you know, had a breakdown." She went on to talk about him until her emotions got the best of her, and she left the stage in tears.

That year Oprah's show didn't even get Outstanding

Director; that honor went to Russell Morash of "This Old House."

After the ceremony, Oprah secretly went on a strict diet to shed the thirty pounds she'd gained since her dramatic 1988 weight loss.

Ironically, Oprah blamed her new weight problems on the "quick fix" liquid diet that helped her achieve the earlier weight loss.

Oprah had stunned her fans in 1988 when she dropped sixty-seven pounds in three months on a four-hundred-calories-a-day liquid protein diet. After the diet she weighed just 130 pounds and wore size ten clothes, but almost immediately she had begun a losing fight to keep off the flab.

In late June, Oprah began a new, gimmick-free diet that included lots of salads and snacks, vowing, "I'll never be fat again."

And she decided to keep her diet a secret to keep her weight problem out of the public eye.

At first, she seemed to be winning, losing a pound a week. And her staff loved it because the once edgy and irritable star had become a pleasure to work with around the set.

Oprah told one close friend: "I loved being slim—but I never got a chance to enjoy it because I started regaining so quickly.

"My body had learned to function on hardly any food, so as soon as I began to eat normally again, I packed on the pounds. I was angry and miserable. I started to hate my own body because I couldn't maintain that super shape that squeezed into size 10 jeans. I started to get depressed."

She was "on a high" after she revealed her new svelte figure on her talk show back in November 1988, but

Oprah soon came crashing back to earth, said her close friend.

"She'd exercise like crazy, watch her calories—the suddenly pig out on chocolate or piles of potatoes. Her weight was like a yo-yo. She'd put it on, lose it, put it on, lose it.

"Her problems really came to a head in 1990. She was busy with so many projects that she had to cut back on exercise and she just didn't have the energy to devote to a diet. Pounds piled up."

Another friend observed that "Oprah found herself grabbing something to eat whenever she got hungry—chips, fried chicken, hot dogs."

Oprah told the friend: "It was easy to lose weight with the liquid diet, but it takes so much energy to keep the weight off. People warned me this would happen, that liquid diets melt the pounds away but they return when the dieting's over."

Once "Brewster Place," the series, was cancelled in May, Oprah had a chance to slow down. "She took a look in the mirror and hated what she saw," said the friend. " 'I was fat again!' she wailed. 'What happened? I can't believe I let myself slide like this.' "

Oprah also felt she'd let down all the women who had been inspired by her startling weight loss—and may have placed false confidence in liquid diets as a result, said another associate.

Instead of being a role model, she started to feel like a failure. Oprah was in a panic, and she decided the only thing to do was once again go to battle against her weight.

"Her new diet is Oprah's own creation. She took what she considered the most sensible aspects of many diets she's tried or read about, and put them all together."

Oprah was following a low-fat, one thousand calories-a-day diet, drinking eight glasses of mineral water a day, and avoiding snacks.

"For breakfast she ate low-fat yogurt and a piece of fruit. Sometimes she would have cereal, like granola, with low-fat milk.

"For lunch, she likes a tossed salad with a light dressing. She might have a turkey sandwich on whole wheat as well.

"In the evening, she had a mixed salad and sometimes a piece of grilled fish with lemon dressing or roast skinless chicken. She's cut out all red meat. If she wants a dessert, it's always fruit."

Oprah had been on the diet about three weeks and had lost three pounds. That was just what she wanted: to lose around a pound a week.

"When her weight was on a yo-yo Oprah was a snapping, snarling dragon lady," the friend said. "But since going on the diet she's regained her sense of humor."

She told the friend: "I feel like I'm back in control again."

And to help her feel in control, Oprah would be doing everything she could to keep this diet a secret. "Oprah doesn't want any publicity for the diet at this time." She told the friend: "I don't want to be in a goldfish bowl so that every time I take a bite of cake you read about it in the newspaper."

As usual, Stedman supported Oprah a hundred percent, telling her, "You're my girl, no matter what you weigh. But if you want to get slim again, you have my total support."

Oprah was determined to get back into those size ten jeans. She told a friend: "I'm tired of battling, battling, battling. I want a sensible diet to become part of my life forever.

"This diet's got to work—I've promised myself that."

Chapter Thirteen
Coping with Success
and Celebrity

You don't have to have laws that say "you can't come here or go sit there in that place" in order to be a slave. The only thing that can free you is the belief that you can be free.

—Oprah Winfrey explaining what she meant by the "slave mentality," 1990

One of Oprah's new ABC projects was "In the Name of Self-Esteem," which aired June 20. The issue of self-esteem has always been important to Oprah, and it has been a critical theme for her talk show. She once told a friend that "Every show I do tries to encourage self-esteem. If we've got that, we've got it all."

"What we are trying to tackle in this one hour," she says, "is what I think is the root of all the problems in the world—lack of self-esteem is what causes wars because people who really love themselves don't go out and try to fight other people. . . . It's the root of all the problems."

The special featured Oprah's conversations with a variety of people about that sense of confident self that is so important to one's happiness.

Among the guests were Maya Angelou, Drew Barrymore, an inner-city teacher, and a woman who was running a treatment center for drug addicts. The consensus was that self-esteem can come from within or be drawn from others.

In July, for her next special, Oprah returned to her Nashville roots with visits with Wynonna and Naomi Judd, K.T. Oslin, Clint Black, and Kathy Mattea.

THE $200,000 COUNTER AND OTHER PLEASURES

Few things Oprah has done in her private life have generated as much press attention as her purchase of a simple table that summer.

On August 5, Oprah and several friends showed up at an auction of Shaker furniture in upstate New York. The somewhat staid crowd of antique dealers and collectors was not prepared for Oprah's down-to-earth style. David Schorsch, a Manhattan antiques dealer who sat behind her at the Mt. Lebanon auction, reported, "She was quite different from what we're used to; whenever she got a piece she'd been bidding for, she was hooting and hollering like mad. It was obvious she was having a great time; she was like a kid in a candy store."

Schorsch, who had consulted with Oprah's great friend Bill Cosby and other celebrities on their antique purchases, told the *Chicago Tribune* that Oprah had paid a record $200,000 for a Shaker tailoring counter which he considered "a masterpiece," and another $200,000 on other pieces that were "not of like quality, but it seemed she was just furnishing, not collecting."

Actually, according to *Maine Antiques Digest*, the bible of the antiques-buying world, Oprah had accounted for some $470,000 in sales that day, and the items would give her Indiana farm a distinctive, elegant look.

Oprah bought a three-drawer work counter with its original red paint, initialed "AW" with "1830" on the back for a record $220 thousand (the *Tribune* under-reported). She also bought an armchair for $9,350 and another for $6,600; an elder's rocker for $8,250; a small oval box with original bright blue paint for $11,000, and a large basket for $4,180, among other items.

"She bought some wonderful things," said Willis Henry, a Marshfield, Massachusetts, auctioneer. "She bought at the top of the market." The work counter was "one of the best pieces the Shakers ever made, one of the finest pieces we've ever sold."

Maine Antiques Digest reported that Oprah bought "the great pieces" on the advice of Dave Driskill, "a renowned American artist who has had major shows at both Colby College and Bowdoin College and whose work is exhibited in galleries from coast to coast."

Henry added that it was "very unusual for a celebrity to come to an auction in person instead of sending a representative, but "It was a pleasure to have her come and be a part of it," he said. "She had a lot of fun. Every time she bought something she loved, she got up and cheered."

Oprah could certainly afford to enjoy every penny she spent. By the end of 1990, she was worth $250 million. She was earning $50 million a year; in the past two years, she had gone on an incredible $35 million spending spree.

"I'm blessed with more money than I could ever use," Oprah told a friend. "I'm lucky. Life's short and I'm going to enjoy every minute of it!"

In the last two years, Oprah had reached deep into her pocketbook to shell out:

★ $2 million to buy and refurbish her Indiana mansion, including a brand-new heated doghouse.

★ $1 million for dazzling jewelry, plus $500,000 for designer gowns and $130,000 for shoes and purses.

★ $200,000 to purchase thoroughbred horses she could not even ride.

★ $500,000 to go on exotic vacations all over the globe.

★ Nearly $500,000 during a whirlwind five-hour antique shopping spree.

★ $4 million for a fabulous twenty-five-room luxury apartment.

Oprah was budgeting $1 million a year for "pocket money" and had a twenty-four-hour driver, hairdresser, and makeup artist. She once gave her best friend, Gayle King Bumpus, $1.25 million, just so the Hartford, Connecticut, broadcaster could be a millionaire, too.

Even Oprah's golden retrievers were treated like kings. Their climate-controlled doghouse also featured an intercom that let her summon them without leaving the house. Total price of the doghouse: $10,000.

Since 1988 Oprah had lavished millions of dollars worth of gifts on friends, relatives, and even complete strangers.

"If you check the dictionary under the word 'generosity,' you'll find Oprah Winfrey's name," declared Gayle King Bumpus.

Other friends have nicknamed her "Oprah Spendfree."

Among Oprah's proudest possessions was her real estate. In addition to the $1 million Chicago condo she had owned for several years, Oprah bought a $4 million, twenty-five-room apartment in a fancy high-rise.

She has converted several rooms into a dream-come-true closet for all her clothes.

"Oprah buys designer clothes the way other people buy T-shirts. For the Emmys she ordered a $10,000 gown. She's amassed $500,000 worth of designer gowns, $80,000 in designer shoes, and $30,000 in designer purses," her pal continued.

Jewels were another of Oprah's passions, and Oprah

likes to wear the real thing. She buys most of her jewelry from Lester Lampert on Michigan Avenue, and by 1990 her collection was worth more than $1 million.

At the same time that she was getting settled in her new condo, Oprah was creating her dream home on her 160-acre farm in Rolling Prairie. Since buying it for $750 thousand, she had already poured more than a million dollars into such improvements as two new guest houses, tennis courts, guardhouses, and a large circular driveway.

"Workers gutted the huge, sprawling mansion and completely remodelled it," said a crew member on the project. "The renovations to the garage alone are costing almost $300,000."

The crew member was immediately impressed with Oprah's attitude: "The first day I went there she was going over the blueprints with one of the architects. She turned to a few of us and said, 'Welcome to Oprah Land! Help me make my dreams come true. If you can build it, I can pay for it.' "

Oprah had also spent nearly a half-million dollars on horses even though she was not much of a horse enthusiast.

"Oprah paid $200,000 for three thoroughbred horses, but she discovered that type of horse is really too high-spirited to ride," said a friend.

But Oprah kept the horses anyway, and spent thousands more to buy quarter horses, which are more even tempered.

Oprah indulged herself freely. She owned her own limo and employed her own full-time driver, her personal Emmy award-winning hairdresser and personal makeup artist. Her five fur coats were worth a total of $1,000,000.

When she wanted to end a vacation a few days early, Oprah once sat, phone in hand, trying to change her flight reservation before it dawned on her that she could afford to hire a plane. She told an interviewer how she could buy sheets without waiting for the January white sale.

"I didn't wait until somebody came to visit," she boasted. "I put them on the bed in the middle of the week."

But even as Oprah pampered herself, she also showered friends, relatives, and complete strangers with mind-boggling generosity.

"Oprah has a heart of gold," said her mother Vernita Lee. "For example, she retired me from my job here in Milwaukee. She sends me $5,000 every month. And she bought me a beautiful $158,000 condo.

"My granddaughter, 14 year old Chrishaunda Lee, lives with me, and Oprah is sending her to an exclusive private school this fall. Annual tuition is $15,000."

Oprah bought her father Vernon a $330,000 house near Nashville and furnished it for $200,000.

Oprah even spent $70,000 remodeling the Mississippi home of her aunt, Susie Mae Peeler, in 1988.

Complete strangers have also been touched by Oprah's generosity. Every year she spends $50,000 to feed the elderly of Alexandra, South Africa.

She has donated more than $2 million to help needy students at such institutions as Morehouse College, Tennessee State University, and the Chicago Academy of Performing Arts. She had her entire $100,000 fee for posing in the Revlon ad donated to Chicago inner-city schools.

And a $20,000 donation from Oprah would soon help open a new shelter for battered women in Inver Grove Heights, Minnesota.

Even her smallest gestures have enriched people's lives.

"Browsing in a Winston-Salem, North Carolina, china shop, Oprah overheard a young bride-to-be trying to buy her first set of dishes and glassware," a friend recalls. "But as the store owner tallied the bill, it was clear she didn't have enough money. The girl left the store in tears—but Oprah took the manager aside and paid for the entire set on the spot. She asked to remain anonymous, but the manager tracked the girl down and told her anyway. She found Oprah and cried, 'This is the happiest day of my life.' ''

Only one person close to Oprah had not been lavished with her generosity: longtime beau Stedman Graham.

"Stedman loves Oprah for herself, not her money—and she admires his independence," said the friend. "He doesn't like expensive gifts, so Oprah bought him a new golf bag and some sweaters. She did convince him to accept a $10,000 gold watch.

"That's the way Oprah is," the friend explains. "She buys things, goes to nice places, she helps people. She has fun spending her money."

"OPRAH SHOW" BLAMED FOR SUICIDE

That August Oprah was devastated by reported charges that she drove a young man to suicide by completely humiliating him when he was a guest on her show.

That angry charge came from the grieving friends and family of Michael La Calamita who hanged himself from a ceiling fan in his Northlake, Illinois, home on July 18, less than two weeks after Oprah and her studio audience ripped him to shreds on her July 6 show.

A therapist who appeared on the program with Michael said it was obvious that the young man was emotionally unstable and she was shocked that Oprah aired the show.

The victim's outraged family had hired a lawyer and was talking about suing.

"I know in my heart that Oprah's show killed my

son," a devastated Michael La Calamita, Sr., told a close family friend. "My boy was exploited by Oprah Winfrey—and she should be crucified."

When the twenty-eight-year-old Mike appeared on a show dealing with the topic "Bad Influence Friends," he became a human target.

Oprah had him sit onstage with an engaged couple who were having problems with their relationship. Mike and the man were close friends, and the woman blamed Mike for being a bad influence on her fiancé. She called Mike an ex-drug user and a big drinker who flirted with other women even though he was married.

During the show, Mike admitted he liked to go out and party while his wife stayed home. With Oprah's prodding, he also confessed he had lots of women friends and that he had a bad marriage.

At one point when the camera zoomed in on Mike, the words "Bad Influence" appeared under his face.

And when a woman in the audience called Mike a "major nightmare," the audience applauded.

"I was surprised Oprah even aired that show," said Dr. Donna Rankin, an associate professor at Loyola University of Chicago and a marriage therapist who was also a guest.

"From the things Mike was saying it was clear that he had severe emotional problems. Obviously, he needed help."

The reaction to the show from Mike's neighbors had such tremendous impact on the young man that his longtime pal Jim Cavanaugh said flat-out: "If that show hadn't aired, I feel Mike would still be with us today."

A family friend revealed: "Everyone in his neighborhood was talking about what a horse's ass Mike made of himself on TV."

The friend said that once, Mike ducked into a store to

pick up a soda and while he was waiting in line, the crowd turned on him. A woman pointed at Mike and said, "That's him. That's the crazy guy from Oprah's show."

Another woman told Mike he was a "low-down male chauvinist pig."

Poor Mike bolted out of the store, jumped in his car, and fled.

"I feel like the whole world is out to get me," Mike told friends. "Everywhere I go people are hassling me about the 'Oprah' show."

Confused and depressed, he confided that "Maybe Oprah and her guests are right. Maybe I am just a bad influence on everyone I meet. All I know is my life is ruined and I don't know where to turn."

Finally, poor Mike killed himself to end the pain and shame.

"But the real nightmare was just beginning for Mike's family," said Mike's friend. "His father found Mike hanging from the ceiling fan. Mr. La Calamita had a heart attack right on the spot and nearly died of the shock."

The friend was convinced that "Even though he survived the heart attack, his broken heart over Mike's death is killing him slowly."

A spokesperson for Oprah said, "I do not know the circumstances which caused Mike La Calamita's death. Only Mike La Calamita or perhaps a psychiatrist would know why he took his own life."

But one thing was clear: Mike's suicide left his family devastated.

"They feel Mike's appearance on 'Oprah' never should have aired," said a family friend. "They have a lawyer and they're talking about suing 'The Oprah Winfrey Show.'

"But they know that money will never replace Mike—

and just the mention of his name brings bitter tears to their eyes.''

No doubt Oprah, too, finds the memory painful. This was one occasion when her instincts failed her, and she misread the extent of poor Mike La Calamita's problems.

"AMERICA'S ALL-STAR TRIBUTE TO OPRAH WINFREY"

That September, Oprah received her own salute from the ABC network. ''America's All-Star Tribute to Oprah Winfrey'' aired on ABC on September 18. On it Oprah received ''America's Hope Award'' from Bob Hope. This was the third year the award had been given to someone in the entertainment industry whose words, actions and deeds best exemplified the attributes of generosity and humanity. Oprah joined entertainment legends Bob Hope, who won the first America's Hope Award in 1988, and Elizabeth Taylor, who was honored in 1989.

That October Oprah and Bill Cosby cohosted the Essence Awards at New York's Radio City Music Hall. The ceremony paid special tribute to Winnie Mandela and, posthumously, Sarah Vaughn. In addition, Leontyne Price, Diahann Carroll, Patti LaBelle, and Whitney Houston were among the honorees.

There was something painfully obvious about Oprah's appearance at these affairs, however: She was nearly bursting out of her dress. Her weight was up again.

In fact, she had a dress made especially for the America's Hope Award—a size ten—and it had been hanging in her closet for three months. All that time she had been telling herself that she would be able to lose the weight— she had done it before. And as the time drew closer, so did the feeling of shame.

OPRAH EXPLAINS THE "SLAVE MENTALITY"

In speeches and press interviews, Oprah had often referred to "the slave mentality" and credited her business partner Jeffrey Jacobs with freeing her of that mind-set so that she could achieve bigger things than she had ever dreamed of. She assured her listeners that they, too, could achieve greatness if they could escape the "slave mentality."

For those who wondered what exactly Oprah meant by that, Oprah had a chance to explain when she appeared on a special edition of the nationally syndicated "Ebony/Jet Showcase" during the weekend of August 24–26.

In a candid one-on-one conversation with cohost Darryl Dennard, Oprah said she was ticked off at blacks who bash other blacks in public, betraying their ancestors who struggled to cast off the physical shackles of slavery so that the generations that followed would be free.

Oprah explained that when she used the phrase "slave mentality" she was really talking about freedom—"freedom to believe that you can really do anything that your mind can conceive."

She hastened to add that she was not using the phrase, "slave mentality" as an indictment of some black people. "No, it's not an indictment of anyone, unless I'm going to indict myself," she said, admitting that she was still bothered by blacks who called her an Oreo (black on the outside and white on the inside).

"It's only saying that you don't have to have shackles," she insisted. "You don't have to have laws that say, 'you can't come here or go sit there in this place' in order to be a slave. The only thing that can free you is the belief that you can be free."

After discussing the "quantum leap" to maturity and

earnings that made her the richest black woman in America, Oprah talked about the roles and contributions of blacks who built the bridge that had allowed her to cross all kinds of barriers to succeed.

"I live my life in such a way that I think the ancestors would be proud. And you know it all sounds rhetorical and lofty, but that's really how I try to lead my life," Oprah said.

Oprah's tone grew more passionate as she launched into a topic that was clearly very important to her.

"The ancestors don't deserve the treatment that we're giving them," she said. "They don't deserve it and I believe that. I see us as a people doing things to ourselves and our children. I see the drug problem. I see abusiveness toward ourselves.

"I see self-hatred that makes us turn against each other and try to pull each other down. I see that and I think that Frederick Douglass did not deserve this. He did not teach the slaves to read by candlelight to see us at our banquets and meeting halls sit and try and tear each other apart. He does not deserve this!"

In conclusion, Oprah returned to another theme that occurs often in her speeches: "Your grandmother and great grandmother did not work in the white folks' kitchen just trying to make enough money so that your mother might be able to have a pair of shoes to wear to school and not be embarrassed. They don't deserve great-grand-children who don't take books to school. They don't deserve it."

THE PAIN OF REGAIN

In spite of her lofty dreams and ambitions, Oprah also had to deal with day-to-day reality. And the latest painful reality was that her weight once again seemed to be out of control.

By November Oprah was forced to admit that the secret diet she had embarked on in July was a failure. She had gained sixty-nine pounds, more than she had lost on her much publicized diet. And it was even straining her romance with Stedman.

Their relationship had become platonic, according to insiders.

And the pair, who used to date four times a week, now saw each other once a week at most.

What's more, Stedman refused to move into the $4 million hideaway that Oprah had bought for them.

"He is embarrassed by Oprah. He feels she's thrown in the towel and lost all interest in controlling her weight," said an insider.

Stedman, a fitness fanatic, used to take pride in Oprah's slimmed-down look. He helped her stick to her diets and exercised with her every day.

But now, the insider said, "He has called off the romance. He's just hanging on to the hope that Oprah will get her weight under control. If she doesn't, he'll be gone for good.

"Oprah's weight has destroyed their relationship."

This was a tragic turnaround for Oprah who had only two years earlier stunned America with her dramatic sixty-seven pound weight loss.

"I'll never be fat again," she had publicly vowed. But it was a promise that she could not keep. Now, according to friends, 5 foot 7 Oprah was up to 199 pounds and still gaining.

"It's so hard—food is my drug and I just can't kick it!" she told a friend.

"Part of me just wants to say, 'Forget it! Let me be

me and let me do what I like to do: Eat!' But part of me hates me fat, hates me for piling on the pounds after promising I would be good!''

And the pounds just kept packing themelves on, because Oprah could not control her growing appetite.

"She's put on 39 pounds in addition to the 30 she regained by July,'' said her pal. "She keeps pigging out.

"We went for lunch and she ordered like a crazy woman—cheeseburger, a large order of fries, a non-diet soft drink and a piece of cheesecake!''

Oprah was caught in a vicious circle, a friend confided. She started overeating when she became depressed over the cancellation of her series, "Brewster Place,'' in May. Gaining weight left her more depressed which led to more overeating.

"Now she's terrified she'll hit 200 pounds,'' said a friend. "Oprah has opened up her 'fat closet' and is back to wearing the clothes she used to wear. And that makes her feel worse.

"Oprah is so frustrated with her weight gain that she was not even trying to diet now. It's a stress situation and she just can't seem to help it.''

"Stedman says I've become a picky and irritable woman, the worst I've ever been, and he's probably right,'' Oprah admitted to a friend. "He knows it's because I'm not happy with myself and my weight.''

"Now her stress is building even more because Stedman had changed his mind about moving in with her. He doesn't want to deal with her mood swings.''

Stedman told a source: "I know she put $4 million into a Chicago apartment for us, but I won't be ready to move in until she tackles her problems. I tell her, 'Baby, lay off the junk food!' But she just looks at me blankly and pops another Cheez Doodle into her mouth.

" 'I love her as much as I can, but the battle must be fought by her alone!' "

The two faced off over Oprah's eating during a charity arts festival in Ann Arbor, Michigan.

"Oprah sneaked away to a nearby hot dog stand," said a witness. "I watched as Oprah wolfed down three hot dogs and a huge piece of cheesecake. Just as she finished the cake, Stedman spotted her. He scolded her and she acted defiant. But he should have been there minutes earlier when she was scarfing down the hot dogs!"

Stedman was still on hand for public appearances like "America's All-Star Tribute to Oprah Winfrey," but Oprah confessed to a friend that "It was a dreary time for us."

He was acting more like an escort, taking her to public events, than like a man she planned to marry. "He's staying away from her and when she talks with him it's mostly by phone. Their relationship has become platonic.

"Unless Oprah does something about her weight soon," the friend warned, "she is going to lose Stedman for good."

Everywhere Oprah went, people were asking her, "How do you feel about gaining the weight back?" In her usual courageous style, Oprah decided to face the weight issue head-on on her November 5 show devoted to the topic "The Pain of Regain," featuring female guests who had also lost and regained large amounts.

After a burst of welcoming applause, Oprah opened the show by addressing the audience.

"You know, there's an expression that goes 'There are only two things in life you can count on, death and taxes.' Well, believe me, you can add this one to your list: 'If you lose weight on a diet, sooner or later, you'll gain it back.'

"The truth of the matter is, I will never diet again. I will certainly never fast. I'll never diet again."

She sounded a plaintive cry: "I would just like to get on with my life and not have this be an issue."

Privately, the weight gain had left her cranky and sullen, and she was starting to think men weren't worth the torture of trying to stay slim.

Fed up with starving herself to look sexy, Oprah threw in the scale. She said she was giving up men, including Stedman, until a guy came along who accepted her just the way she was—fat but happy!

"From now on I'm living this life for Oprah, not for some man," she told a close friend.

"Women diet to keep their men, everybody knows that. But I've decided men can go to blazes.

"Why should I spend the rest of my existence worrying about some silly man? If he doesn't want me the way I am, he can take a hike.

"The charade is over. I'm going to be the Oprah I always wanted to be: fat and sassy!"

Publicly, Oprah said she did the show because "everywhere I go people ask me, 'How do you feel about gaining the weight back?' I thought I'd address it myself."

But according to insiders, Oprah, who loved to eat, really was just sick and tired of going through hell just to look terrific for Stedman or any man.

That's why she chose croissants over cuddling . . . rigatoni over romance.

"Oprah is really angry over the way Stedman pulled away from her after she started regaining her weight," said one close source. "She told me, 'Men are the only reason women starve themselves and work out until they're ready to drop.' "

Now that she had made her decision, Oprah seemed

happier than she had been in the past two years, said a pal.

"I've never seen Oprah so peaceful. She told me, 'I've accepted the fact that I'm not going to be slim again.' "

Oprah had also put on hold her dream of someday having children.

She told an insider: "I don't want anything to do with men now and that includes starting a family with one.

"To hell with guys. I'd rather be fat and happy than miserable with someone who can't accept the real me!"

But that was all for public consumption. For Oprah had a secret she did not want anyone to know: She was back on her diet after all.

Although Oprah swore to her TV audience on November 5 that "I'll never diet again," she secretly started another weight-loss program just five days later.

And her commitment to slim down patched up her broken romance with Stedman. In fact, the two of them were slimming down together. Fitness buff Stedman had recently become alarmed when he realized he packed on thirty-five pounds himself.

"Oprah sat him down and said, 'Stedman, let's beat this fat thing together! Let's go on a diet.' "

But Oprah was staying away from quick weight-loss methods like the liquid diet that allowed her to slim down to 130 pounds in 1988. Instead she put together her own sensible plan.

She and Stedman were having yogurt or cereal for breakfast; for lunch they ate a light salad or fish; dinner consisted of vegetables and fruit, and at night they snacked on raw vegetables.

Oprah and Stedman grew even closer as they fought the flab together. And their romance, which had fizzled last fall, was going full-blast again.

259

Stedman had even moved out of his Chicago apartment and into Oprah's place across town, according to a close source.

No matter what her size, Oprah still wanted to look her best. It hurt her deeply when the October 20–26 issue of *TV Guide* included her among Mr. Blackwell's "Worst Dressed," and by December she had released her long-time wardrobe advisor, Jennifer Jacobs (wife of Jeffrey), and decided to dress herself.

"Oprah's eyes almost popped out of her head seeing herself linked with Roseanne Barr and the cartoon character Marge Simpson as the trashiest dressers on TV," revealed one set insider.

"She said, 'I'm just so humiliated I could lie down and die.' "

Oprah ordered up clips of the shows she had done over the past three years and watched them carefully, analyzing each outfit she wore on every show.

"She went into shock when she saw how short some of her skirts were and how chunky they made her legs look," the insider reported. "She was appalled at how she often wore big belts that cut her in half and made her look all hips and bosom."

Oprah realized that her wardrobe adviser had been putting her in clothes so brightly colored they made her look heavier. And so tight they practically looked painted on.

"I've seen sausages that weren't as stuffed as I looked!" Oprah told the insider. "Now I realize the outfits made me the laughingstock of TV!"

Two weeks later, Jennifer Jacobs was out the door. Oprah also reassigned her longtime personal makeup man to working only on her talk show guests.

"The problem with Oprah's make-up was that he was putting her in loud colors to coordinate with her too-loud outfits," explained a friend of the star.

Oprah hired New York makeup expert Reggie Wells to do her makeup.

"Her makeup artist is using more rich earth tones—nice blues, camels, golds, browns and greens," said her personal hairdresser, Andre Walker.

Oprah's previous hairstyle swept around her face, making her features look too full. Her new style, according to Walker, "is blown up as straight as you can get it.

"It's cut very blunt, one length, with a bit of layering in the front."

Oprah started sporting fresh new outfits on the show. Her clothes were now the right size, and the too-tight look was gone forever.

She was wearing jumpsuits that concealed her weight . . . turtlenecks to conceal her double chin . . . more loose-fitting outfits . . . classy two-piece suits cut so they cleverly concealed her hips . . . and solid colors instead of wild patterns.

New makeup man Wells was advising Oprah to wear colors such as gray and camel that went well with her skin tones. He even accompanied her on clothes shopping trips, and she ordered him to tell her when an outfit didn't look just right on her.

MERRY CHRISTMAS

That Christmas Oprah set another record for generosity to her staff by giving her producers dream vacations.

Each of her producers received two round-trip tickets to go anywhere in the world for two weeks, along with $10,000 and free accommodations.

In return, her longtime executive producer Debra Di Maio gave Oprah a flock of sheep for her farm at Rolling Prairie.

As she faced the end of the year, Oprah could look

back on a tumultuous, challenging period. For better or worse, the psychic predictions that had her in a personal and professional partnership with Arsenio Hall had not come to pass, but Stedman Graham had stood by her through thick and thin, literally.

She had weathered the disappointing cancellation of "Brewster Place," possibly the first public failure of a broadcasting career that began when she was only a teenager, and she was already on to exciting new projects such as the well-received ABC documentary "In the Name of Self-Esteem." She had developed a new interest: collecting the elegantly simple wood furniture and household furnishings of the Shaker Community.

And she had been widely honored in the industry (even if she was shut out of the Emmys that year) and the black community.

Her greatest problem was her weight, and somehow she was just beginning to realize that the root causes would have to be confronted, examined, and dealt with. Her main task would be to build her strength for that enormous undertaking.

To deal with her present, to be all that she could be, she would have to face the most painful issues of her past.

Chapter Fourteen
Facing the Dark Issues
of the Past

I've been dieting since 1977, and the reason I failed is that diets don't work. I tell people, if you're underweight, go on a diet and you'll gain everything you lost, plus more.

> —Oprah Winfrey discussing her most recent weight gain, 1991

Oprah celebrated an especially happy thirty-seventh birthday in January 1991: She had just signed a new contract with King World to continue hosting and producing "The Oprah Winfrey Show" through the 1994–95 season. Terms were not disclosed, but it was obvious that Oprah would continue to be one of the highest-paid people in show business.

That month, *Art & Antiques* magazine included Oprah, along with Madonna and actor Steve Martin, in its annual list of the United States' top one hundred collectors.

Not that everything was perfect. The failure of the "Brewster Place" series had cost her $10 million, and now that the show had shut down, the beautiful state-of-the-art production facilities at Harpo Studios were idle.

A "HONEYMOON" IN PARADISE

But that March Oprah whisked Stedman off on a fabulous $10,000-a-day honeymoon in the Caribbean.

The word on the street was that Oprah had secretly arranged the romantic getaway because Stedman was getting cold feet about tying the knot. Although he'd already agreed to marry Oprah, he had not come through with a formal proposal and engagement ring on Valentine's Day, as she had expected.

"Oprah was staggered and heartbroken on Valentine's Day when Stedman told her he still wasn't convinced she was ready to cut back on her super-busy career, settle down and have babies," confided a friend of the star.

"He said he needed more time to think about their future together."

So Oprah decided to give him a taste of how wonderful married life would be with her.

"In sheer desperation, Oprah hit on the amazing idea to take Stedman away on a pre-marriage honeymoon. She wanted to convince him of her commitment and show him they could be happy together."

Oprah chose sun-kissed Necker Island, a privately owned paradise in the British Virgin Islands. It was a favorite vacation spot of Princess Diana, Mel Gibson, and other celebrities.

The island had only one large house, a fantastic ten-bedroom stone villa atop a seventy-five-foot bluff near the shore. It was one of the most beautiful homes in the entire Caribbean, boasting spacious high-ceilinged tropical rooms with spectacular views of the ocean.

Visitors were pampered by a staff of nineteen servants, including maids, chefs, and waiters, who catered to their every whim.

Necker Island cost Oprah $9,000 a day to rent, and additional expenses set her back another $1,000 a day.

But Oprah considered the secluded island worth every penny. Because for more than a week, she and Stedman had the time of their lives.

Guards prowled the island's shorelines and patrolled the seas around it to repel prying eyes.

Oprah spent hours in the Jacuzzi, locked in Stedman's arms. Together they played tennis, swam, and even tried wind surfing. They went deep-sea fishing, and Oprah even caught a shark.

When her fishing line went taut, Oprah yelled: "It's a big one! It's a big one!"

Eventually, Oprah pulled the fish to the side of the boat, and saw it was a six-foot shark. "How about that!" she screamed.

But she had the line cut and freed the big fish.

"Then Oprah turned to Stedman and said: 'I let the shark go but there's no way I am going to let you go that easily!' She threw her arms around him and they kissed passionately," an observer reported.

Oprah also used the vacation to try to get fitter.

At nine o'clock in the morning, she was lifting weights and riding an exercise bike.

Some days she and Stedman played tennis on the villa's private court. Other days they went hand in hand for a walk in the hills on the island, then came back and swam in the pool before lunch.

One afternoon Oprah tried her hand at wind surfing. Another day she water-skied.

At sunset the couple could be seen sitting on the patio, sipping exotic rum-based drinks. Afterward, they dined on lobsters, sea bass or shrimp, all of which Oprah loved.

On several evenings, Oprah had a calypso band

brought in by boat from a neighboring island. While the music played, she and Stedman danced into the wee hours of the morning.

"Halfway through the 'honeymoon,' Stedman obviously was having a terrific time. He was unbelievably playful and grinning from ear to ear," the observer reported.

"It sure looks like Oprah's plan has succeeded," an optimistic friend gushed. "And she and Stedman will soon be a happily married couple."

"I'LL NEVER DIET AGAIN"

In a cover story in *People* magazine, Oprah was candid about her most recent weight gain.

"I've been dieting since 1977," she said, "and the reason I failed is that diets don't work. I tell people, if you're underweight, go on a diet and you'll gain everything you lost plus more."

She was taking a new approach, Oprah told *People*. "Now I'm trying to find a way to live in a world with food without being controlled by it, without being a compulsive eater. That's why I say I will never diet again."

She had given a lot of thought to the painful subject. "My greatest failure was in believing that the weight issue was just about weight," she said. "It's not. It's about not being able to say no. It's about not handling stress properly. It's about sexual abuse. It's all about the things that cause other people to become alcoholics and drug addicts."

Oprah also acknowledged that because she had fallen into the classic traps of the dieter, failing to make permanent changes in her eating and exercise habits, the pain of regain was inevitable.

"I didn't do whatever the maintenance program was,"

Oprah admitted. "I thought I was cured. And that's just not true. You have to find a way to live in the world with food."

At last, Oprah saw that she had used food to medicate herself through stressful situations.

But just a few weeks later, Oprah was spotted at a fancy New Orleans restaurant, wolfing down a double order of soft-shell crabs and crawfish etouffe. And she topped all that with three desserts: a chocolate eclair, crêpes maison, and jelly-filled crêpes.

It might be considered cruel to constantly report on Oprah's eating excesses, but she was the one who made them a public issue. Perhaps it was part of her ongoing self-therapy: It's possible that she hoped the pressure of public scrutiny would help her control her appetite. Unfortunately, if that was her hope, it wasn't working.

OPRAH TURNS ACTIVIST

As already noted, Oprah has always said that the major turning point of her life came when, after years of abuse by relatives in Mississippi and Milwaukee, she was sent to live with her father, Vernon Winfrey, in Nashville for good. That winter of 1991 she reached another critical turning point in her personal and professional journey. This was a major stopping point in the journey she had begun with her spontaneous admission live on the air in 1985 that she had been sexually abused at the age of nine by a nineteen-year-old cousin and at the age of fourteen by a favorite uncle.

Some would say that it was by chance that winter that Oprah turned on the evening news and learned of the horrifying murder of four-year-old Angelica Mena in Chicago. The child had gone from her mother's apartment on the second floor to visit an aunt on the first floor and was never seen again. Little Angelica had been molested, strangled, and thrown into Lake Michigan by a man with two previous convictions for the kidnapping and rape of children. He had just moved into the apartment next door to her mother.

In Oprah's vision of the world there is no such thing as chance. Everything happens for a reason, and there had to be a reason why this tragic story came to her attention at that particular time.

The tragedy touched Oprah in deep and profound ways. There was, of course, the simple horror of it, but there were also, no doubt, the parallels to her own experience as a sexually abused child.

She had to do something. She had to make a stand.

Oprah began her stand on March 13 by devoting an entire ''Oprah Winfrey Show'' to the problem of child abuse.

On the program, Oprah appeared outraged. ''Our children in this country are not safe,'' she told her audience. ''They're not safe at the hands of strangers. Oftentimes they're not safe at the hands of relatives and friends and even their own parents. One of every six violent crimes in this country is committed against a child. And I think it's time for all of us to decide to do something about it.''

Oprah also announced that in the same month she would be hosting a television special called ''Nine.'' She explained that the special would be about being a child, ''especially what it's like to be a 9-year-old child today for many children. And for many children, it's not a pretty picture.''

Oprah showed her audience clips from the special, and introduced her audience to children who appeared in it; children whose young lives had seen crimes and abuses no one, especially a child, should ever see. One boy had been set on fire by an angry playmate; a girl had killed her abusive father; another had seen two men murder her mother, her little sister, and two friends.

At one point their emotional testimony almost became too much for Oprah. "I don't know about you all," she said to her audience, "but I am really—I'm tired of hearing about the abuse. I'm tired about crime against— hearing about crimes against children. I'm tired of the molestations. I'm tired of people who have committed crimes against children getting off."

Next, she introduced her audience to Andrew Vachss, a New York attorney and author who has dedicated his life to fighting crimes against children, both in the court-room and through his novels. She asked him: "When are we going to do something to change this?"

Vachss painted an even more frightening picture of child abuse rampant in America.

Oprah was outraged. "So Angelica is murdered, and this city and across the country there are hundreds of other children murdered in the same day and none of us hear anything about it, because it's so common?"

Even after the shows aired, the tragedy continued to haunt Oprah. She could not put the story of little Angelica out of her mind. She could not forget the stories of all those other wounded children. She had been there. She had suffered in the same way. She shared their pain, and she had to do something about it.

Oprah vowed to take a stand for the children of this country. Andrew Vachss encouraged her, suggesting the idea for a national registry of convicted abusers. He also gave her some important advice: "Start with something do-able. Don't try to change the world tomorrow."

"EVERYBODY'S WORRIED ABOUT OPRAH"

Meanwhile, since returning from her Caribbean vacation with Stedman, Oprah's weight had soared. She was heavier than ever at 205 pounds, and her doctor had ordered her to lose weight or face a serious health crisis.

Friends reported that she weighed more now than at the beginning of her 1988 fast and, worse, she had given up all pretense of trying to control her weight. She was gorging herself on high-calorie foods and had completely stopped exercising.

As a result, Oprah was at risk of heart disease, stroke, diabetes, high blood pressure, and knee joint problems and had been told by her doctor to lose at least thirty pounds.

Her plans for a September wedding had been put on hold. She feared being a fat bride.

"Everybody's worried about Oprah, no one has ever seen her this heavy," a source close to the talk show host disclosed.

"And Oprah doesn't seem to be able to do anything about it. She doesn't exercise, she doesn't watch what she eats. It's like she's totally given up.

"She wheezes after a 30-foot walk down a corridor.

"Oprah recently signed a contract extension through 1995. Now she's got the pressure of keeping her show a hit for the next four years. And faced with stress, Oprah eats.

"She told me, 'I can't set up movie deals, do the show and try to put together a TV series *and* diet all at the same time.'"

According to a close associate, Oprah had stopped any pretense of control since returning from the Caribbean in March. "Now she eats desserts at every meal," the associate claimed. "She snacks in between.

"She's got a business empire to run with almost 200 employees. She needs to be healthy and being that fat ain't healthy!"

That's just what Oprah's doctors reportedly told her when she went for a physical.

"She tipped the scales at 205 pounds and the doctor shocked her by saying she had to lose at least 30 pounds," a friend revealed.

"He told her if she didn't comply, she was asking for all sorts of health problems, including high blood pressure, heart problems, and back and knee joint problems. Especially at her age, 37, the heart can't take the added weight."

A person who is more than fifty pounds overweight, like Oprah, is at a major risk of heart disease, stroke, diabetes, arthritis and other serious ailments, confirmed Dr. Donald S. Robertson, who runs the Southwest Bariatric and Nutrition Center in Scottsdale, Arizona.

"Someone who should be 130 to 140 pounds but instead is up at 190 or more is playing with a potential killer," he said.

Yet even her doctor's stern warning to lose weight failed to hit home with Oprah.

She told a friend: "I know I've been gaining a great deal of weight, but frankly I don't give a darn. I feel fine and fit and plan to live to be 100, regardless of my weight.

"But there's one area I'm sensitive about. I don't want to be a fat bride and have people snicker. So I've made it clear to Stedman that right now marriage is out. I'm not prepared to make the changes a man might want— like losing weight."

Just how much weight Oprah had packed on was clear to viewers when Dolly Parton, who is a petite 105 pounds, guested on a recent show.

"Tiny Dolly with her skinny waist sat next to Oprah

who dwarfed Dolly,'' said one insider. ''Oprah was too fat to cross her legs as she and Dolly chatted.''

But that hasn't slowed Oprah down one bit.

''She's been seen enjoying all the entrees at the Eccentric and she snacks like crazy during taping breaks in her show,'' added the insider.

''At this rate, by 1995 she'll tip the scales at over 300 pounds—or something worse will happen. All of us are worried about Oprah.''

In late May, a desperate Oprah visited the posh Cal-a-Vie spa in Vista, near San Diego. The exclusive fat farm cost $3,750 a week per person and only took twenty-two guests a week. Instructors taught visitors how to be healthy for life.

The spa seemed the ideal place for Oprah because it emphasized fitness, not dieting. Her meals were composed of very low-fat, low-sodium and low-cholesterol foods. The emphasis was on vegetables, fruit, seafood, and poultry.

Cal-a-Vie was known for its exotic relaxation therapies, such as seaweed body wraps, aromatherapy massage, and hydrotherapy.

At the spa, Oprah's day started with a 6:00 A.M. hike before breakfast, followed by aerobics, weight training, pool exercises, stretching, and yoga.

''Cal-a-Vie is not a fat farm. We help people promote a healthy lifestyle,'' Debbie Zie, the spa's marketing and publicity manager told interviewers. ''Oprah really likes the program and has a great time. She participates in everything.''

Oprah lost only five pounds but left happy, saying she was excited about taking a ''love boat'' cruise with her beau, a source at the spa confided.

''Then she started humming the theme from TV's 'Love Boat.' ''

A MEANINGFUL EMMY

Before the cruise, however, Oprah would be attending the Daytime Emmys at New York's Marriott-Marquis Hotel on June 27. This event was marked by something new. As host Bob Barker put it: "This is a very special occasion. For the first time in 18 years, the telecast about the people who make up daytime TV gets a chance for a prime-time celebration."

Last year's upset winner of Outstanding Talk/Service Show Host, Joan Rivers, introduced that category with a montage of old clips showing talk show greats of the past.

"And could they talk," she said. The group included kids saying some of the darndest things on "Art Linkletter's House Party," Jack Benny giving the silent treatment to Merv Griffin, and Muhammad Ali telling David Frost, "You're not as dumb as you look!"

This year, "The Oprah Winfrey Show" swept the field, taking Outstanding Host, Outstanding Program, and Outstanding Director.

Accepting the Outstanding Program award for her production team, executive producer Debra Di Maio thanked Oprah's "once-in-a-lifetime" spirit, while Oprah herself thanked Truddi Chase, a victim of sexual abuse who also suffered from multiple personality disorder, as she accepted her Outstanding Host award.

It was the episode with Oprah's interview with Truddi Chase that had been submitted to Emmy's judging panels.

"During the show," Oprah said, "a lot of victims of sexual abuse were able to release some of their personal shame." It was a moment that Oprah could take great personal pride in.

The Outstanding Program award was shared by Ray Nunn, senior producer, Oprah herself as supervising producer, and David Boul, Mary Kay Clinton, Rudy Guido, Dianne Hudson, Alice McGee, Sally Lou Oaks, and Ellen Rakietan, producers. Outstanding Director went to Peter Kimball.

SAILING IN THE MEDITERRANEAN

Her weight problems did not keep Oprah from whisking Stedman off on a splashy $45,000-a-day "love boat" cruise in the Mediterranean that July 2. Oprah, Stedman, and friends flew to Nice, France, and hopped into two limos for the short drive to San Remo, Italy, where they boarded the yacht *Talon*.

And they had the time of their lives aboard the lavish 128-foot-long yacht. She and Stedman shared a large, plush master suite that had its own marble Jacuzzi.

And the seven-day cruise was so romantic it convinced Oprah she had made the right decision in dropping her plans to wed Stedman.

"We've got no reason to get married right now. It's sexier living together!" Oprah told a friend after the cruise.

"We love each other and we'll be together forever. Someday I may walk down the aisle, but not now."

Oprah, now sharing a Chicago apartment with Stedman, added: "Living with Stedman is so romantic. It's like we're constantly courting each other."

On the cruise Oprah took along her hairdresser, two pals, and Stedman's fifteen-year-old daughter, Wendy.

The three-deck yacht was so huge it could entertain one hundred people at once. There were four guest staterooms in addition to the master suite, and a master chef was aboard to prepare fancy meals. The dining room glittered with Tiffany silver, Wedgewood china, and Baccarat crystal.

276

As usual, generous Oprah picked up all expenses, even providing gifts for her guests. The final tab for the week was $315,000 or $45,000 a day.

"The night they boarded the *Talon*, Oprah and her guests celebrated with a beautiful dinner," the star's friend disclosed.

Later that evening, as the yacht lay at anchor in the bay, Oprah and Stedman took a moonlight walk on the deck by themselves.

"They held hands, and Oprah snuggled against Stedman's side as they leaned on the rail. They exchanged sizzling kisses several times," said an insider.

The *Talon*'s first port of call was Portofino, Italy, where Oprah immediately went on a lavish shopping spree.

"In one store she saw a collection of 18th century European jewelry and she bought it all for $60,000. She gave half of the antique jewelry to her friends," said an insider.

The *Talon* sailed on to the Italian ports of Varazze and Portovonere, where Oprah and Stedman went sightseeing.

"They kissed and clung to each other as they spent two hours strolling through the old Roman amphitheater in Portovenere," said an insider.

Each time the yacht docked, Oprah went jogging. In the evening, she and Stedman dined in the finest local restaurants, sampling all sorts of fare.

"Oprah never binges," said the insider. "There was too much love play going on between her and Stedman for her to think about overeating."

But Oprah did have one moment of green-eyed jealousy when the yacht stopped at St. Tropez.

"When she and Stedman went to the beach, Stedman glanced at some topless girls," an insider reported.

"Oprah grabbed his arm and gave him a withering look that clearly said, 'How could you do this to me?'

"Stedman turned his eyes away and whispered to Oprah: 'Honey, you're better than a hundred of these girls all wrapped into one.'

"Oprah smiled and immediately forgave him for looking."

As the yacht sailed from port to port, Oprah and her friends played backgammon, enjoyed the on-board sauna, and went fishing.

In the French port of Saint-Jean-Cap-Ferrat, the star and her party hopped on jetskis for some high-speed fun.

The yacht anchored in Monaco's bay the next day. Oprah and her guests had a ball playing in the clear blue water. Even though her weight was up to two hundred pounds, Oprah felt relaxed enough to don a one-piece swimsuit and try waterskiing, said the insider.

"She's not a swimmer, but she rode the water well."

As her shopping continued, Oprah spent $50,000 on antique statues and urns for the Chicago apartment she shared with Stedman.

In addition, she plunked down another $80,000 for exquisite antique crystal glasses, rare old books, new clothes, and more.

The cruise ended back in San Remo on July 9. At that point, Oprah's hairdresser and two pals flew back to America. But Oprah and Stedman and Wendy flew to Rome for more fun.

Wendy checked into a luxury $682-a-night suite at Rome's upscale Excelsior Hotel, while her dad and Oprah cozied up in a deluxe $965-a-night suite.

Later, Oprah told a friend: "What a wonderfully romantic way to end our cruise!"

Walter Ferrare, concierge at the hotel, told the press:

"Stedman and Oprah are a very romantic couple and appear to be deeply in love. Oprah told me, 'It's my best vacation ever!' "

The next day, July 10, Stedman had to fly back to Chicago on business. Oprah looked sad to see him go.

Reportedly, there were tears in Oprah's eyes as she kissed Stedman goodbye, and told him: "I love you so much, Steddy, I've never felt closer to you.' "

Wendy flew home a couple of days later, leaving Oprah alone.

"Oprah missed Stedman so much that she called him and begged him to come back early to be with her," said her friend.

"Stedman rearranged his schedule and flew to meet her in Switzerland on July 15."

Oprah had a great time on her cruise, but it cost her a fortune.

She shelled out $50,000 to lease the yacht and spent another $75,000 on airfare, limos, and a load of other expenses.

In addition, Oprah spent a whopping $190,000 during her shopping sprees, which brought her total expenditures to $315,000.

"Sure it was expensive. But I have the money," Oprah told her friend.

And did she! The star's income had reached $38 million a year, which averaged out to $104,000 a day. So Oprah's cruise cost her only about three days' pay.

Oprah continued to share her wealth. In September she donated $100,000 to buy books for the new Harold Washington Library, named for the late Chicago mayor. "Books were my path to personal freedom," Oprah said in a statement. "I learned to read at age 3 and soon discovered there was a whole world to conquer that went beyond our farm in Mississippi."

OPRAH CAPTURES A MURDER SUSPECT

Oprah has contributed a great deal of understanding and education through her talk show, but few are aware that she has even helped capture a murder suspect, who had eluded police around the world for three years.

Handsome model John Hawkins, twenty-eight, had been on the run since police in Glendale, California, charged him with murdering Ellis Greene in 1988 to collect $2.5 million in insurance money.

Even after "America's Most Wanted" profiled the shocking case three times, police failed to capture Hawkins. But then Oprah stepped in and featured the crime on her talk show, then televised in thirteen countries.

The result: An informant in the Netherlands recognized Hawkins and turned him in.

"Knowing that I helped rid society of a criminal made me feel very proud of my show," Oprah told a close friend.

The mother of the murder victim, Darlene Greene, added: "I am forever grateful to Oprah for catching my son's alleged killer. Thank God for Oprah. My son can finally rest in peace."

Hawkins's luck ran out when the "Oprah" episode aired in the Netherlands, and a woman there recognized the fugitive as a former lover with whom she'd sailed the Mediterranean.

She phoned the local TV station that aired "Oprah," and they passed the information to the police. Two weeks later, Hawkins was nabbed when he docked in Sardinia. And police say they have finally gotten a criminal whose lust for money led him to conspire with two other men, Melvin Hanson and Dr. Richard Boggs, to commit murder.

Here's what happened, according to authorities:

Hawkins and Hanson were co-owners of a sportswear store, and Hawkins modeled the store's clothing line in TV ads. After Hanson took out a huge life insurance policy and named Hawkins as the beneficiary, they decided to fake Hanson's death and collect.

So Hawkins picked up thirty-one-year-old drifter Greene in a Glendale bar and took him to Dr. Boggs's office—where he was suffocated.

Dr. Boggs then listed the death as due to natural causes and identified the dead man as Melvin Hanson. However, police became suspicious and compared the corpse's fingerprints to those of Hanson on a driver's license. They didn't match.

Hanson and Dr. Boggs were arrested. By then, however, Hawkins had collected about $1 million in insurance money and was on the lam.

Police say that over the next three years he traveled throughout Canada, the West Indies, Britain, Italy, France, Greece, Spain, the Netherlands, and possibly Mexico. He often used aliases.

No one could catch him, until Oprah entered the picture!

Her producers asked John Walsh to bring some of his toughest cases from "America's Most Wanted" and profile them on her show.

"The John Hawkins profile was the first we did on 'Oprah.' And without a doubt that was the reason he was captured," said Walsh.

The "Oprah" episode featuring Hawkins aired in the United States in late May, then it was broadcast in Europe on July 14.

That's when the call came in from an anonymous Dutch woman who said she had sailed with Hawkins. Police asked the U.S. Naval Investigative Service for help in tracking him down.

"The Dutch woman happened to watch the 'Oprah' episode and recognized John Hawkins," said Rod Miller, head of the Navy agency's Los Angeles office. "The woman became angry at Hawkins when she learned from the show that he might be bisexual. She was scared of catching AIDS.

281

"Our service has agents in almost every port of the world. We were told to look for a red catamaran near Sardinia.

"On August 1 our officers spotted a catamaran matching the description given us. We then notified the Italian police, who arrested Hawkins on an international fugitive warrant.

"Because of the 'Oprah' show being broadcast in the Netherlands, Hawkins was apprehended."

Jerry Treadway, a fraud supervisor for the California Department of Insurance who was working with police on the Hawkins murder-for-insurance scam, agreed it was Oprah who made the bust possible, saying: "I give her show full credit for capturing Hawkins!"

OPRAH'S NEW DIET SECRET: A "DIET COP"

Oprah returned from the Mediterranean cruise with a new resolve, and that September, determined to slim down from her record 205 pounds, Oprah hired Rosie Daley, a top chef, to act as a "diet cop" who would make sure she dropped fifty-five pounds.

Oprah lured the chef away from the Cal-a-Vie spa to prepare mouth-watering treats on a tasty diet program she could stick with. And it was working beautifully. In just six weeks, she had dropped twenty pounds.

Oprah met chef Daley when she spent nine days at the spa in May, and she was so impressed by Rosie's low-calorie gourmet dishes that she convinced her to move all the way to Chicago to become her personal cook and nutritional consultant.

Rosie prepared all of Oprah's meals, serving delicious low-fat dishes in Oprah's apartment. She traveled with the star when Oprah visited her Indiana farm, packed lunches for Oprah to eat at the studio, and phoned ahead to restaurants to help select Oprah's diet meals. She was on call twenty-four hours a day.

With Rosie, Oprah was convinced that she would shed a total of fifty-five pounds and reach her target weight of 150.

"When I buy antiques I get advice from experts, and when I need to hire directors or designers I find out the best people, but with my weight I was struggling to do it myself," Oprah told a close friend.

"I realized I needed to get experts to help me. I like to eat, but I don't want my weight out of control. So I decided to hire a dietician/cook—and found Rosie."

Oprah was hoping her secret "diet cop" would finally bring victory in her on-again, off-again battle against the bulge.

"I never want to return to my old eating habits," Oprah told an insider. "And by having someone 24 hours a day to monitor what I eat, and prepare only healthy foods for me, I think I'm at last on the right track."

The insider disclosed: "Oprah's menu is high in complex carbohydrates, such as fruits, vegetables, pasta, rice and grains.

"Gone are the cream sauces, the foods laden with butter, salt and shortening. The portions of calorie-rich foods are smaller, but you don't go hungry because you fill up on the bulkier, calorie-light foods such as vegetables and grains.

"It's not a quick weight-loss plan—it's basically a long-term 1,000 to 1,200 calorie-a-day diet.

"Breakfast might be fruit, such as melon or grapefruit, or a cereal made from buckwheat and served with low-fat milk.

"Lunch is either a soup, salad, pasta or seafood.

"Dinner consists of an entree with a vegetable, soup and a dessert of fresh fruit or concoctions like low-cal banana parfait or apple cake, made with low or no sugar.

"Rosie encourages Oprah to drink lots of mineral water. And an hour before the evening meal she prepares an herb tea and juice cocktail for Oprah."

Oprah was paying the rent on Rosie's $1,790-a-month Chicago apartment, in addition to her salary. And each morning the nutritionist arrived at Oprah's apartment to fix breakfast, pack a lunch for Oprah to take to work, and then prepare dinner, said the close friend.

"She also cooks meals in advance and freezes them for the weekends and for when Oprah and Stedman wanted to be alone.

"When Oprah has to eat out, she and Rosie plan in advance what she's going to eat. Rosie will even call ahead to the restaurant to see what kind of things Oprah can eat, like broiled fish or salad.

"Stedman is delighted. He told Oprah: 'This is the best decision you've ever made. The food is great and you look wonderful.'

"And Oprah told me, 'I've never been happier. I've dropped 20 pounds in just a few weeks. And I'm getting plenty to eat.'

" 'I'll never get into those skinny jeans I wore on my show. But that's O.K. I don't want to wear those fat woman clothes either.' "

OPRAH SETS A DATE?

That October rumors abounded that Oprah had finally set a date and she intended to be a June 1992 bride.

Stedman had already bought Oprah an $8,000 engagement ring, and they had decided to exchange vows at her TV studio with a galaxy of stars in attendance.

Supposedly, Oprah was inspired by Elizabeth Taylor's decision to wed construction worker Larry Fortensky. Their marriage convinced Oprah it was possible for an ordinary husband to live in the shadow of a superstar.

"Liz has made me think about what I really want, and

I want to be married to Stedman," Oprah allegedly told an insider.

Although Stedman ran a thriving public relations firm, he was nowhere near as successful as Oprah, who raked in $38 million a year.

"Oprah has always worried that once Stedman becomes her husband he'll simply become known as 'Mr. Oprah Winfrey.' She knows it can be difficult for a man to live in a woman's shadow and she was afraid the tension might cause the marriage to crumble," confided the insider.

As Oprah and Stedman were taking a long walk on her Indiana farm in late September, she told him she was finally ready to marry him, reported the insider.

"Stedman put his arms around her, gave her a big kiss and said, 'How does June sound?'

"Tears came to Oprah's eyes. She smiled softly and said, 'I always wanted to be a June bride.' "

Stedman was planning to give his bride-to-be the engagement ring at Christmas, confided the insider.

"Oprah told me they'll get married in Chicago at the Harpo Studios, which she owns and where 'Oprah' is taped. That way they can decorate it any way they want and control security.

"Her matron of honor will be her best buddy Gayle King. Oprah's dad Vernon will give her away. Stedman's daughter Wendy will be a bridesmaid."

Just how likely was this romantic scenario?

Well, Oprah and Stedman had been dating since 1986, and they had made plans to wed in early 1989. After those plans fell through, they reset dates for Christmas 1990 and for September 1991. Each time, however, Oprah backed out.

Now the wedding was on again. And this time it was

a sure thing, according to the source, who insisted: "Oprah told me, 'I can't wait.' "

"WE WANTED TO DO A DEAL WITH OPRAH"

That fall, Oprah also joined forces with five other co-producers to bring *From the Mississippi Delta* to an off-Broadway theater, marking her debut as a New York theater producer. The play, by newcomer Dr. Endesha Ida Mae Holland, chronicled a woman's rise from the streets to a Ph.D.

And in November, Dennis Swanson, president of sports, daytime and children's programming for ABC, announced that Harpo would produce all four of ABC's "Afterschool Specials" during the 1992–93 season.

The deal sprang from the agreement announced in May 1990 by Oprah and ABC that called for Harpo to become involved in producing shows for the network.

Now Harpo would produce four original "Afterschool Specials" that would include a drama, a documentary, and two reality-based shows similar in format to a town meeting.

Swanson was the very executive who had first brought Oprah to Chicago when he hired her to host "AM Chicago" back in 1984.

"The audience is obviously there for Oprah at that time, and I would think that the affiliates will be pleased that, in one way or another, they'll get Oprah," said Ame Simon, director of "Afterschool Specials" for ABC. "We wanted to do a deal with Oprah, and we wanted to do something new with the specials to bolster the audience levels. We have a lot of respect for what she does, and we think that the new shows will provide a new way of dealing with issues."

286

Chapter Fifteen
Ms. Winfrey Goes
to Washington

This is my first effort at the federal legislative level to help protect children from child abuse. . . . I will lobby and work on this issue with the same energy I devote to my television career, and the Congress of the United States and the legislatures of the 50 states will be hearing from me . . .

—Oprah Winfrey in her testimony before the
Senate Judiciary Committee, 1991

Oprah was still thinking about little Angelica Mena and her horrible murder. And in thinking about it, she had to recall her own years of abuse. For so many years she had suppressed the memories, unable to discuss them with her family. Even after sharing the experiences and the pain with her talk show audience, there was still a part of her that would not heal. She realized now that it was the fundamental fact of her life, something that was at the root of her longtime problems with her weight and her relationships. Long ago, she had exhorted an audience of enthusiastic women to "Consult the spirit within you first, and seek the truth. Get yourself straight first."

Now she wondered: Had she really and truly gotten straight with herself? Or was there still more work to be done in that area?

And the answer came: a new road opened up to her,

beyond the paths she had already blazed in the worlds of entertainment. She was being called to public service.

There was still much, much more that she could do about the horrendous scandal of child abuse.

That November, Oprah opened up in a way she had not before. She spoke before the Chicago Bar Association which had invited her to participate in its Justice for Youth campaign.

"I really can think of no greater purpose in life than to be a voice for the children, the children who wish to be heard, but whose cries and wishes and hopes often fall upon deaf and inattentive ears."

From that eloquent beginning, Oprah praised the Association's daunting work to transform the Cook County juvenile justice system. "I'm a really spiritual person," Oprah said, "and I know that it is just spiritual law that you can't save a life without uplifting your own, and every time you remove a child from an abusive home, you rescue a child from neglect and emotional humiliation.

"Every time a child is saved from the dark side of life, every time one of us makes the effort to make a difference in a child's life, we add light and healing to our own lives."

Oprah was clearly well-informed about the specific shortcomings of the Cook County system, but what she criticized most of all was their lack of commitment.

"In my opinion, we seem to have declared war against our children," she said. "The stories about abused children reveal a nation really at odds with itself."

She talked about the specific inadequate programs for children who have been abused in their own homes, by their own family.

"I know what I'm talking about," she told the Bar Association members. "I know it because I blamed myself for most of my adult life. You lose your childhood.

People often say you lose your innocence, but I know you lose your childhood when you're abused.

"Jeff, my partner, and I have this saying, I say most people have a guardian angel, I have a team of guardian angels, and they've been working for me for a long time to bring blessings into my life.

"And I was, luckily, blessed that the system in Milwaukee, Wisconsin in 1968 was already overworked and overcrowded before I was sent to a detention home. And it's very interesting. As I was preparing the words to say to you last night, it's the first time I thought about it.

"I've said many times before that I was raped when I was 9 years old by a 19-year-old cousin, and then repeatedly sexually molested for the next five years after that.

"So by the time I was 14, I was really, really in the throes of acting out the abuse in other negative ways. I was, as my mother used to say, 'runnin' the streets.' I ran away a couple of times. I didn't want to be at home.

"I was literally looking for love in all the wrong places and getting myself deeper and deeper in trouble.

"And my mother, who was on welfare and had two other children at the time, didn't know what to do. She had no parenting skills. So her only alternative, she thought, was to put me in a detention home for girls."

Oprah revealed that she had not thought about that episode for many years, until the night before her speech. She told them how she recalled the humiliating interview process and how confused she was.

"I knew I wasn't a bad person, and I remember thinking how did this happen? How did I get here?"

And then luck, or her guardian angels, intervened, and the system was too crowded to take her. Her exhausted mother packed her off to live with her father in Nashville.

"Children cannot stand alone; none of us do. There's not a one of us in this room, no matter how smart we are. . . . No matter how diligent or persistent you have been, there is not a one of us who made this journey towards success by ourselves.

"Somebody helped you; somebody helped me, and we have to help the children. We have to make the system better." She must have been thinking of little Angelica Mena as she went on: "Nothing, I don't know of one thing that angers me more in this world than hearing the story of a child being abused or assaulted or raped or murdered by someone who had a previous conviction for child abuse and then got out. Plea-bargained. Served eight months, was released and came out to molest and murder another child. Well, that was Angelica Mena's story."

She recounted the details of the horrifying murder of the little girl.

"And I remember seeing that on the news that evening and I wept for the frightened four-year-old Angelica, and I thought about her muffled cries. . . . And I wept. I wept for us, society, that seems to talk so much about but cares so little, really cares so little, about the children, that we would allow a man with a history of violence against children, once convicted, to serve eight months, go free and kill the four-year-old next door."

Oprah announced that since April she had hired former Illinois governor James Thompson and the law firm of Winston and Strawn to draft a National Child Protection Act of 1991. If passed, the law would establish a national registry of those who have been convicted of child-abuse crimes to prevent them from going from state to state and having access to children. The registry would enable employers to screen child care workers for histories of abuse or other serious crimes.

"This act, we hope, will be the centerpiece of a national plan of action to identify predatory child abusers."

Already, Senator Joseph Biden (D., Del.) had agreed to be the primary sponsor of the bill. "This is not Geraldo Rivera," said Biden. "This is something Winfrey does from the heart."

"And if the bill is passed, and one child is spared, I'll be grateful," Oprah said. "I know that children cannot stand alone." She concluded with a plaintive cry: "Children cannot stand alone, so I ask you, will you take a stand for the children or will you turn your back as you often do, knowing I'm your sons and I'm your daughters, too?"

Oprah was finally coming to terms with her past in a creative way.

Around this time, she found herself driving out to her Rolling Prairie Farm with two girlfriends for a relaxing weekend. And in talking about the past and mutual experiences, Oprah suddenly saw her childhood experiences in a whole new way.

Until then, "I always said, 'If I had not talked about what happened to me at school, it wouldn't have happened.' I thought, well it was a conversation about kissing, and maybe that's what aroused him, and he thought because I was talking about kissing boys, that meant that I wanted to kiss him. And that's what my uncle had told me: 'You started it.'"

"I INTEND TO MAKE THIS MY SECOND CAREER"

A few weeks later, on November 12, 1991, Oprah took her new crusade to the United States Senate. Accompanied by former governor Thompson, Jeffrey Jacobs, and Debbie Di Maio, Oprah first met privately with Senator Biden and his staff to discuss their research, ideas, and draft bill language.

Next, she testified before the Senate Judiciary Committee, which was holding hearings on the issue of child abuse and considering legislation to help protect children.

Oprah called for the enactment of legislation to create a national database which would permit child care organizations to determine if child care workers had been convicted of child abuse or other serious crimes.

Her testimony was the first step in her effort to spearhead a national plan of action to protect children from predatory child abusers.

In her eloquent way, Oprah cited statistics that said there were more than 2.5 million reports of suspected child abuse and neglect each year in this country, many of these by repeat offenders.

"But the experts tell me, and I know from my own personal experience and from the mail I have been receiving ever since I went public with my own history of abuse, that the statistics tell only part of the story," Oprah said.

"There are millions upon millions of silent victims in this country that have been and will continue to be irrevocably harmed unless we do something to stem this horrible tide.

"I am speaking out on behalf of the children who wish to be heard, but whose cries, wishes and hopes often fall upon deaf or inattentive ears," she said.

"Every time a child perishes, a little piece, tiny, almost invisible piece of society, a portion of humanity dies."

Once again she referred to the tragic story of Angelica Mena, recounting it for the senators.

"I wept for us, a society that cares so little about its children that we would allow a man with two previous convictions for kidnapping and rape of children to go free after serving only 7 years of a 15-year sentence, to kill another innocent little 4-year-old girl."

Oprah told them that she had vowed the night she first heard the story of Angelica Mena, and later when she had child advocate Andrew Vachss on her show, "to do something, to take a stand for the children of this country.

"When I was abused, I blamed myself," Oprah told the senators. "I blamed myself for most of my adult life. You lose your childhood once you've been abused. My heart goes out to those children who are first abused at home and have absolutely no one to turn to.

"This is my first effort at the federal legislative level to help protect children from child abuse," Oprah said, but she assured the senators that "I will lobby and work on this issue with the same energy I devote to my television career, and the Congress of the United States and the Legislatures of the 50 states will be hearing from me and anyone who cares to join me in this project for weeks, months and years to come."

After Oprah's impassioned testimony, Committee Chairman Biden told her: "I look forward to your announcement to run for public office." Strom Thurmond, the South Carolina Republican who once set a filibuster record for speaking twenty-four hours and twenty-seven minutes against civil rights, held Oprah's hand, calling her "a great woman."

"I am committed to using all of my will to follow through on this legislation, and on the issue of child abuse," Oprah told the committee. "I intend to make this my second career."

The response of those on Capitol Hill was unanimously favorable. Rep. Patricia Schroeder (D., Co.) said, "Usually these celebrities come in with their scripts, and then you never see them again. But she has done a lot of study."

Rep. Don Edwards (D., Ca.) said, "She's not only charming and modest, but she wouldn't be the star she is unless she was very sensitive to people and knew where they were coming from on the inside. She knows the things people fear and the things they love. She's astonishing, really, and she's good for the country.''

Only a few hours after her moving testimony before the Senate, Oprah was being interviewed at a restaurant in Washington's Union Station. She joked that the project was costing her a lot of money, but assured everyone that ''I used to write checks all the time. And I make decisions to give money based on my gut, like I make all other decisions in my life. I'm an instinct player and I still write a lot of checks. That's the easiest thing somebody like me *can* do, I think, is write a check.''

But it was clear that Oprah was now deeply committed to doing much, much more than writing checks.

''I don't believe that is effective in changing a life,'' she said candidly. ''And that's what I really want to do—change a life. I've paid lip service to it for years. I've gone around and done speaking engagements. I get on my show and say, 'We really ought to do something.' '' Her voice took on a mocking edge. '' 'How can we let this happen, people?' And that's all I'd say. And then I went home and continued my life. As everybody else does.''

Oprah clearly understood just what kind of responsibilities she was taking on in what she called ''my new career as a child advocate.

''It takes money, it takes energy, it takes a lot of your time,'' she told the gathered press. She should have been back in Chicago taping shows that very day. It was a ratings period.

''But I made the commitment because it's part of my own healing. I think it does no good for me to have had all of this horror in my life and not be able to grow from it.''

Reporters from *USA Today* asked Oprah: ''Do you

think there will ever be a time when you don't blame yourself?''

She was able to answer: ''I think I'm not blaming myself today. I really do. I think that was the last shred for me. Like a darkness lifted because I don't have to carry that anymore.''

Unfortunately, unlike most things with which Oprah is involved, this episode does not have a happy ending. With Oprah's support, the National Child Protection bill sailed through committee, but sank in Congress when it became part of a crime package that included the ''Brady Bill'' gun control proposal, which was bitterly opposed by the powerful National Rifle Association.

Oprah took little comfort in that the legislation had ''almost'' passed. ''Almost,'' she said, ''doesn't save a child.''

AN EMBARRASSING INCIDENT

It is certainly a mark of stardom when a magazine features you in a celebrity look-alike contest, and so Oprah was thrilled when she was included in such a contest in *Ladies' Home Journal*. The winner was chosen from over four thousand contestants who sent in their photos, and Jacquin Stitt, thirty-two, a clerk with the Flint, Michigan, Water Department, won a free trip to Chicago to appear on ''Oprah.''

Stitt was looking forward to meeting Oprah and greeting her with: ''Girlfriend, I'm so tired of people telling me I look like you.''

But it was soon revealed that Stitt, who also ran a female-impersonator production company, was ''going through some changes,'' i.e., a sex change, and in fact had been born a man.

Contest officials were unruffled, and *Journal* editor

Myna Blyth assured the press that "We don't believe in sexual discrimination."

For her part, Oprah was a good sport and said she looked forward to having Stitt on her show the following May.

SLIMMING DOWN FOR THE HOLIDAYS

In early December, Oprah chartered a private jet to fly to the sun-kissed Caribbean island of St. Kitts for a relaxing getaway with Stedman Graham. But paparazzi found them and circulated photos showing a slimmed-down Oprah.

Oprah now weighed 170 pounds, thanks to "diet cop" Rosie Daley. Even though Rosie wasn't looking over her shoulder during the five-day vacation, Oprah religiously watched what she ate.

What's more, she endured an exhausting exercise session that included thirty-five minutes of muscle-burning stair climbing.

And it was paying off. Oprah was finally getting her shape back.

"I've lost over 35 pounds with Rosie's help. I'm exercising. I'm eating smart. I'm not pigging out. And I'm still determined to get down to 150 pounds," Oprah told a close pal.

"I'll never get into skinny jeans again. But I want to get to a normal weight—slowly and sanely. A few pounds at a time."

Oprah's fun holiday began when Stedman, who had business on St. Kitts, invited her to go along and she jumped at the chance.

Stedman paid for their plush $2,000-a-day beachfront suite at the luxurious Four Seasons Resort on nearby

Nevis Island, where they stayed from December 1 until December 6.

And even though the resort boasted two fine restaurants with delicious food, Oprah ordered sensibly from room service.

On Monday night it was a chilled appetizer made with snapper, lobster, shrimp, grilled pineapple and chili sause, followed by a main dish of grilled lobster with tarragon lime butter. She had fresh fruit for dessert.

On Tuesday, she ordered a healthy breakfast of juice, granola with skim milk, dried fruit, bran muffins, and tea.

For lunch, Oprah had an island fruit plate and a lobster club sandwich. She passed up both French fries and potato chips.

For dinner she had Caribbean seafood gumbo with lobster and a main course of grilled fish with fresh fruit for dessert.

On Wednesday night, Stedman convinced Oprah to try a famous local restaurant called Old Manor.

Oprah stuck to her diet, ordering coconut shrimp with rice, salad and local fruit.

The next day, Oprah, clad in multicolored spandex pants, an orange T-shirt, and pink and white Reeboks, walked into the resort's fitness center at 10:00 A.M.

Noticeably thinner than she appeared on TV, Oprah exercised nonstop for an hour and a half.

She pedaled a stationary bicycle for fifteen minutes, climbed a Stairmaster for thirty-five minutes, and patiently plodded on a treadmill for twenty-five minutes, then finished with fifteen sit-ups.

At first, Oprah listened to her Walkman while she worked out. Then she watched the rape trial of William Kennedy Smith—and she turned the fitness center into a mini version of her talk show.

When the alleged victim gave her testimony, Oprah yelled, "Just tell the truth."

Then, in a more sympathetic voice, she told everyone within earshot, "If she tells the truth and stops being afraid, it'll be O.K. No woman deserves to be raped."

Soon after, people working out began to offer their opinions on the trial, and Oprah listened just as she did on her show.

And not once during her workout did Oprah have to slow down or catch her breath.

"She worked on the Stairmaster for a full 35 minutes without pausing," an eyewitness reported. "Even some of the men didn't stay on the Stairmaster half as long as she did. When they quit, Oprah picked up the pace, pumping her legs faster."

By the time Oprah had finished her workout, it was raining outside. So she draped a towel over her head, grabbed her red duffel bag and Walkman, then headed back to her suite.

On their last night in Nevis, Oprah and Stedman went to a new restaurant called Miss June's, a cozy spot with just ten tables. Oprah and Stedman kicked off their shoes and sang along with the restaurant's guitarist before calling it a night at 10:30 P.M.

They checked out of the resort Friday morning, then sped back to St. Kitts on the resort's high-powered launch.

In St. Kitts, Oprah, wearing a flowing white pantsuit with matching visor, shopped at an art gallery. She spent $11,920 on twelve paintings in twenty minutes, said gallery owner Rosie Smith Cameron.

When she walked out of the gallery, Oprah, whose syndicated show was carried to the islands on cable TV, was mobbed by local people who recognized her.

Then she and Stedman visited a local landmark, the

Brimstone Hill Fort, and ate lunch at historic Ottley's Plantation Inn.

"Oprah had curried asparagus soup, coconut shrimp in a coconut shell and lobster quesadillas. She said she didn't have time for dessert," said owner Ruth Keusch.

When she got home, Oprah told a good friend: "It was a nice getaway. I relaxed, and I was good on my diet. But I've never seen such temptations! The restaurants [were] so delicious I could have gained back all 35 pounds in one sitting.

"But I stuck to the fish and fruit and ate sensible portions. I'm proud of myself."

Right now, losing weight was Oprah's top priority. It was even more important to her than finalizing her marriage plans to Stedman. She was determined to drop to the 150-pound mark by counting calories and continued her ninety-minute daily workout.

"I'm going to stick to my diet and exercise program," she promised a close friend. "I made it through those island temptations and I'm stronger than ever."

And Oprah was stronger than ever because she had finally faced down her demons.

Chapter Sixteen
Living in the Moment

I'm a truth seeker. That's what I do every day on the show—put out the truth. Some people don't like it, they call it sensational, but I say life is sensational.

—Oprah Winfrey, 1992

As 1992 opened, Oprah could afford to face the future with strength and optimism. She was the country's most successful talk show host and one of its most admired women, with annual earnings of $30 million.

A visitor to a taping of the talk show was struck with her confident, consummate professionalism, but in a moment of uncharacteristic candor she confessed to an interviewer: "I'm beginning to think I'd have done myself a lot more good if I had been on a psychiatrist's couch all these years instead of doing my therapy on TV."

After a brief lull following cancellation of the "Brewster Place" series, things were humming at Harpo Studios. Many commercials were being created there. Nike filmed its Bo Jackson and Michael Jordan spots there, and Tom Selleck's new feature film was shot on its soundstage.

Oprah usually arrived at the Harpo Studios at 6:00 A.M.

for makeup and wardrobe before taping two shows. After taping, she personally shook hands and said goodbye to her more than five hundred guests.

"It's more memorable than an autograph," she explained. She had stopped hugging years ago. It always made her uncomfortable.

The rest of the day was taken up by meetings: story meetings, meetings with attorneys, meetings with advisors, meetings with accountants. She still signed every check personally.

She was usually the last person to leave the studio at night, sometimes even staying over in the apartment she kept there.

A visitor to Harpo Studios around that time found Oprah behind her gleaming and immaculate mahogany desk. With its peach and beige flocked wallpaper and thick soft carpet, her private office had clearly been designed to provide Oprah with a serene retreat. The visitor noted the vase of cut flowers, stacks of art books, and a collection of framed photographs of friends like Quincy Jones and Maya Angelou.

Oprah showed the visitor a dog-eared script for a screen adaptation of Toni Morrison's Pulitzer prize-winning novel, *Beloved*. The script had been written by Akosua Busia, who had appeared with Oprah in *The Color Purple*.

"It's such a great first draft that even Toni Morrison herself has written me and said so," Oprah said. She revealed that she planned to star in the film as Sethe, the escaped slave haunted by her murdered daughter.

She was determined to confront her long-standing personal problems. It was not that she was unhappy. On the contrary, there were areas of her life that brought her deep personal fulfillment. But others were troubled, and

Oprah was bent on resolving them. For one thing, in spite of her achievements, Oprah was still struggling with feelings of low self-esteem and vulnerability.

"All these years I have done show after show about low self-esteem, but because I was on TV, was famous, was making pots of money, I never thought I might be talking about *me*," she revealed. "In truth, I was in denial about the problem despite all the signs of it."

She was still ill at ease with compliments or praise. "I don't receive love as well as I give it," she acknowledged. "Actually, I don't receive anything as well as I give it. Which is true of most people suffering with low self-esteem. We don't think of ourselves as worthy of receiving."

She had also been unable to take an extended vacation. When she and Stedman took a month-long hiatus in the Caribbean in 1991, she discovered that she could not relax.

"I felt compelled to read, to do something that made me feel productive. I discovered I didn't feel worth a damn, and certainly not worthy of love, unless I was accomplishing something. I suddenly realized I have never felt I could be loved just for being."

Only now was she coming to understand that she was still carrying around the baggage of her childhood sexual abuse. "I never moved on," she said. "I still haven't. I was, and I am, severely damaged by the experience. All the years that I convinced myself I was healed, I wasn't. I still carried the shame, and I unconsciously blamed myself for those men's acts."

The saddest thing, Oprah said, was that she continued to blame herself. "Something deep within me feels I must have been a bad little girl for those men to have abused me."

Oprah credited her new role as a children's rights activist and her recent workshops with John Bradshaw for helping her confront her painful past.

With the help of Bradshaw, she had been "healing the wounded child within by acknowledging my hurt and guilt as well as the rage I now feel toward those men for what they did to a nine year old child. I was *not* responsible. No child is. Those men abused me, a *baby*, and there is nothing more despicable."

Now Oprah felt passionately that she was reclaiming herself.

It was the abuse, too, that fueled Oprah's longtime need to maintain total control.

"It's all about fear, all my problems, even my weight," she admitted. "When I'm heavy, I feel safer and more protected, although I don't know what I'm trying to protect any more than I know what I'm so afraid of. Food for me is comforting. It also calms me. I find its results, however, very distressing and a real monkey on my back."

Publicly, at least, Oprah was sticking by her statement that she would never diet again. "I meant it because I now understand my eating and weight gains are symptoms of underlying emotional problems that dieting won't cure," she said. "Beneath my added poundage are buried feelings and my fear of feeling whatever they may be. That's the real issue and not the weight."

How ironic and how sad that a woman who was famous for encouraging her guests to share their innermost feelings still could not deal with major areas in her own life.

Yet Oprah knew that if she could just allow herself to get past the fear and feel whatever that pain was, she would finally be free of it and the weight, because she would be free of the need to protect herself.

Forget the people who claimed they preferred her

plump. She loved being thin. She loved how she looked. These days, when she looked in a mirror, she sometimes wondered aloud, "Who is that woman?" Surely she was not the real Oprah.

A TRUTH SEEKER

Even critics like Geraldo Rivera had come to respect Oprah. "There's a sincerity in Oprah," Rivera finally admitted. "Television is a brutal lie detector. You can fool the audience once or twice. But year after year, then the audience can look into your soul." Clearly, the audience had looked into Oprah's soul and found it true.

Oprah's longtime friend and mentor Maya Angelou put it differently: "Usually a television person tries to pull in the audience. But there's something about Oprah that makes audiences reach out and pull her into them."

Oprah was even saluted by America's best-loved evangelist Billy Graham, with reservations. "I admire her because she listens," he said. "However, sometimes when I see people on the show and the desperate problems they face, I want to cry out to them, 'turn to God.' "

Oprah had her own insights into the enormous popularity of her talk show. "I'm a truth seeker," she said. "That's what I do every day on the show—put out the truth. Some people don't like it, they call it sensational, but I say life is sensational."

For Oprah's thirty-eighth birthday that year, her staff at Harpo Studios surprised her with a male stripper who peeled down to the skimpiest of red bikini briefs.

That night, Oprah celebrated with Stedman, who took her on a romantic carriage ride along Lake Shore Drive, ending up at the Eccentric where 150 guests were waiting to celebrate with her over some of her favorite foods: meat loaf and mashed potatoes with a touch of horseradish. About that time, Oprah also put her 219 East Lake Shore Drive condo up for sale. She had never lived in it and was fed up with construction delays. Also back on the market, the restored 1957 Mercedes 190SL convertible. Stedman had given up trying to teach Oprah how to drive with a stick shift.

Oprah had fallen in love with Telluride and splurged on a house for $1.4 million and eighty additional acres nearby where she planned to build a dream house in the next two years. Meanwhile, she'd make do with the existing house which had three master bedrooms, each equipped with its own Jacuzzi and massive fireplace, and eventually make it a guest house.

SIX KEYS TO OPRAH'S SUCCESS

Dennis Kimbro, author of *Think and Grow Rich: A Black Choice*, interviewed Oprah and reported that "of all the people I interviewed, Oprah epitomizes the best qualities of the successful person."

He offered these keys to her success:

★ *Persistence*. Oprah never let the word "no" bother her. "If she believes in a project and encounters resistance, she'll find people who believe along with her to help see her through," said Kimbro.

★ *Self-Discipline*. Once Oprah believes in something she always follows through to the end.

"For Oprah, self-discipline means not letting outside distractions get in the way of goals," said Kimbro. "When it's time to work, she works."

Kimbro noted that at one point, Oprah was doing her talk show while acting in and producing the series "Brewster Place." "Doing just one of those jobs would be enough to exhaust most people," he said, "but Oprah's self-discipline allowed her to work 30 hour days and remain as upbeat and enthusiastic as if she'd just returned from vacation.''

★ *Faith in Yourself.* Kimbro believed that Oprah's deep optimism and faith in her own ideas had become the basis for her pushing ahead when others have said, ''It just won't work.''

''For example, many people have tried to discourage her from setting up her own production company,'' said Kimbro.

''They said very few women were successful at producing. But Oprah knew she had what it takes to be a great producer, and she persisted until naysayers had to admit she was right.''

★ *Inner Peace.* ''Oprah relies on God for guidance and knows He works in mysterious ways,'' reported Kimbro. ''So if a project fails, she doesn't allow it to discourage her because she knows it's all part of God's great plan. She simply picks herself up and tries again.''

★ *Spreading the Wealth.* ''Oprah gives back more than she receives. She knows that what goes around, comes around,'' said Kimbro.

''For example, Oprah gave four-year scholarships to a group of students entering her alma mater Tennessee State University. But she told them they had to maintain a 3.0 grade point average or risk losing the money.''

★ *Realization That There's More to Life Than Money.* ''Even though Oprah enjoys the fruits of her success, like cars and jewels, she knows she could do without them,'' Kimbro reported.

''I've seen Oprah at home, happy as a cat in blue jeans and a sweatshirt, curled up on the couch with a good book.''

Added Kimbro: ''By putting into practice Oprah's keys to business magic, you can increase your own chances of success in achieving your goals in life.''

THE BOOK

That April, Oprah was reportedly about to sign a $6 million deal with the prestigious New York publishing house of Alfred A. Knopf for her memoirs.

But as usual with an Oprah project, there was some controversy. Richard Johnson, gossip columnist for *The New York Daily News,* reported that Oprah had made it clear to her literary agents at CAA that she didn't want people of color excluded from the project. She did not want her first publishing venture to be an all-white affair.

Somehow, according to Johnson, the message got lost in the translation. When a top editor in New York offered to edit the book, the editor was told, "Oh, she won't work with you. You're not black."

In fact, Oprah's credited "ghost," Joan Barthel, was white, while her editor, Errol MacDonald, was black.

Also in April, Oprah cohosted the Fifth Annual Essence Awards with Denzel Washington in New York. And she was about to embark on two new and exciting television projects, one "soft," one "hard."

"OPRAH: BEHIND THE SCENES"

Oprah has often said that she would not be in business if not for Barbara Walters.

"From the very first interview I did," she says, "I was imitating Barbara."

But Oprah soon learned that the best style is your own, and dropped the Barbara pretense when she got to "AM Chicago."

But now she was following Barbara's lead into prime-time television with a collection of celebrity interviews.

"There's always room for the next level of personal

development," she explained to Bruce Ingram of the *Los Angeles Times*.

The first of four prime-time specials focusing on the world of show business, "Oprah: Behind the Scenes" would air that May.

It was a funny situation for a star who admitted, "I've always been terrified of meeting celebrities."

"It's fun and interesting to remove the fame shield from people and look at a part of their lives that's not normally exposed," Oprah said.

How celebrities dealt with fame fascinated her. "If you come to fame not understanding who you are, it will define who you are," she said. "It shouldn't change you. If you're a jerk, you just get to be a bigger jerk. What fame does is magnify who you are and puts that on a platter for the whole world to see."

Oprah did not go into the project intending to get the stars to open up. She was trying to get to their essence, not any startling revelations.

Besides chatting with them about everday life, Oprah would provide a glimpse of the celebrities at work. For the first show she dropped in on Meryl Streep and Goldie Hawn on the set of *Death Becomes Her,* their upcoming comedy about the quest for eternal youth.

She also caught up with Dustin Hoffman who was playing a thief in a new film, *Hero.*

And she visited Grammy winner Michael Bolton backstage at a concert. Bolton had good reason to be fond of Oprah. After appearing on her talk show, sales of his album *Time, Love and Tenderness* shot from fifty thousand to five hundred thousand weekly.

"The wonderful thing about this medium," Oprah told interviewers, "is that it allows people to know they're not alone. That's one of the greatest fears in life. Most people think in the midst of crises they're the only ones who have ever gone through it.''

Oprah acknowledged that there could be a downside to her success. The worst part was ''having people write and say things that aren't true.''

Oprah was still putting money into causes she believed in. When director Spike Lee's epic production of *Malcolm X* ran into trouble that May, she joined prominent black celebrities like Bill Cosby, Earvin (Magic) Johnson, Michael Jordan, Prince, and Janet Jackson in coming to the financial rescue.

She declined to reveal just how much money she kicked in. ''I told him I would give him the money because if I were in a similar situation, I hoped someone would do the same for me,'' she said.

Director Lee said that without their help he would have been forced to shut down postproduction on the film.

''SCARED SILENT''

Disappointed but undiscouraged by Congress's failure to pass the legislation that would have created a national databank of convicted child abusers, Oprah kept her commitment to speak for abused children.

''Every bad relationship I've ever been in is the result of my having been abused,'' she said while preparing ''Scared Silent: Exposing and Ending Child Abuse,'' a documentary in which both victims and perpetrators told their story. ''Scared Silent'' made prime-time television history that September by airing on three networks, CBS, NBC, and PBS, simultaneously. Her own network, ABC, unwilling to preempt the lucrative ''20/20,'' aired it two nights later.

Shortly before the documentary aired, Oprah featured some of the subjects of ''Scared Silent'' on her talk show.

Among them was a woman who confronted the stepfather who abused her. ''Seeing her be able to do it was a powerful thing,'' Oprah said later. She added that she had never been in therapy. ''Being on television has been my therapy. When you help other people, you get help.''

In the documentary, Oprah introduced six tales of child abuse, adding her own story: ''I'm Oprah Winfrey, and like millions of other Americans, I'm a survivor of child abuse. I was only 9 years old when I was raped by my 19-year-old cousin. He was the first of three family members to sexually molest me.''

Oprah acknowledged that for years she was racked by self-reproach because, enjoying the attention, she had allowed the illicit fondling to continue. ''A lot of the confusion and guilt,'' she has said, ''comes to the child because it feels good.'' She adds, ''Every bad relationship I've ever been in is the result of my having been abused.''

Having convinced the highly competitive networks to shelve their rivalries for one weekend to air a documentary for the public good, Oprah still had hopes for the national databank of child molesters.

She was still lobbying Congress, but if that failed, she told *People* magazine that she was considering gathering ''a million mothers'' of children who have been abused, along with adult survivors of abuse, and mounting a march on Washington.

''WITH STEDMAN'S HELP, I'VE LEARNED TO BE TRUE TO MYSELF''

Stedman had seen Oprah through fat and thin, but mainly he just plan saw *her*, and that was the most important thing to Oprah. He was her rock, and Oprah knew it.

"He is the first man I have ever known who truly wants me to be not only the best I can be, but *all* I can be. He knows in the past I caved in to pressure because I felt I hadn't the right to say no. Because I always felt just being Oprah wasn't enough. I had the need to always please others, to win their approval, and to be admired. Often at my expense. No more. With Stedman's help, I've learned to be true to myself."

It was especially comforting that her millions meant nothing to him. "Stedman knows that I'm not impressed by money, although surely I once was," Oprah acknowledged. "Now that I have all the *things* I once thought would make me happy, they have little meaning for me. Experience, and not just a little heartache, has taught me money buys convenience and conveniences. I'm not knocking it either, but life's true meaning is about the time you spend comfortably with your mate—and with yourself."

Oprah seemed to be coming to terms with her relationship with Stedman Graham, but she could still get testy when hit with the "Marriage Question." Sure, she would always say, they would probably get married *someday*. But for now. . . .

"I'm allowed great personal freedom in the relationship right now," she said, "and I think that if I'm married, as good as Stedman is, I think that his expectation of what I should be would change. I really do. 'Cause I think he's pretty old-fashioned in that respect. You know, that a 'wife' ought to be home sometimes, and I'm not ready for that right now."

As for the children she used to talk about and the ticking of her biological clock: "It's getting loud," she acknowledged, "but there are so many little black children out there . . . if I reach the point where the clock has gone dead on me, I will just adopt children."

Then, too, there was the question of whether Oprah really wanted to get married or whether she only felt she should because society expected it of her.

"Frankly, a piece of paper legalizing what Stedman and I have together couldn't make it any better than it already is. So, unless we decided to have children, it wouldn't bother me if we never got married."

Oprah would not consider having children without the benefit of marriage. She recalled all too well what it was like to be an illegitimate child. "Also, with a child but without a marriage, how could I speak before the thousands of teenagers I address each year and advise them not to bear children unless they are married? It doesn't matter that I am near forty and can well afford to take care of a hundred as easily as one child without a husband. I would still feel the hypocrite."

Still, she waffled about having a child. Did she want a child of her own? Sometimes she thought so, yes, she did want to have that experience; at other times there was so much else she wanted to do. Raising a child was a serious business.

"You have to be emotionally mature and responsible," she said. "And I'm not sure I'm describing me when I say that, at least not yet. But I'm getting there . . ."

"DIET COP" FLOP

Unfortunately, by that May, Oprah's "diet cop" could no longer keep her from blowing up again.

Oprah had packed on twenty pounds in the past two months and friends and coworkers were reportedly afraid to tell her point-blank that she needed to slim down.

Just a few months earlier, she had been down to 160 pounds, but now she had topped 180 and was headed toward two hundred pounds again.

She had stopped exercising on a regular basis and was back to snacking on Cheetos. She couldn't stay away from the fried chicken, macaroni and cheese, and the peach cobbler she loved.

"Nobody around Oprah dares to look her in the eye and tell her, 'Hon, you're getting fat again,' " a close friend said.

"They're afraid of hurting her feelings or getting fired. And her really close friends fear that if they point out to Oprah something she already knows—that she's getting heavier—she will become depressed, despondent and start eating more."

Even Stedman was not commenting on Oprah's latest weight gain. He told the friend: "All I can do is tell her I love her just the way she is. Oprah has too much self-esteem to continue on this path. Sooner or later, she'll realize she needs help and she will get it."

According to Dr. Darwin Dennison, professor of health behavioral sciences at the State University of New York at Buffalo and a developer of safe weight-loss programs, Oprah's friends were not doing her any favors by not confronting her about her weight problem.

"The help of loved ones and co-workers is needed to help a person lose weight and keep it off," Dr. Dennison said.

Oprah had stopped joking about being fat. In fact, she never mentioned it at all. "Who knows how hard she's crying on the inside," an associate remarked.

The big reason for Oprah's weight gain was that she was working a tremendously hectic schedule and was under terrific stress, the source confided.

"She's working 12-hour days, not getting home until after 8 o'clock at night. She's too tired to exercise. She just wants to put her feet up and munch on something."

Rosie Daley, the "diet cop" who had helped her drop from 205 pounds to 160 by preparing low-calorie meals, had not been able to help Oprah lately.

Oprah's fans loved her fat or thin. Her staff loved and respected her, and her friends would always be there for her.

"But they know how much she suffers physically and emotionally when she's fat. And they know that if she continues to get fatter and fatter she could die.

"For her own health and happiness, they wished Oprah would lose the weight once and for all."

That June, a proud Oprah collected her third Emmy for best talk show host at the Daytime Emmy Awards. And she publicly credited her longtime beau.

"Thank you, Stedman, for putting up with all the long hours," she said.

After six years together, Oprah could still say, "Stedman's the best thing that has happened to me. I want to spend the rest of my life with him. But I love him too much to marry him."

Later that night, the lovebirds celebrated with a candlelight dinner in her suite at the Waldorf-Astoria.

But by June 26, when Oprah was in Las Vegas to present the American Academy Achievement Awards to Oliver Stone and other outstanding Americans, it was painfully obvious that Oprah's weight had ballooned to a deadly two hundred pounds.

One observer reported that "When Oprah attended a reception at the Hoover Dam, she looked positively miserable.

"It was a hot night and most of the guests, who included Dolly Parton, Barbra Streisand, Demi Moore and Kevin Costner, were in shorts or light slacks and T-shirts.

"But Oprah wore a long-sleeved floor-length dress long enough to hide the fat she's put on," the observer noted.

After the reception, the guests had to walk about one hundred yards across a parking lot and a street to get to dinner. For Oprah, it was like a death march, said the observer.

"She would walk six feet and pause with Stedman by her side," said an eyewitness. "She was sweating profusely."

At that point, Oprah seemed to stumble. Stedman stopped in the street while she caught her breath. Oprah blamed the heat. "But it was obvious her swollen ankles were beginning to bother her and she had trouble breathing. She was constantly wheezing," the eyewitness said.

The following night, Oprah showed up at an awards ceremony wearing a two-piece satin suit looking as if she was poured into it.

But Oprah's pals were more concerned about her health than her looks.

Packing on those extra pounds could be deadly, warned Dr. Donald S. Robertson.

"Someone like Oprah, who should be 130 to 140 pounds, but instead is up to 190 or more, is playing with a potential killer," said Dr. Robertson. "Obesity is a major risk factor for coronary disease, stroke, diabetes and any life-threatening ailment you can think of."

Although Oprah was still employing Rosie Daley, the only one losing weight was Stedman who had dropped thirty pounds on her diet. But he did not push Oprah to follow his lead.

"Stedman loves her the way she is," said a friend. "He just wants her to be happy."

The friend agreed that Stedman had made Oprah "happier than ever," but also warned, "She's afraid that if they get married, Stedman will be labeled 'Mr. Oprah Winfrey'—and that would destroy him.''

Though associates would not rule out a wedding sometime in the future, Oprah told her pal, ''The only reason we would marry is to have children. I do want two children. But not now. There are still too many things to do—and I enjoy the courtship.''

Friends said that she had lots to enjoy, because Stedman Graham was a very thoughtful and loving man.

''He still sends her flowers. He leaves romantic notes by her bedside. And when he leaves for out-of-town trips they spend hours on the phone,'' said one close associate.

''Stedman loves to give her massages and Oprah adores them. She especially loves to have her toes massaged. And when she's stressed out from a hard day, he takes her head in his hands and gently massages her temples to relax her.

''The best thing about Stedman is that he doesn't argue. As everyone who watches Oprah's show knows, she loves to argue. But if Stedman and Oprah disagree about something, he calmly discusses it, then suggests they just cool off for a while. He's the easiest-going man on earth.''

Now that she had put the new apartment back on the market, Oprah was concentrating on turning her home into *their* home.

She was doubling the size of her three thousand-square-foot apartment to make it into a permanent love nest.

''She bought the apartment below hers for close to a million dollars,'' a friend reported. ''She'll have a spiral staircase to connect the floors. There will be offices for each of them, two guest bedrooms, a workout room for Stedman, a lounge for houseguests and a beautiful master bedroom.

''Oprah loves Stedman very much,'' said the friend. ''She really is creating a place that's theirs.''

That summer, it was reported that Stedman was considering a talk show of his own. He taped a pilot for "Sports Lifestyles," an interview show with ex-athletes, at the Harpo Studios with Harvey Ketchum, formerly of the Milwaukee Bucks and the Philadelphia 76ers.

SEX HARASSMENT SCANDAL AT THE SHOW

Although Oprah carefully screens the people who work for her at Harpo because they truly are her family, her behind-the-scenes staff is not immune from the same kinds of problems that are discussed on the show. The following story is an example of backstage life imitating the on-air "Oprah Winfrey Show."

That summer an outraged Oprah axed her show's producer after his terrified ex-girlfriend charged him with making sexually harassing phone calls and threatening her.

Producer Ray Nunn was set to answer harassment charges in court and was served with a restraining order to stay away from and stop calling the ex-girlfriend.

According to the complaint the ex-lover filed in court, some of the calls were even traced by the phone company to Nunn's office at Harpo Productions.

She accused Nunn in court papers of "telephone harassment . . . threats . . . stalking [me] on May 10 and June 30 of this year and making 'threats repeatedly to people who are close to me.' "

She added, "In the past he has been violent, bruising me and removing phones from walls so I can't call [my] family."

What's more, the attractive blonde told friends that the producer also placed her name in a sleazy personal ad requesting sex.

The producer's ill-fated relationship with his ex-girl-friend began in 1985 when she was president of a press club and he was an ABC bureau chief. In 1990, when he got a job as senior producer with Oprah, she went with him to set up house in Chicago.

During that time, the woman met Oprah many times and even visited her during Oprah's Caribbean vacation on Necker Island.

"We all have gone on trips together," the ex-girlfriend said. "Last year when all the producers were given free trips, I went with him to Europe and I saw Oprah on her boat in Monte Carlo."

But six months ago, the couple split and the girlfriend moved out. Shortly afterward, she began getting the harassing calls—up to thirty in one twenty-four hour period. It was an eerie echo of shows Oprah herself had done on abuse and harassment, such as "Telephone Terror Victims."

"He threatened me," the ex-girlfriend confided to a friend. "Other times it was just hang-up after hang-up, dozens a day."

The frightened woman filed a telephone harassment charge and went to court against Nunn on June 30. "I thought if I got the judge to tell him to stop he would stop. I was being very naive," she told a friend.

The judge issued a restraining order and the woman dropped the criminal charges when Nunn promised to leave her alone. But she told her friend that he broke the order the same day.

After weeks of harassment, the shaken woman made a frantic call to Oprah's offices pleading for help. After Oprah investigated the alleged fatal attraction phone calls by Nunn, she exploded:

"I will not stand for this. I will not allow that to be done from my very own company headquarters. There's no excuse for this kind of behavior. Nunn is gone and that's all there is to it.''

Oprah, long an advocate for abused women and children, was especially moved by the ex-girlfriend's plight because she had been terrorized, too. ''I went through harassing phone calls myself,'' Oprah told an insider. ''I know the fear and the terror.''

Oprah gave her producer a face-saving out—his contract was not renewed when it expired that month.

''Ray Nunn's employment contract with Harpo Productions expires at the end of August,'' Colleen Raleigh, Oprah's spokesperson, declared. ''It has always been our understanding that Mr. Nunn would be moving on to other projects at this time. The present situation is a personal matter between himself and his former girlfriend.''

Nunn blamed his ex-girlfriend's charges on ''a domestic squabble that got out of hand.'' Although he admitted he phoned her ''a few times,'' he says he never threatened or stalked her. He also insists that he wasn't fired by Oprah and that the charges had nothing to do with his leaving the show.

The woman confided to a friend: ''I felt like I was in the middle of an Oprah show.''

''I'M GOING TO BE THE WORLD'S HAPPIEST BRIDE''

Just when it looked as if Oprah was resigned to the single life, she made a stunning announcement on November 6 on her best friend Gayle King Bumpus's Hartford, Connecticut, talk show: She and Stedman were engaged!

Sources say that the two were alone at Oprah's Indiana farmhouse in mid-October when Stedman shocked her by suddenly popping the question. And she shocked him by accepting.

Oprah had backed out of marrying Stedman several times during their six years together. But this time she was finally going to be his bride, and it was all thanks to her new diet guru Geneen Roth, who had changed her life.

Geneen's teachings had given Oprah the confidence to accept herself, stop being self-conscious about her weight, and strive for what would make her truly happy.

And Oprah realized that what she wanted most was to marry Stedman and start having babies right away.

According to friends, Stedman proposed in a handwritten note. He was asking for a prenuptial agreement because he did not want a penny of Oprah's millions.

"I'm going to be a June bride. And the world's happiest bride," Oprah told a friend.

Insiders said that Stedman had carefully set the stage for his latest proposal. He gave Oprah's household help the night off so that the two lovers could be alone.

"He cooked the evening meal—a chicken dish—and the two sat down at the kitchen table in her farmhouse.

"Then Stedman handed her a handwritten note and said, 'Read it, please, darling.'

"Oprah quietly read the note. All the words she'd wanted to hear from Stedman were there on the page. He told Oprah how much he loved her, that he wanted to spend the rest of his life with her, that he wanted her to be his wife.

"Tears fell down Oprah's cheeks. Then she said, 'Yes, yes!'

"She jumped out of her chair, ran over to Stedman, put her arms around his neck and gave him a huge kiss. She was crying and laughing at the same time.

"Stedman told me, 'I was shocked and thrilled when

she said yes. I'd expected her to drag her feet again. I hadn't even gotten the ring yet.'

"He'd picked out a lovely yellow pear-shaped diamond ring for $17,000, but hadn't placed the order for it."

Oprah asked Stedman to keep their engagement a secret for a while because she wanted to get used to the idea of being "Mrs. Stedman Graham." He agreed to not breathe a word.

But on November 6, while being interviewed by her best friend Gayle King Bumpus on WFSB-TV, Oprah suddenly blurted out the news.

Stunned Stedman told a pal: "My jaw just dropped! But after blabbing her secret to the whole world, Oprah can't back out now. No more cold feet. We're on our way to the altar and I'm walking on air!"

Oprah's public announcement seemed to prove that *this time* she was dead serious about tying the knot.

"She announced it for two reasons," a friend said. "First, she feels really comfortable with herself and her love of Stedman. And second, she wanted to help Gayle by giving her a scoop."

Said an insider: "Stedman wants to sign a prenuptial agreement. He told her: 'I don't want anyone thinking I married you for your money.

" 'If this doesn't work out, I don't want to walk away with anything but a broken heart.' "

Vernon Winfrey got the news about his famous daughter from a customer in his Nashville barbership, and at first he was skeptical.

"Don't believe everything you read in the papers," said Vernon. But the customer insisted that the story was true. Oprah had said it herself on TV.

"I was so surprised you could've knocked me flat with a sneeze!" said Vernon.

Vernon added that he was not upset about not being told by Oprah. "Stedman's a nice guy. I know they want to have children, and I'm looking foward to her making me a grandpa."

Vernon even had a wedding present in mind. "I don't know if she has any peanuts up there," he told reporters. "She used to like peanuts. I might give her some peanuts."

A NEW GURU

Oprah's new diet advisor Geneen Roth, author of *Breaking Free from Compulsive Eating* and *Feeding the Hungry Heart*, had shown Oprah the way to the altar. She had boosted Oprah's self-confidence and helped her find out the real reason she had never been able to control her weight.

Weeks earlier, a friend had given Oprah a copy of Geneen Roth's book, *When Food is Love*. She read it, then *Feeding the Hungry Heart*, and saw herself described to uncanny perfection on many pages.

"Oprah was so impressed, she requested Geneen appear on her program and lead a seminar on weight and appetite control," reported Geneen's business manager, Maureen Nemeth.

"Geneen spoke to Oprah several times on the phone before flying to Chicago in October to tape the show. They became very good friends."

Reportedly, Oprah told Geneen that she was going to follow all Geneen's ideas that applied to her.

On her November 4 show, a prelude to Geneen's appearance, Oprah's guests were seven other women who, like her, were overeaters because of emotional turmoil.

She talked about her own battle to slim down and about how she came to realize her food problems stemmed from being raped by her cousin and molested by her uncle in her childhood.

"What caused me to be continually sexually abused was being in a family that I didn't think would support me if I told," she confessed to her guests.

"And also the shame that resulted from being sexually abused . . . the shame and the guilt and the fear . . . I realized I stuffed all those feelings."

And it was those pent-up emotions, said Oprah that triggered her overeating.

Oprah told Ellen Shuman, a newcaster for WCPO in Cincinnati and one of Oprah's seven guests, that "Geneen has changed my life. And with her help, I'll change my figure—forever!"

On a recent show Oprah had talked about her struggle and confessed: "I don't understand why Stedman can love me so at this weight because I think, 'You could have any thin girl you wanted.' "

But now Oprah realized Stedman loved her for herself. And her friends were convinced that with Geneen Roth's help, a new, slim Oprah would be walking down the aisle in June.

"Geneen told me this won't be dramatic. I won't suddenly appear in size 10 jeans. But if I listen to my body and eat only when I'm hungry, eventually the weight will come off."

It would be a major challenge. Oprah now tipped the scales at 210 pounds, her fattest ever. But Oprah was convinced that she had finally uncovered the reason for her complsive eating.

She told a TV audience that the shame of being sexually abused as a child caused her to turn to food for comfort. And she had Geneen Roth to thank for that revelation.

Oprah's biggest obstacle to shedding pounds has been that she is a binge eater, according to friends.

"She tries to diet, then she goes off the wagon," a friend said. "She can't stay away from the foods she loves—macaroni and cheese, yams, barbecued ribs, all the soul food."

Stedman had been incredibly supportive, telling Oprah he loved her at any weight. "Oprah is the most beautiful woman in the world to me," he told a friend. "I only wish she'd hear me when I tell her so."

OPRAH A HOMEWRECKER?

Tragically, just as Oprah was finally contemplating wedded bliss, her best friend Gayle was filing for divorce from William "Bill" Bumpus after ten years of marriage. And an angry Bill Bumpus blamed Oprah for the breakup.

Oprah had lavished costly gifts on his wife and phoned her every day, making him feel like an outsider and a failure, according to a friend.

Bill told the friend, "Gayle makes Oprah No. 1, not me, and I can't stand that!"

Oprah didn't mean to hurt them, and it wasn't malicious, Bill knew, but "she ruined our marriage with her generosity and her insistence on taking up so much of Gayle's time.

"There probably are lots of husbands who complain about their wives watching Oprah. But at least they can turn off the television set," Bill Bumpus growled.

"They don't have Oprah calling at all hours of the day and night, they don't have her buying their wives expensive presents. They don't have her giving their families things they can't afford.

"I can't take it anymore."

Bumpus, a thirty-four-year-old assistant state attorney in Hartford, Connecticut, earned about $50,000 annually, nowhere near enough to buy his wife the things she got from multimillionaire Oprah.

In a fabulous gift that made headlines, Oprah had even given Gayle $1.25 million in cash, just so the two friends could both be millionaires.

On Bill and Gayle's fifth anniversary, Oprah treated them to an all-expenses-paid trip to Europe on the Concorde.

And after Gayle had two children, now ages five and six, Oprah agreed to pay for a nanny "for as many years as you want" so Gayle could continue at her job as a Hartford TV anchorwoman.

Oprah also treated her best friend of sixteen years to fantastic vacations, ran up $500 monthly phone bills calling her every day, and flew her to Chicago just to get her hair styled by Oprah's personal hairdresser.

"Oprah gives Gayle anything she wants, and Bill just can't compete with that," said an insider.

"Bill and Gayle have been having problems for a year now. Oprah has tried desperately to counsel them.

"She even brought them to her farm in Indiana recently to try to convince them to work things out.

"Oprah begged them to stay together. With tears in her eyes, she pleaded: 'Think of the children, my little godchildren. They need a mother and a father.' "

But her pleas didn't work.

As the marriage deteriorated, Bill started staying upstairs whenever Oprah visited Gayle at home, said the insider.

"And Oprah told me: 'When I call for Gayle, Bill often won't give the message to her. He can be cold and distant.'

"When Oprah flew to Hartford in November to make

the announcement on Gayle's local show that she and Stedman had gotten engaged, the real purpose of the trip was one last-ditch effort to save Gayle's marriage.''

But it didn't work. Just three days after Oprah's November 6 announcement, Gayle filed for divorce, citing ''marital discord.''

Gayle and Bill have agreed to joint custody of their son and daughter, said the insider. Property records show that Bill signed over his share of their $1 million home to Gayle for $1.

Gayle was ''heartbroken'' over her split with Bill, a Yale graduate and former police officer, said the insider. ''She really loves Bill, but she loves Oprah, too.''

''Gayle said, 'It's not fair that he's blaming Oprah. He's threatened by her wealth and power. All she wants to do is help us because I'm her best friend. I wish he could see that.' ''

Now Oprah was trying to help her best friend through her marital crisis. She invited Gayle and her children to spend Christmas with her at her Indiana farm, then go skiing with her over the New Year's holidays at her new getaway place in Telluride, said the insider.

''And Gayle has thrown herself into planning Oprah's June wedding to Stedman.

''Gayle said, 'It's grief therapy. I want at least one of us to be happily married.' ''

OPRAH TAKES TO THE SLOPES

Temporarily shelving her many responsibilities, Oprah jetted off to her new getaway home in snowy Colorado for a holiday skiing spree. And she had a ball.

Oprah looked like she had found heaven on earth as she grinned, laughed, danced, cozied up to Stedman, and skied, skied, skied until her companions were exhausted.

And for Oprah the real fun part was that the pounds began melting away like snow in the spring.

Friends said Oprah's frenzied skiing was part of her plan to slim down before her scheduled wedding next June.

"Oprah ran her friends ragged on the slopes. She's gone exercise crazy," said an eyewitness.

Her friends just couldn't keep up with her. She loved to ski fast and she left them behind.

Stedman did not even bother to keep up. He stayed inside, warming his toes by a fire.

Oprah even told one Telluride friend, "When I'm here, even my fat feels beautiful! And that makes me feel great, like I can do anything. So I ski, dance, listen to music, laugh with friends.

"I'm having fun and the best of all, I'm losing weight."

Oprah told another friend: "God has been good to me. I'm very grateful this Christmas. It's the best Christmas of my life."

Chapter Seventeen
In the Heart of the
Learning Curve

I am in the heart of the learning curve. I feel there
are important discoveries yet to be made.
—Oprah Winfrey's only comment on her sudden
cancellation of her autobiography, 1993

The new year 1993 started auspiciously for Oprah with a prediction from Chicago psychic Irene Hughes who forecast the 1991 Chicago flood. Hughes predicted that Oprah would tie the knot with Stedman live on her talk show as their friends and family packed the audience. At the end of the ceremony, Oprah would announce that she would be away from the show on a four-month honeymoon abroad.

In fact, on the eve of 1993, Oprah and Stedman ushered in the new year together by attending the wedding of one of her show's producers, Ellen Rakietan, to financial consultant Peter Kupferberg at Chicago's posh Four Seasons Hotel.

Oprah swept in wearing a black mink coat over a gorgeous low-cut gold gown, tottering on 3½ inch high heels.

Oprah and Stedman, handsome in a black tux and bow tie, held hands throughout the Jewish ceremony.

The reception, held in the hotel's cavernous ballroom, featured a band and immense buffet tables loaded with smoked salmon, pizzas, pasta salads and other delicacies.

Oprah and Stedman sipped champagne and mingled with the guests. Then they took to the dance floor, where she wrapped her arms around his neck while he held her around her waist.

After fifteen minutes, Oprah and Stedman sat down and dined on stir-fry chicken and vegetables, according to another wedding guest. After they ate, a new band came on with four singers who did a Temptations medley. Oprah pulled Stedman onto the dance floor, but they just clowned. Observers were surprised that Oprah was not much of a dancer.

During the song, "The Way You Do the Things You Do," Oprah waved her arms and sang along, pointing at Stedman.

When the lovers saw in the New Year at midnight, Stedman held Oprah close, and the two shared a long kiss.

Oprah told a guest, "Seeing how happy Ellen and Peter were, I wanted to jump in my jet and rush off to Vegas and get married.

"But I've always wanted a big special wedding, so we agreed to wait. It's only a few more months."

On New Year's Day, Oprah and Stedman flew to Phoenix, Arizona, to attend a bull-riding event Stedman had promoted. They were overjoyed that a sellout crowd of seventeen thousand showed up.

Oprah arrived in jeans, a cowboy hat and cowboy boots, and appeared on-camera when ESPN taped the event for a later showing.

Oprah even met the granddaughter of the event's sponsor and spent nearly an hour holding the child on her lap.

Oprah cuddled the little girl, and told her tenderly: "One day soon I'm going to have a daughter just like you."

According to an insider, Oprah and Stedman kicked off the new year by making a marriage pact, with both agreeing to make sacrifices to keep their love and upcoming marriage strong. They sat down together and sorted out their obstacles.

Oprah agreed to cut back on her speaking schedule and concentrate only on her talk show and TV specials.

Stedman agreed to cut out some of his public relations assignments and limit himself to promoting sports event.

Oprah agreed to accompany him on most of his business trips.

And Stedman agreed to have a child with Oprah. He'd been reluctant to have children, but gave in to Oprah's insistence that they have a baby within a year of their marriage.

She told him, "I've always wanted to be a mother. My biological clock is ticking and I want to get started on a family right away."

There was speculation that Oprah planned to turn one room of her Chicago apartment into a nursery. She would have a second nursery at Harpo Studios so she could spend more time with her baby.

"And I want a bilingual nanny so my baby can learn another language," she confided to an insider.

In another clause of their unwritten marriage pact, Oprah agreed to learn to cook for Stedman so they could spend more time alone.

Oprah had never liked to cook. (Remember her sister Patricia's description of Oprah's macaroni and cheese?)

Now her personal chef Rosie Daley was teaching her to fix a few things like spaghetti.

Oprah had quit binging and was down to 190 pounds. Friends believed she would reach 150 pounds by her wedding day.

THE INAUGURATION

Just when it seemed that Oprah had done it all, she could still make news. And while 1993 was still young, she was about to make a lot of it.

One of the greatest moments in her life came that January when Oprah joined a galaxy of celebrities for the inauguration of President Bill Clinton in Washington. Oprah got to see her friend and mentor May Angelou read the inauguration poem she had written especially for the event, and to hobnob with celebrities like Jack Nicholson, James Earl Jones, and Bill Cosby. Diana Ross graced the crowd with ''God Bless America,'' Aretha Franklin belted out a tune at the Lincoln monument, and Oprah read a moving passage from Thomas Jefferson to the crowd.

Of course, being Oprah, she immediately generated controversy when she was spotted at the inaugural wearing a fur coat, which riled some of the poitically correct.

An assistant in public relations at Harpo Productions tried to clear the air by issuing a statement that Oprah's coat was merely a nubby tweed, so nubby that it could understandably be mistaken for fur. But asked whether that meant Winfrey was anti-fur and would never wear fur, the aide hedged: ''Well, I wouldn't exactly say that.''

Longtime Oprah-watchers doubted that she was about to give up her minks and sables. She had worked too hard for them. Besides, the winters in Chicago are a lot rougher than the winters on the Potomac.

THE BRIDE-TO-BE

After the inauguration, Oprah settled down to preparing for her scheduled June wedding by trimming her waistline and her calendar.

She had lost twenty pounds since announcing her engagement to Stedman Graham last November, and they had agreed to try for a baby right after the wedding. She was also cutting back on personal appearances so that she and Stedman could spend more time together.

Oprah had even managed to drop pounds during the holidays, a time when most people overindulge and gain weight.

She was being seen in public in blue jeans for the first time since her dramatic 1988 weight loss.

Oprah and Stedman were looking at the second week of June for their big day, and the latest plans called for Stevie Wonder to sing at the wedding.

MICHAEL JACKSON TALKS TO OPRAH WINFREY

News junkies tried to find out more about Oprah's wedding plans when she and Stedman attended a television industry convention in San Francisco. Oprah confided to George Christy of *The Hollywood Reporter* that they had considered getting married in Europe, "but we're Americans, and decided we should wed here."

But Oprah confessed that she couldn't even think about the wedding until after her ninety-minute Michael Jackson special on February 10 on ABC. "It's live, and I love that edge," she told Christy. "I'm counting on Michael to talk."

Yes, the reclusive and eccentric "King of Pop" had agreed to give Oprah his first interview in fourteen years.

And Oprah confessed that "When I got the confirmation for the interview, I went dancing barefoot on my snow-covered porch in my pajamas."

After the interview was announced, Oprah complained that people wanted her to ask about the wrong things. "Everybody wants to know his sexual preference, but I don't think that's anybody's business," she said. "I wouldn't ask *anybody* that." Otherwise, she expected to pose all the questions everybody wants asked. At last Jackson fans would learn whether he really slept in a coffin or had bleached his skin, as rumored.

Oprah was asked if Jackson wanted to pre-approve the questions. "Absolutely not," she told Karen Thomas of *USA Today*. What about when Jackson expressed concern about possible "bad pictures"? It was, Oprah assured Thomas, a showdown of two control-freaks. And as a public figure with a very publicized weight problem, she told him he was arguing "bad pictures" with the wrong woman.

Oprah also told Thomas that at first Jackson was not sold on the at-home interview approach. "He kept thinking of other places . . . he said, 'We're not going to do that looking at-all-my-cars kinda thing, are we?' "

Oprah told him: "If you're not willing to talk about everything, then you shouldn't talk at all."

Jackson's response, said Oprah, got her a little "lumped." He said, "I'm scared, but I'm going to be brave."

"Oprah Live with Michael Jackson: 90 Minutes with the King of Pop" broadcast from Jackson's ranch, "Neverland," in Santa Ynez, California, and provided viewers with a rare glimpse into the private and mysterious celebrity's life. It was seen by an estimated ninety million viewers in sixty countries. It was to be a one-on-one interview except for a brief surprise visit from Elizabeth

Taylor, who had encouraged Michael to do the interview with Oprah.

But ninety minutes of live television with a notorious recluse was a risky proposition, and Oprah admits that "five minutes before we went on the air, my knees were trembling so bad I thought my whole body was shaking."

Viewers got to see a side of Michael Jackson they had never imagined as he showed Oprah around his secluded ranch, including his zoo and movie theater. He confessed that he had been in love only twice—once with Brooke Shields and once with "another girl"—later identified as Tatum O'Neal.

Jackson also revealed that he suffered from a bizarre skin disorder, vitiligo, that had turned his skin white.

But he was less forthcoming about rumors of plastic surgery. He insisted he had only two cosmetics procedures. Later, an expert insisted that he had undergone at least eight.

In fact, Jackson was less than candid about a number of things.

He lied to Oprah and the world when he claimed the press made up a 1986 story saying he slept in an oxygen chamber to extend his life.

Jackson claimed that a photo showing him lying inside the pressurized bubble had actually been shot while he was merely checking out a chamber in a hospital's burn unit.

But after the show, it was revealed that Michael himself had supplied the photo exclusively to a tabloid through his then manager Frank DiLeo and his plastic surgeon, Dr. Steve Hoefflin.

DiLeo had even phoned the tabloid with the original story idea and said: "Michael specifically insisted that the word 'bizarre' be used in the story to identify him."

Dr. Hoefflin gave the tabloid two Polaroid photos.

341

One showed Michael napping in the chamber; the other showed the star and Dr. Hoefflin standing beside the machine.

And when DeLeo was told later that the Polaroids were not suitable for reproduction, he set up a second photo shoot and gave the tabloid better pictures.

DiLeo was even quoted in the tabloid article as saying Michael "really believes this chamber will purify his body, and that it will help him accomplish his goal of living to be 150."

But the story of Michael's "chamber of life" was far from over. He actually tried to buy one of the devices, called a hyperbaric chamber, from the manufacturer, Sechrist Industries. And he hired a magician to create a bizarre replica without the oxygen, but loaded with such smart options as a phone, TV, VCR, and CD player.

Michael dubbed his bubble-domed contraption "King Tut's Tomb," and it was designed to be a spectacular stage illusion that would dazzle his fans. The star actually took it on the road for rehearsals, but vandals ripped off his VCR and CD and scratched KKK on the dome. It was repaired but never used on stage.

During Oprah's interview with Michael Jackson, he also blasted a report that he once tried to buy the remains of the Elephant Man for $500,000.

"Another stupid story," said Michael. "No, I have never asked for the Elephant Man. Where am I going to put some bones?"

But David Nunn, curator of the museum at Royal London Hospital Medical College where the Elephant Man's remains are kept, clearly remembered Michael's secret visit to the museum and how "fascinated" Michael had been by the skeleton.

"After that, Jackson's manager Frank DiLeo wrote the

dean of the college and offered half a million dollars for the skeleton," said Nunn. "Of course, the offer was refused."

Michael Jackson also dismissed as "crazy" stories that he demanded to be called "King of Pop." But a few months later it would be revealed that he had insisted Paramount Studios refer to him as "Michael Jackson: King of Pop" in all upcoming print and TV ads hyping his new song for *The Addams Family Values* movie.

True or false, Oprah's chat with Michael Jackson drew the fourth-highest Nielsen ratings among entertainment programs since 1960. It was one of the most-viewed entertainment programs in television history. Oprah would call it "My finest hour in television."

For everyone involved with the Jackson interview, the short-term news was all good. The day after the ninety-minute interview aired, ABC estimated that ninety million people had watched at least part of it, making it one of the most-viewed entertainment programs in television history.

The broadcast attracted a whopping fifty-six percent of the people watching television in the United States at that time. Even though many shows have had higher ratings than Oprah's interview with Michael Jackson the actual number of homes they reached—36.5 million—was the fourth highest for an entertainment program since records began being kept in 1960.

The only entertainment programs to reach more households were the final episode of "MASH" in 1983, at 50.1 million; the *Who Shot J.R.* episode of "Dallas" in 1980, at 41.5 million, and the nuclear-war TV movie "The Morning After" in 1983, at 38.3 million. In fact, it had been widely accepted that the multichannel, cable-glutted TV landscape had made it impossible for any

TV entertainment to draw those kinds of numbers in the 1990s, but Oprah and Michael Jackson shot that theory to blazes.

How? By giving the public what it wanted, an up-close and personal look at a hard-to-get superstar.

Jackson would sell a lot more copies of his *Dangerous* album, while Oprah instantly vaulted past everyone else to become the hottest television personality in the country.

Whatever she wanted to do next, she was sure to find plenty of eager partners, participants, sponsors and distributors.

OPRAH AND STEDMAN SEEK COUNSELING

But just as Oprah was basking in the glow of her record-breaking, international success, her on-and-off wedding was off again.

That March, Oprah told a pal that she had put off the wedding because she had not had enough time to plan for the lavish ceremony. But friends insisted Oprah simply had cold feet.

Stedman, hurt by the delay, took off to celebrate his forty-first birthday on a pricey Amazon cruise . . . without Oprah.

A June wedding was out of the picture, and it looked like the earliest they would walk down the aisle would be that fall.

To get ready for the big day, Oprah and Stedman had been viewing eight hours of videotaped marriage counseling from a therapist Harville Hendrix, who had appeared on "The Oprah Winfrey Show" eight times.

"Oprah and Stedman are going through my video workshop, hour by hour, and page by page of my manual,'' reported Hendrix. He added that Oprah had approached him about the course.

"Stedman has been resisting this, but I was told he has finally gotten interested."

Oprah was dragging her feet about getting to the altar with Stedman, and friends suspected her feet were pretty cold.

Perhaps Oprah had figured that by announcing her engagement she would be forcing herself to get on with the wedding. But she was finding that it was harder than she thought to give up her independence.

"She's scared like any bride," a friend said. "The only difference is that she can hide behind her career."

In the wake of the ratings bonanza from her interview with Michael Jackson, Oprah was busy planning future specials and arranging a birthday bash for Maya Angelou.

"Even though Oprah said she was going to cut back on her career, she can't help herself," an insider revealed.

Stedman told the insider: "I'm hurt by the delay. But I understand this is a hard change for Oprah to make. I'm patient."

He headed off to the Amazon with a group of business friends on a $20,000, fourteen-day cruise from Manaus, Brazil, that would take him away for his birthday, March 6.

The trip had been planned before his engagement. But he expected to cancel it because he'd be busy with wedding plans and he would gladly have called it off to get married.

Bride-to-be Oprah wanted to sure that the scars of her childhood abuse did not wreck her chances for a happy married life with Stedman. That was one reason she had been following the advice of marriage counselor Hendrix.

Hendrix, who has a doctorate in psychology and religion from the University of Chicago, has written two books on improving relationships. He has also devised an eight-hour video workshop and an accompanying manual to help couples.

"Oprah is aware that her pace at getting married has been affected by her own childhood fears," said Dr. Hendrix. "The tape helps them understand their childhood so they can see that what leads to fights and criticisms is rooted in childhood needs.

"Once they establish what that childhood need is what is showing up in their relationship, the rest of the workshop helps them devise a process by which they can begin to meet each other's needs.

"Oprah and Stedman are preparing for life together. And they can't miss having their dreams come true as long as they never stop their full and open communication."

Oprah's dream of being a 150-pound bride was also on its way to becoming a reality.

Observers reported that she was keeping her eating under control, and she was down to 180 pounds and is getting more comfortable with her body.

The wedding was set for the fall, but it still may be the world's longest engagement.

Shortly after that, Oprah was seen dining out with friends in San Francisco. She ordered a dozen oysters plus crab cakes, tuna tartar and mushrooms with sauteed rice in truffle sauce. Then she turned to her friend and chirped: "I'm eating lightly because I'm on a diet."

"THE BEST DIET I'VE EVER BEEN ON!"

There was another reason Oprah was slimming down. She was hard at work on her autobiography, writing it with the help of Joan Barthel. And she believed writing it was the therapy that had helped her drop a whopping fifty pounds in seven months.

"Writing my autobiography has been the best 'diet' I've ever been on!" she announced in May.

"Facing the pain and shame of my life, looking it right in the eye and putting it on paper, lifted a burden from my heart. I discovered I didn't need food to make me feel better—I felt good without it."

Oprah told a friend that working on the book with Joan Barthel had helped because it "forced me to face the ugly, sad, painful parts of my life."

While writing the book she often woke up in the middle of the night recalling the pain of being raped by a cousin at age nine, or the sadness of losing a premature baby at age fourteen. Sometimes the anger she had at people who hurt her or hadn't protected her from being abused surfaced and she was furious.

"But she realized she had been carrying all these feelings around for years. And as she expressed them in her autobiography, she felt herself letting go and actually felt a weight lift from her head," her friend confided.

"The hardest thing to write about was her pregnancy at age 14. It was also very painful to talk about being fat and the pain and ridicule and lack of self-esteem that involved," her friend elaborated.

Sometimes Oprah got terribly hungry while writing those chapters. Slowly she realized that she was using food to stop herself from feeling all the pain and anger and shame.

That's when she began to see why she ate even when she wasn't hungry. And she called her best friend Gayle King or cuddled up next to Stedman rather than eat something.

Oprah began to eat less and less. Fruit for breakfast, a nice salad for lunch, and chicken or fish for dinner. And she ate for the right reason—because her body needed fuel, not to cover up painful memories!

It was a slim Oprah in a clinging flowered dress who taped a show beside one of the covered bridges that gave their title to the best-selling *Bridges of Madison County* that May.

HONORING MAYA ANGELOU

That April, Oprah threw a sixty-fifth birthday party for Maya Angelou on the Wake Forest campus in Winston-Salem, North Carolina. Among the guests at the exclusive affair: Cicely Tyson, Gladys Knight, Quincy Jones, and Julius Erving. Oprah was happy to tell her guests that Alfred A. Knopf, her publishers, would be throwing a major party for her at the bookseller's convention in Miami that May.

A few days later, Oprah and Stedman attended a Good Friday service at the Trinity Baptist Church in Chicago, then headed for her farm in Indiana for a quiet Easter weekend.

Oprah was about to make big news again.

THE BOOK

Even before Oprah had written one word of her autobiography, booksellers were touting it as one of the biggest best-sellers of all time. "They could move 2 million copies, *easy*," said one editor at a rival publishing house.

Knopf, Oprah's publisher, already had orders for 750,000 copies and wouldn't say anything about the book's contents, except that it would be on sale in September. So, it was with enormous enthusiasm that booksellers greeted Oprah Winfrey when she arrived in Miami to address the American Booksellers Convention.

Her publisher had arranged the full-star treatment: a special private dinner that Saturday night at International Place and a coveted spot as featured breakfast speaker before 1,800 booksellers that Monday.

Oprah told the gathered booksellers that her forthcoming autobiography, *Oprah,* would bring "people who don't ordinarily buy books . . . into your stores."

Stunning in an aqua silk suit, Oprah assured booksellers that her book would not be a celebrity tell-all since "I haven't done all that much" in the romantic sense and besides, "You don't know them!"

The book had been an attempt to "try to make sense of my life," Oprah said, and revealed that one of the most difficult topics she addressed in the book was the issue of her weight. Writing the book had been the equivalent of "ten years of therapy."

She assured her audience that her book would truly empower people.

The happy booksellers went home from their convention secure in the knowledge that in a notoriously unpredictable business they had a guaranteed best-seller coming up that September.

In the afterglow of the ABA convention, Knopf had increased the first printing from 750,000 copies to a nice round one million.

The book was being closely watched by the publishing community for a number of reasons. For one thing, it was the biggest venture yet by Knopf, regarded as the most elite of American publishers, into the world of celebrity autobiography.

It also marked what was believed to be an unprecedented contractual development: the first time an author

349

was able to demand equal partnership with a publisher. In effect, Oprah was copublisher of her own book—a situation that would have been a tremendous windfall for her if it had scored big.

And then, suddenly, just three weeks after the convention, and a mere three months before *Oprah* was to go on sale, it was announced that Oprah had indefinitely postponed the book.

"I am in the heart of the learning curve," Oprah said. "I feel there are important discoveries yet to be made." That was it. She said no more about her reasons.

David Streitfeld of *The Washington Post* called it "the most dramatic last-minute cancellation of a book since *American Psycho* was dropped by Simon & Schuster three years ago as 'a matter of taste.' "

Colleen Raleigh, Oprah's spokeswoman, was only slightly more forthcoming: "After speaking to everyone at the ABA, she just realized it wasn't ready yet," said Raleigh. When asked whether the book would ever be published, Raleigh said, "I don't want to say either way."

"I've never seen this before in all my years in publishing—someone with a major book like this, particularly an autobiography, withdrawing it so close to publication," said Arlene Friedman, editorial director for the Literary Guild and the Doubleday Book Club, both of which had chosen *Oprah* as a main selection.

Friedman, who had seen seven chapters of the book, had found it "moving and very revealing."

But Oprah had second thoughts. A friend told *The Washington Post* that "the book had no heart in it. She was dissatisfied with the product."

And a little later, Oprah told the *Chicago Sun-Times* that "The book, as written, does a really great job of chronicling the events of my life, but I wanted it to say more. I wanted to offer some insight, some clarity and some wisdom that might benefit other people.''

Charlotte Hays, a columnist for *The New York Daily News*, offered another theory, that Oprah had second thoughts once her fiancé Stedman Graham voiced his discomfort over some of the more personal material.

Knopf's publisher, Sonny Mehta, assured Hays that the book had been written, and only editing remained to be done. He said that the book would eventually be published, but that Knopf was not giving Oprah any kind of deadline. Hays also reported that Oprah's editor, Erroll McDonald, was high on the manuscript and deemed it a great read.

It was reported that Stedman himself had exploded after reading the book. He apparently believed that publicly exposing painful details of her life could destroy their happiness just as they were getting ready for their wedding.

When he read the manuscript on June 13 at Rolling Prairie, Stedman angrily told Oprah, ''You can't do this! You're dredging up all the unhappy moments of your past when I want us to focus on the future!

''I won't stand by and watch you reveal your soul to every person in America while we're trying to start a new life together!''

Two days later, Oprah cancelled the book.

But in spite of Stedman's objections, just working on the project had helped Oprah—by making her realize she was dealing with painful memories. Writing it had forced her to confront all her demons and to stare them down.

Ultimately, Oprah concluded that all her pain, all her problems over the years arose because she did not value herself. She worried too much about what other people would think of her. In fact up to the time she cancelled the book she was worrying what her publisher and booksellers would think of her when she told them she was not going to go through with it. They might be angry with her. They might not like her anymore.

But in the end Oprah had to listen to her inner voice, the only voice beside Stedman's that she has ever truly trusted. And that inner voice told her that the book so enthusiastically greeted at the American Booksellers Association convention in Miami was not at all the book she wanted to publish.

Her life story was never the most important thing she wanted to tell. What Oprah had always had in mind was a book that would help others to learn from what she had learned.

"I wanted to write a book that would empower people," she later told Laura B. Randolph in *Ebony*. "A book that would connect the dots of my life in such a way as to give it meaning and in the process offer some sense of wisdom for other people in their lives. But I didn't have the clarity or the insight yet where I thought I could do that."

Stedman, too, did not see how the book she had written fulfilled the goals she had set for herself. "Well we have all the details of your life," he told her, "but who is this going to help? I thought you wanted to write a book that would empower people."

But Oprah is anxious today to dispel any idea that Stedman squelched the book.

"He didn't say anything was too explicit or shouldn't be said," she insists. "He said it wasn't powerful enough . . . I prayed and cried . . . I feel bad about disappointing people. I went back on my word. But I finally said [to myself], 'Congratulations. You have always done what other people expected of you, and now you've done something for yourself.' "

There was an amazing postscript to this story. A few

weeks after Oprah pulled the book, Hays reported that "According to the publishing buzz, Oprah never, astonishingly enough, signed a contract with Knopf. In retrospect, such an omission could have been a warning signal of Winfrey's ambivalence about the project."

And anyone trying to make sense of Oprah's decision only had to look at her remarks in the past. She has always been frank about trusting her instincts.

"If something feels right, I do it," she has always said. "If it feels wrong, I don't. It's really very, very simple, but you've got to be willing to take your chances doing stuff that may look crazy to other people—or not doing something that looks right to others but just feels wrong to you."

And an interesting coincidence: Oprah was not the first celebrity to pull her book after all. Only a year before, Barbara Walters, the very newswoman on whom Oprah had once patterned herself, told Putnam's to cancel her life story after she read the first draft. "She had been very, very forthcoming," said someone familiar with the project. "In the end, when she saw her story in type, she just wasn't ready to do it." Perhaps Oprah felt the same way.

Around Knopf they had taken to referring to the most famous best-seller that was never published as *Noprah*.

HARPO HAUNTED?

Not all Oprah's secrets were locked up with her book. That summer it was revealed that the Harpo Studios were haunted, and that Oprah herself had been the victim of poltergeist pranks right in her own office.

"There are ghosts here," Oprah confided to a close pal. "My studio is haunted."

Many of Oprah's employees were also convinced that spirits roamed empty studio hallways nearly every night, and they had actually seen one they dubbed the "Gray Lady."

"I can say for sure there are spirits walking the halls," revealed security guard Robin Hocott, who worked the overnight shift at Harpo Studios for three years.

Workers reported they heard whispering voices, children laughing, someone sobbing, turn-of-the-century music, the clinking of glasses toasting, and even marching footsteps.

In 1991 Oprah had confessed on her show that she had seen a spirit in her home. Now she admitted to a few close friends that she herself had been a victim of Harpo Studios' ghosts.

Lights that she turned on when working late suddenly went off if she left her office for just a few seconds. Files she left on her desk were mysteriously moved to other rooms overnight.

"I know it's ghosts," Oprah told her friend. "No one was in my office overnight. No one could have moved them."

Although Oprah didn't want word of the chilling events to get out, it is impossible to suppress the strange happenings that plagued Harpo Studios when darkness falls.

The unexplainable has been happening there since 1989, when Oprah officially opened the huge four-building production facility.

At first, security guard Hocott heard strange crashing sounds throughout the studio and when she went to investigate, found nothing amiss. "Then things started happening three nights a week," she said. "One evening after midnight the phone rang on my desk. It was a producer working late in her office who told me she'd just heard the sound of laughing people right outside her office door."

Hocott rushed to the location to find the producer locked in her office, very shaken. "She told me that when

354

the laughter startled her, she immediately opened the door and the hallway was empty. She could hear voices, but couldn't see anything.''

When Hocott mentioned the strange happenings to other guards, she learned they were having the same experiences.

"There's a lobby staircase where we always heard footsteps going up and down. And not just a few—hundreds!" said Hocott. "It was as if Oprah's audience was leaving the studio. But it was after midnight!

"There were sounds of people whispering and glasses clinking together, like someone toasting.

"Doors would open and slam shut.

"I'd try to chase down the source and hear children laughing and giggling in the distance.

"One particular night, I began to smell a strong odor of violets, like a cologne your grandmother would wear, then the sound of someone sobbing. A chill ran through me.''

On many nights, guards hear "Gay Nineties" music in darkened areas of the studio, and it's not from any radio, said Hocott.

One security guard revealed she and other employees have seen a ghost. "We call her the Gray Lady," said the guard.

"She's a woman in a long flowing gown and ornate hat. We've seen her on security monitors. The first time we thought it was someone lost in the building. But a guard walked down the corridor to direct her and there was no one there.

"Other guards have seen the woman in the halls. She floats rather than walks and is always a shadowy figure.''

"Oprah" staffers claim that they have reported the strange happenings to supervisors, but were told the word from Oprah and her top executives was to keep things quiet.

Harpo Studios' spirits are peaceful, say employees. Although some workers have quit because they're frightened, most have just gotten used to ghosts as company.

An expert believes that the spirits may be victims of a tragedy that happened July 24, 1915, near the present site of Harpo Studios.

"That day, 2,500 people crowded on to the steamer *Eastland* for an outing and the boat capsized on the Chicago River.

"More than 800 men, women and children died and one of the buildings, now part of Oprah's studio complex, was a former armory that served as a temporary morgue for victims.

"We've had many reports of spirit activity around the site where the steamship went down," said researcher and lecturer Richard Crowe, who's been investigating accounts of ghosts in Chicago for twenty-five years.

The studio sounds of laughing adults, giggling children, clinking glasses, and music all jibe with the festive mood *Eastland* passengers were in as they boarded, says Crowe.

The Gray Lady's garments sound like what a woman would wear on a summer day in 1915. And the sobbing certainly could be a spirit who died in the tragedy, crying over the loss of life.

Said Crowe: "The spirits of the *Eastland* are very active."

And it looks like they're permanent guests of Oprah Winfrey.

THERE ARE NO CHILDREN HERE

If she was concerned about the ghosts, Oprah gave no sign of it. She could not be concerned with a tragedy that happened in 1915, when her mind was on the difficult lives of contemporary children.

By July, Oprah was in the middle of producing and starring in "There Are No Children Here," a made-for-television movie based on Alex Kotlowitz's national best-seller.

Part of the project would be filmed on the Harpo soundstages, and part would be filmed at the Horner Houses, the West Side public housing development where much of the book was set. Neighborhood residents were hired as extras.

Oprah had been transfixed by the true-life story of the Rivers brothers, Lafayette and Pharoah, growing up in a Chicago housing project where drugs, shootings, and gangs are a way of life. She had owned the film rights since 1989, and ABC had tentatively scheduled it for the 1993–94 season.

Besides being executive producer, Oprah was playing the mother, LaJoe, a woman determined to save her sons from the streets.

"I'm really excited that she's playing LaJoe," said Kotlowitz, a former newspaper reporter who spent several years at Horner researching his book. "It will bring the film that much more attention."

The West Side was a rough neighborhood. One afternoon, a young man was shot in the leg a few buildings away from where Oprah sat between takes on a director's chair under a large black and red umbrella.

Although she was unavailable for press interviews, Oprah made herself accessible to the people of Horner. She had won their hearts long before announcing she was coming to the housing project, but she erased whatever wariness remained when she said she was donating her salary from the movie to a scholarship fund for the Henry Horner Housing Project.

"She made us feel right at home," one Horner resident said, forgetting for a moment that it was Oprah who was visiting, perhaps a credit to Oprah's unmatched people skills.

That summer brought some mixed messages for Oprah about the state of her work. A study by *Satellite ORBIT* magazine reported that her chatting took up 33.2 percent of the talking time on her show in contrast to Phil Donahue's 22.2 percent and Joan Rivers's 29.4 percent. The talk show host who talked more than Oprah on their shows was Montel Williams, who gabbed away 40.5 percent of his show.

That didn't interfere with Oprah being named the nation's most popular talk show host in a nationwide Harris poll. Thirty-one percent of adults surveyed said they preferred her talk show, giving her a twenty-point lead over Phil Donahue. Regis Philbin and Kathie Lee Gifford were right behind at number three. Geraldo Rivera tied with David Letterman for fourth.

UPROAR OVER OPRAH'S GURU

In August Oprah once again came under fire for one of her more controversial talk show topics. She found herself blasted by top doctors for promoting a New Age medical guru who preached self healing—which the outraged physicians warned was putting her viewers' lives at risk.

On July 12, Oprah devoted an entire hour to the teachings of Dr. Deepak Chopra, an Indian-born physician promoting his new self-help book, *Ageless Body, Timeless Mind*.

Oprah seemed fascinated as Dr. Chopra discussed his convictions that the mind can heal the body and help reverse aging. The guru, whose disciples include Michael

358

Jackson, also talked about the miraculous benefits of herbs, meditation, and other New Age practices.

There was nobody on the show to dispute the controversial Indian guru, who practices a modern version of ayurvedic medicine, which goes back six thousand years.

The bizarre practices of ayurvedic medicine have included treating constipation with a milk-urine mixture; improving male potency through 216 different kinds of enemas including some concocted from animal testicles, and wearing crystals to achieve wealth and longevity.

"Within 24 hours of Dr. Chopra's appearance on 'Oprah,' sales of his book went through the ceiling," said a spokeswoman for his publisher, Random House. "The book was selling out in stores across the country."

But doctors also went through the roof!

"Oprah should be ashamed of herself," said Dr. William Jarvis, president of the National Council Against Health Fraud. "She's endangering the lives of her viewers by having Dr. Chopra appear on her show."

Dr. Jarvis charged that the danger was that people in Oprah's audience with serious diseases might turn their backs on legitimate medical care and follow this ayurvedic path.

"If they do," said Jarvis, "Oprah shares some of the responsibility for what can happen to these people."

Dr. Jarvis, a professor of health promotion at California's Loma Linda University, added:

"By giving Dr. Chopra a forum, without having someone on the show to give the other side, Oprah gave Dr. Chopra and ayurvedic medicine a publicity bonanza."

Dr. Jarvis was deeply puzzled by Oprah's decision to have Dr. Chopra on the show. "Why would she want to help someone like Dr. Chopra?" he asked. "I see him as a huckster."

Dr. Chopra doesn't consider himself a con man, but

someone who is merely teaching the truth: The mind can heal the body.

"I believe Oprah is embracing these techniques," declared the physician, former chief of staff at New England Memorial Hospital and the author of five other books on self-healing.

"She told me she had been studying my books for a long time. Oprah sought the truth in what I had to say."

Dr. Chopra said that he was introduced to Oprah by Michael Jackson, a mutual friend. "I've been working with Michael as a doctor for a few years, teaching him various mental techniques and stress management," he explained.

Critics charge that Dr. Chopra's books are packed with useless "psychobabble," but he denies that accusation.

"In my books I teach that we human beings are the only species who consciously influence the biological expression of aging. That's because we are the only species who are aware of the fact of aging," Dr. Chopra explained.

"We're also the only species aware of the fact that we are aware. Awareness in itself is the flow of biological information. Through our own awareness we can harness its power and utilize this biological information for the good of our bodies."

On Oprah's show, Dr. Chopra said that thoughts create chemicals in the body. When you think good thoughts, your body creates chemicals that fight diseases.

Bad thoughts have the opposite effect, he said. "Anger causes inflammatory disorders . . . depression is correlated with cancer . . . guilt also is correlated with cancer."

To demonstrate the power of the mind, he had Oprah hold a string with a washer-like object tied to the bottom end.

"Mentally have the idea it's moving back and forth . . . it'll start moving," he told her.

As the pendulum began swinging, Oprah exclaimed: "Oh, my heavens."

"Oprah is enthusiastic about Dr. Chopra's teachings," said a friend. "So far her health has been good, and she's eager to get any information to help her stay that way."

But medical experts warned that happy thoughts alone can't fight serious illnesses. And they point out that some of the ayurvedic medicine practiced by Dr. Chopra is suspect at best.

For example, he has advised washing the eyes out with saliva to improve vision.

The prestigious *Journal of the American Medical Association* blasted Dr. Chopra two years ago and said he charges patients $1,400 for two twenty-minute sessions.

In one session, patients are told to listen to their heart during meditation; in the other, they receive a secret "health mantra" to repeat, said the *JAMA* article.

In addition, the article alleged that Dr. Chopra had collected hundreds of thousands of dollars from the sale of ayurvedic medications, herbs and other items connected to the practice.

Dr. John Renner, director of the Consumer Health Information Research Institute, also took Dr. Chopra to task two years ago—for dispensing his saliva-in-the-eyes advice.

"This is a dangerous procedure with no proven benefit and much possible harm," said Dr. Renner. "Some bacteria present in the mouth can actually cause corneal ulcerations. This [saliva] procedure makes as much sense as drinking one's urine, another treatment in ayurvedic medicine."

Although Dr. Chopra has legions of followers, some

experts charge he's using his medical credentials to get rich.

"He is using Oprah and Michael Jackson to give himself a respectability he doesn't deserve," fumed Patrick Ryan, founder of TM-Ex, a support group of former cult members.

And Chopra's "Oprah" appearance represents a potential threat to her viewers, warned Dr. Renner. "Oprah, in effect, endorsed Dr. Chopra to millions of her followers—and talk shows are not the place to be getting medical advice.

"If someone with a serious medical problem checked into the nearest ayurvedic clinic rather than go to a doctor—and got very ill or died as a result—Oprah would have to share some of that responsibility," continued Dr. Renner.

"She had a responsibility to present the other side to Dr. Chopra, and she did not," said Renner. "And that is irresponsible."

MORE GOOD WORKS

Oprah and Elizabeth Taylor had long ago formed a mutual admiration society. Oprah admired Elizabeth enormously, especially after the ailing star attended an AIDS Benefit performance at the Cirque du Soleil, a famous circus, in Chicago. "Liz was risking her life to help people with AIDS," Oprah told a friend. "She needed to be in bed. But she refused to take the easy way out."

The valiant star had recently developed pneumonia, while stricken with bronchitis, but she had promised to appear, along with Oprah, Woody Harrelson, and comic Rosie O'Donnell. In spite of her doctor's warnings and her husband's objections, Elizabeth flew to Chicago on July 31.

When Oprah learned that Elizabeth was ill, she was so worried that she advised the actress to forget about the show, said an insider.

"Oprah, who was already scheduled to be there, offered to take her place as hostess. But Elizabeth insisted she owed it to her fans to show up," this insider revealed.

"I was touched by her courage," said Oprah later. "She's a lot more than just a star. Liz is a caring, courageous human being and I'm proud to know her."

PSYCHIC PREDICTIONS

Oprah's hopes may have been buoyed that summer when famed Los Angeles psychic Maria Graciette, who predicted the Manson murders, forecast that Oprah would quit her talk show to open a network of free clinics to help abused women.

And down on her Indiana farm, Oprah was called in to help a cow give birth. The vet was late, but the cow couldn't wait, so Oprah and a farmhand brought the calf into the world. Oprah was a nervous wreck at first, but made it through her midwife crisis.

THE WEDDING IS OFF

That August the rumors were all over the country: Oprah was supposedly reeling in shock after Stedman called off the October wedding, allegedly because Oprah had broken her promise to spend more time with him.

Oprah had made an appointment with designer Oscar de la Renta to look at wedding gowns. She was consulting an almanac to determine what week the autumn leaves would be the best color. Suddenly, everything was off.

According to an insider, Oprah's dramatic weight loss played a big role in wrecking her marriage plans.

"After losing 60 pounds, Oprah was bursting with energy and her self-confidence was at an all-time high, so she began taking on more and more projects," the insider told us.

But as she increasingly ignored Stedman, he steamed . . . and finally exploded during the first weekend in August.

They were at Oprah's Indiana farm where only a few months earlier Stedman had proposed, when he dropped his bombshell, said the insider.

"He told Oprah: 'You promised me you'd cut back on your schedule so we'd have more time together alone, just the two of us. And what happens? You're busier than ever!'

" 'I don't want to go through with the wedding. I won't marry you until you put me first.'

"Oprah was shocked. She didn't realize Stedman had been quietly seething over her not spending more time with him, so she was taken by surprise."

Now Oprah was facing a big dilemma.

"She wants to keep her career as a talk show host, producer and actress," said an insider. "But she also wants to marry Stedman, her main man for over six years, and start a family."

However, Stedman knew that if he married Oprah right now he would be playing second fiddle to her career, said the insider.

"'I don't want to rush into this wedding and six months later be in marriage counseling because we never see each other," Stedman told a friend.

Back in January, Oprah had agreed to cut back on

personal appearances and other engagements so she and Stedman could be together more often.

Things seemed to be going smoothly between the couple, and recently pals became convinced the two were going to wed soon.

Oprah and Stedman were calling close friends in July to get their home addresses, and everyone expected wedding invitations to be in the mail.

Oprah was also seen out shopping for china and looking at wedding gowns.

"But she's slowly gotten involved in more and more work," said the insider.

"And when Oprah and Stedman are alone on her farm, she's either on the phone checking on new movie and TV projects or reading scripts."

Oprah, who had also loaded herself down with speaking engagements and appearances at benefits, didn't even have time that summer to take her usual vacation with Stedman. He was deeply hurt, said the insider.

And when he returned after two weeks in Europe, Oprah couldn't see him. She was too busy producing and starring in her upcoming TV movie "There Are No Children Here." Stedman also was upset by recently printed false rumors that Oprah had given him forty percent of Harpo Productions.

An insider said that Stedman believed his ultimatum would force Oprah to cut back on her work, and that they would eventually tie the knot.

But meanwhile, Oprah was struggling to find some way to balance everything. It was hard, but she didn't want to lose him.

Oprah has become rather philosophical about her on-again, off-again wedding.

"The truth is I'm in no hurry," she says today. "In spite of all the worldly pressure for me to have a wedding,

365

I no longer feel what I felt many years ago—that I had to have a man in order to make myself whole.''

She even admits that the idea scares her. Will Stedman's expectations change? Will he start to want her to come home and cook dinner? Will she want to?

So far, however, Stedman has assured Oprah that marriage simply means that he is there for her . . . and she will be there for him.

It was anybody's guess as to what would happen next. But one thing is sure: There wouldn't be a wedding this year.

OPRAH IN THE RUNNING

Even with her wedding plans shelved again, Oprah was not through making news for the year.

That August, she amazed the world by completing a thirteen-mile race, after losing sixty pounds.

''People told me running would be fun. When I first started training, I said, 'What's fun about this?' But today was a lot of fun,'' Oprah said. ''That last mile was tough, but the goal was to finish.

''I may not have finished first in this race, but I won nonetheless. I'm in the best shape of my life and I couldn't be happier.''

That's what a jubilant Oprah Winfrey told a pal after she celebrated her victory over obesity by running a grueling thirteen-mile road race.

The star had lost sixty pounds since last November and now weighed in at 150 pounds. She showed off her new svelte figure when she completed the half-marathon in hilly San Diego, California, on August 15, and she vowed: ''I'll never be fat again!''

Oprah was positively amazing. A few months before, she could barely walk. And now she was runing a half-marathon!

"I believe that if I put my mind to something I can do it," she told a friend. "The last mile was the longest mile of my life. But I wasn't going to run 12 miles and quit. Besides, I had my own video camera crew along with me. Who wants to poop out on videotape?"

In recent months, Oprah had been exercising hard with personal trainer Bob Greene.

The trainer started her out gradually using a treadmill and Stairmaster and eventually lengthened her runs. She was now running ten miles a day at least four days a week in Chicago.

She did not want anyone to know she planned to run in the marathon, so she entered under the pseudonym of Bobbi Jo Jenkins and swore the race director Neil Finn to secrecy. But once Oprah showed up with a video crew, bodyguard, and trainer, her cover was blown and she became the most famous of the 5,019 entrants.

Oprah had also taken to playing tennis with Stedman when they escaped to her Indiana farm. They had put their wedding plans on hold since Stedman thought she was involved in too many activities.

But he was taking the break from wedding planning philosophically. He told a friend:

" 'She's got some things that she needs to get done before we can settle down. But I sure would rather have her run a marathon than eat a whole peach cobbler!' "

Oprah selected the America's Finest City run in San Diego for her first race because of the mild climate.

It was a pleasant sixty-five degrees when Oprah set out with five thousand other runners at 7:00 A.M. She ran with five of her staff members, including her trainer and her bodyguard, and was suited up in black cycling shorts and a white tank top. Oprah's official number was 2923.

"The course was real challenging. You started off on rolling hills and then there was some punishing downhill," said Terry Nevinger, an editorial assistant who ran just ahead of the star. "The last mile was all uphill.

"Oprah finished at around 2 hours and 16 minutes. That's a pretty fast clip for a first-timer!"

She finished an hour behind the race's winner, Maria Trujillo, thirty-three, of Salinas, California, who won the women's division in 1:16:17.

"Oprah made a point of waving to people as she ran by," said race participant Greg Leavey. "People instantly recognized her and went out of their way to cheer her on. You could see the effect it had on Oprah. She kept thrusting her fist in the air and yelling, 'Ya-hoo!' "

Another eyewitness disclosed: "Oprah had apparently trained well, because around the halfway point she started passing many other runners as she moved up to join the leading third of the pack.

"The last mile was an obvious ordeal for her: She was breathing heavily, but remained strong, not even slowing down until she crossed the finish line."

Stedman was waiting for Oprah when she triumphantly completed the race.

"You did it, baby!" he said proudly as she fell into his arms. "I'm proud of you."

Oprah was especially proud of her weight loss—the biggest since her much-ballyhooed 1988 fast, because this time she did it without resorting to a fad or liquid diet.

"I've learned there isn't any shortcut to getting thin," Oprah told a friend. "You have to exercise and eat moderately. And it takes time. This wasn't like my liquid diet where I dropped a lot of weight quickly. This was slow and painful!"

Oprah's next goal would be to run a full twenty-six-mile marathon. She told a friend: "I'm staying at this weight. I may not run forever, but I'll never get fat again!''

Oprah said she had lost fifty pounds in five months of training. ''I decided a long time ago that I have to be healthy by the time I'm 40,'' said Oprah, whose fortieth birthday was five months away.

It would be nice to believe that this time Oprah will keep the weight off. But, remember, when Oprah was once asked ''If you had one day in which you could be bad, and there would be no consequences, what would you do?''

And she answered: ''I would *eat everything humanly possible* without one single iota of guilt, without thinking about calories. I'd just enjoy it and take great pleasure from all the grease on the potatoes.''

Her next stop: The Chicago Marathon in October.

OPRAH'S FUTURE

That October, there was another nice surprise. For the first time Oprah headed *Forbes* magazine's list of the forty top earning entertainers for 1993. The article reported that ''The Oprah Winfrey Show'' was now seen in ninety-nine percent of U.S. TV markets and in sixty-four countries, generating over $170 million in revenue. Oprah's two-year take: $98 million.

''I know when this is all over, the Master isn't going to ask me how many things I owned,'' she says frequently.

She is and always has been frankly into control.

''Oprah owns her show and controls her money,'' says Jeffrey Jacobs. ''There's no board of directors, no committees. Every final decision is hers.''

Jacobs likes to share a story about Oprah. Not long ago, they stood in the aisle of a Kmart near her Indiana farm trying to decide whether to buy a $7.95 doormat decorated with cats or one festooned with cows. "She couldn't decide. Then she realized—she could buy both. We have a joke between us," he says. "She still has both feet on the ground; she just wears better shoes."

OPRAH'S SURPRISE

In her candid interview with Laura B. Randolph for *Ebony* magazine, Oprah showed that she is still full of surprises. Among the surprises for the two million readers of *Ebony* were Oprah's revelations about her relationship with her mother. Confident that she was following the Biblical instruction to honor her parents, she had provided them a better economic life than they would have otherwise enjoyed.

But emotionally, she admitted, she did not feel connected to either of them. Oprah claimed that her mother, like herself when she was a teenager, had named several people who could be responsible for her pregnancy, a charge that Vernita later heatedly and bitterly denied.

Oprah seemed to mean to give Vernon a backhanded compliment, saying that he was the only father she had ever known, that he had taken her in and taken responsibility for her when he didn't have to. "My father saved my life at a time when I needed to be saved," she acknowledged, "but we're not, like, bonded."

Oprah seemed to remain ambivalent about her feelings for her mother. On the one hand, she revealed that while writing her now-cancelled autobiography she had discovered that her mother had lived with her for the first four-and-a-half years of her life. Vernita had not left an infant Oprah to be raised by her mother on the farm. But Oprah said that even after seeing pictures that show her with her mother in those early years, "as far as I'm concerned it's somebody else's child."

An obviously stll-bitter Oprah also said that from the time she left Milwaukee until she became a television star, she had no contact with her mother. For seven years there was nothing between them. Now she asked, how was she supposed to feel when her mother showed up? What was a daughter supposed to feel?

As for what the future holds for Oprah, we can take a clue from her advice to the graduating class of Spellman College, the distinguished women's college in Atlanta, in the summer of 1993: "Think like a queen," Oprah told them. "A queen is not afraid to fail. Failure is another stepping-stone to greatness."

Epilogue
How Oprah Lives on $5,416 a Day

I still have my feet on the ground, I just wear better shoes.

—Oprah Winfrey

By the end of 1993, Oprah Winfrey was worth $250 million and earned a mind-boggling $5,416 for every minute she was on TV—and she spent it almost as fast.

Oprah is a notorious jewelry lover and clotheshorse who goes on $40,000-a-day buying sprees. She's a generous boss who rewards her employees with all-expenses-paid exotic vacations and picked up the tab for their lavish weddings. And she's still a generous humanitarian who writes six-figure checks for charity.

What's more, Oprah has spent millions on television stations, her restaurant, her private jet and mansions in Colorado, New Mexico, and Indiana, plus an apartment in Chicago that is bigger than most houses.

In October, *Forbes* published its list of the forty Top-Earning Entertainers, and Oprah was at the top of the top, with a 1993 income of $52 million, outdistancing her mentors Steven Spielberg, second at $42 million, and Bill Cosby, third at $26 million.

Oprah Winfrey, the self-described "little nappy-haired colored girl" from Mississippi is now the world's highest-paid entertainer.

In 1975 she was earning $15,000 a year as a TV news anchor in Nashville. Today she earns that in less than three minutes on the air.

In 1993 she collected $52 million for doing two hundred shows that ran forty-eight hours apiece, not counting commercials. She was on the air a total of 9,600 minutes.

Oprah is a part owner in the Granite Broadcasting Corp., which controls six TV stations, and she owns a thriving restaurant in Chicago, the Eccentric.

She owns a Challenger 601-3A jet that costs $1.4 million a year to operate. On the ground, she frequently travels by limo and owns a $100,000 BMS.

Like Elvis, she likes to give cars as gifts.

When Stedman's daughter, Wendy, recently graduated from high school, Oprah presented her with a Jeep for which she had just paid cash.

But she does not lavish a lot of money on Stedman. He doesn't want her money, and she understands that.

Stedman does share Oprah's four luxurious homes, including the baronial Chicago condo.

Oprah has combined two three-thousand-square-foot apartments into a fantastic two-story six-thousand-square-foot pad worth over $2 million.

Oprah spent $500,000 last year remodeling her $3 million home at Telluride, Colorado, which includes a stone Jacuzzi for ten people.

She's never forgotten her roots on the farm, and that's why she likes to relax at her $2 million farm in Rolling Prairie, Indiana. She's also building a fantastic mansion near Santa Fe, New Mexico.

Homes are not the only thing Oprah collects these days. She has begun amassing rare first edition books, valuable black dolls, and owns $1 million in art.

She has a first edition of *Gone with the Wind* by Margaret Mitchell and books by Harlem Renaissance poet Langston Hughes, Mark Twain, Emily Dickinson, and Robert Frost.

When Oprah was a little girl, black dolls were rare. Today she collects the valuable antiques.

Oprah is also the proud owner of several paintings by artists Romare Bearden and Allen Stringfellow. Their works can sell for many thousands of dollars in exclusive art galleries.

Oprah can't get enough clothes and jewelry.

She recently purchased a black cashmere turtleneck sweater, a black cashmere blazer, and a gray wool and cashmere blazer at the fashionable Ultimo shop in Chicago for a whopping $14,500. (Yes, that's about what she earned in a year at her first broadcasting job!)

She bought a Chanel suit for $3,750.

And in the middle of August, after her latest big weight loss, Oprah's assistant Andre Walker came into Chicago's chic Escada boutique and bought upward of $40,000 worth of new slim-fitting clothing.

Oprah has claimed that she had only one pair of shoes when she was growing up in Milwaukee. Now she has five hundred pairs of shoes in her closet.

On TV she wears solid gold jewelry so big and heavy it looks fake . . . but it's not.

Most people buy costume jewelry that looks like the real thing. But in Oprah's case she'll buy a $5,000 solid gold necklace which looks like a $39 department store knockoff.

One of Oprah's most expensive hobbies is weight loss.

During her most recent battle with the bulge she spent a staggering $142,000 to lose sixty-five pounds—or nearly $2,200 a pound!

In order to slim down from 210 pounds to 145, she needed a full-time staff to help her.

She paid her personal trainer Bob Green and her personal chef Rosie Daley more than $50,000 a year apiece. It also cost her $25,000 for them to travel with her.

Oprah spent $5,000 for exercise equipment; $3,500 to join the exclusive East Bank Health Club in Chicago where she can work out daily; $1,000 on athletic shoes; $2,000 on workout attire, and $5,000 on massages.

That comes to a grand total of about $142,000. But that's not all she spent.

Once Oprah got down to her new slim self she had to buy nearly $100,000 worth of new clothes.

But it was well worth it, audience members agreed when she unveiled her new body at the September 10 taping of her show in Miami.

Not only has Oprah lost weight, but she looks strong and fit. She looks fantastic.

Oprah doesn't just indulge herself. She's incredibly generous to the people who work for her.

People are still talking about the Christmas she took her producers and publicist to upscale New York stores and let them buy *anything* they wanted.

Oprah says: "It feels good to be able to do things like that with no strings attached, just because I can!"

She has focused much of her philanthropy on education. She has given millions to the United Negro College Fund. She has also given to breakfast programs and shelters for battered women.

Most recently, Oprah has committed herself and her millions to fight the evils of child abuse and lobbying for legislation to combat it.

As her longtime best friend Gayle King Bumpus puts it: "You can look up the word generosity in the dictionary and you will find Oprah Winfrey's name."

378

Notes & Sources

1989
Description of apartment, *NYTM*, 6/11/89
Women of the Year for 1988, *Ms. Magazine*, Jan/Feb, 1989
Salute from Maya Angelou, *Ms. Magazine*, ibid
Her ministry, TV/TM, 6/11/89

"The whole celebrity fame thing . . ." Ann Hodges, *Houston Chronicle*, 1/16/89

"No matter how rich . . ." Confidential source, 12/22/87

"Baby, all you *have* to do . . ." *NYTM*, 6/11/89

"You are their hope . . ." *NYTM*, 6/11/89

"Oprah, you must keep alive! . . ." *NYTM*, 6/11/89

"I am very, very proud . . ." Ann Hodges, *Houston Chronicle*, 1/16/89

Birthday, *Chicago Tribune*, 1/29/89

Puppy, Confidential source, 1/31/89

Stedman's family, *National Star*, 1/24/89

Hot dog dream, Confidential source, 2/28/89

Rolling Prairie farm, *National Star*, 2/7/89

AWED conference, Liz Smith, *NYDN*, 2/17/89

Oprah Winfrey's speech: as reported by Anne Eaton, *National Star*, 3/14/89; Ellen Pober Rittberg, *NYDN*, 3/5/89

The Eccentric: Colman Andrews, *Los Angeles Times*, 6/25/89

Silverware story: Bill Brashler, *Ladies' Home Journal*, August 1991

Brother Jeffrey Lee interview, Confidential source, 3/14/89

Phone-in poll: *National Enquirer*, 5/2/89

Psychic prediction: *National Enquirer*, 7/4/89

Letterman episode, Confidential source

Golden Door Spa: *National Star*, 4/4/89

Easter miracle, Confidential source, 5/30/89

"Gayle keeps me grounded . . ." Kay Gardella, *NYDN*, 6/2/89

Stedman Rumor; Confidential source, 6/6/89

Tough Love: Confidential source, 12/19/89

San Francisco: Confidential source, 7/18/89

Black theater: *Houston Chronicle*, 8/16/89

Rape Treatment Center: *Miami Herald*, 9/26/89

1990

Water Tower Place: *National Star*, circa 1/90

Shawn Robbins: Confidential source, 1/2/90

Geraldo Rivera: Confidential source, 1/16/90

Whoopi Goldberg: Eric Sherman, *Ladies' Home Journal*, May, 1990

"I feel blessed . . .": *National Star*, circa 1/90

Personal trainers: *National Star*, 3/6/90

"Stedman is ideal for me . . .": Susan Littwin

"Oprah is a slob . . ." Confidential source, 3/27/90

"It's hard to put into my mind . . ." Michele Greppi, *NYP*, 3/16/90

"With 200 talk shows to tape . . ." Mark Caro

"We invested $20 million . . ." George Christy, *The Hollywood Reporter*, 10/18/91

Jose Velez: *National Star*, 5/8/90

Union shop: *Chicago Tribune*, 2/16/90

Reuben Cannon: Michael Post, *Baltimore Evening Sun*, 1/11/90

Brewster Place: Kay Gardella, *TV Guide*, 12/2/89; Susan Littwin, *TV Guide*, 5/5/90

Debra Di Maio wedding: *National Star*, 4/17/90

Polish TV: *Los Angeles Times*, 7/25/90

Visit to Vernon Winfrey: Susan Littwin, ibid.

Vail airport: Confidential source, 2/6/90

Stedman: Confidential source, 3/27/90

Brewster Place: Dorothy Gilliam, *Washington Post*, 5/7/90

Self-esteem: Barbara Grizzuti Harrison, *NYTM*, 8/11/89

$200,000 chest: *Chicago Tribune*, 8/8/90

Oprah's spending: Confidential source, 9/11/90

Stedman and diet: Confidential source, 11/6/90

Jennifer Jacobs: *Chicago Tribune*, 12/4/90

Oprah's new look: Confidential source, 1/8/91

1991

Top 100 Collectors: *Art & Antiques*, March 1990

Harpo Studios: Bill Brashler, *Ladies' Home Journal*, 8/91

Honeymoon, Confidential source, 3/26/91

"I've been dieting since 1977 . . .": *People*, 1/14/91

New Orleans: Confidential source, 2/3/91

Angelica Mena: "Oprah Winfrey Show," 3/13/91

Oprah and Dolly: Confidential source, 6/10/91

Cal-a-Vie, *National Star*, 4/7/92

Love Boat, Confidential source, 7/30/91

Talon cruise: Confidential source, 7/30/91

"Books were my path . . .": *LA Times*, 9/18/91

"Diet cop": Confidential source, 9/17/91

June wedding: Confidential source, 10/22/91

"Afterschool Specials": *LA Times*, 11/7/91

Senate testimony: press release from Ruder-Finn, 11/12/91; *Washington Post*, 11/13/91; *USA Today*, 11/13/91; *Houston Chronicle*, 11/26/91

Lookalike: *People*, 4/29/91

St. Kitts: Confidential source, 12/24/91

1992

Telluride: *Palm Beach Post*, 3/29/92

Harpo office: *LA Times*, *TV Times*, 5/17–23/92

Beloved: *USA Today*, 5/19/92

Geraldo Rivera: *USA Today*, ibid.

Maya Angelou: *USA Today*, ibid.

Billy Graham: Confidential source, 12/31/92

Birthday party: *National Star*, 2/25/92

Back on the market: *Chicago Tribune*, 1/28/92

Six Keys to Success: Confidential sources, 2/11/92

The Book: Richard Johnson, *NYDN*, 4/29/92

Oprah: Behind the Scenes: Bruce Ingram, *LA Times*, *TV Times*, op. cit.

Stedman: Alan Ebert, *Good Housekeeping*, 9/91

Fame shield: Diane Joy Moca, *NYDN*, 5/19/92

Malcolm X: *LA Times*, 5/2/92

Scared Straight: Peter Johnson, *USA Today*, 9/3/92

"A million mothers": *People*, 9/7/92

Weight: Confidential source, 5/12/92

Candlelight dinner: Confidential source, 7/14/92

Apartment: Confidential source, 7/14/92

Sports Lifestyles: *NYP*, 7/15/90

Engagement: Confidential source, 11/24/92

1993

Ellen Rakietan wedding: Confidential source, 1/26/93

Inauguration fur: *Ft. Lauderdale Sun-Sentinel*, 1/23/93

Wedding plans: Confidential source, 1/26/93

Michael Jackson: George Christy, *The Hollywood Reporter*, 2/2/93

Questions: Karen Thomas, *USA Today*, 2/10/93

Plastic surgery: Confidential source, 3/2/93

Elephant man: ibid.

King of Pop: ibid.

Neilsen: *Chicago Tribune*, 2/12/93; *LA Times*, 2/12/93

Wedding plans: Confidential source, 3/16/93

San Francisco: ibid., 3/30/93

Maya Angelou party: *USA Today*, 4/7/93

Book: *Chicago Tribune*, 6/25/93; Charlotte Hays, *NYDN*, 6/21/93 & 6/30/93; *People*, 7/5/93

Satellite ORBIT poll: Confidential source, 7/20/93

Harris poll: *NYDN*, 7/5/93